LOST IN THE HIMALAYAS

LOST
in the
HIMALAYAS

JAMES SCOTT
JOANNE ROBERTSON

MAINSTREAM
PUBLISHING

EDINBURGH AND LONDON

First published in Great Britain in 1994 by
MAINSTREAM PUBLISHING COMPANY (EDINBURGH) LTD
7 Albany Street
Edinburgh EH1 3UG

First published in Australia in 1993 by
Thomas C. Lothian Pty Ltd
Agent Harry M. Miller and Company Management

ISBN 1 85158 623 7

A catalogue record for this book is available from the British Library

Typeset in Stempel Garamond by Servis Filmsetting Ltd, Manchester

Printed in Great Britain by Butler & Tanner Ltd, Frome

This book is dedicated to all those people throughout the world who gave their support and prayers to us whilst James was missing in the Himalayas

Dum spiro spero – whilst I breathe I hope

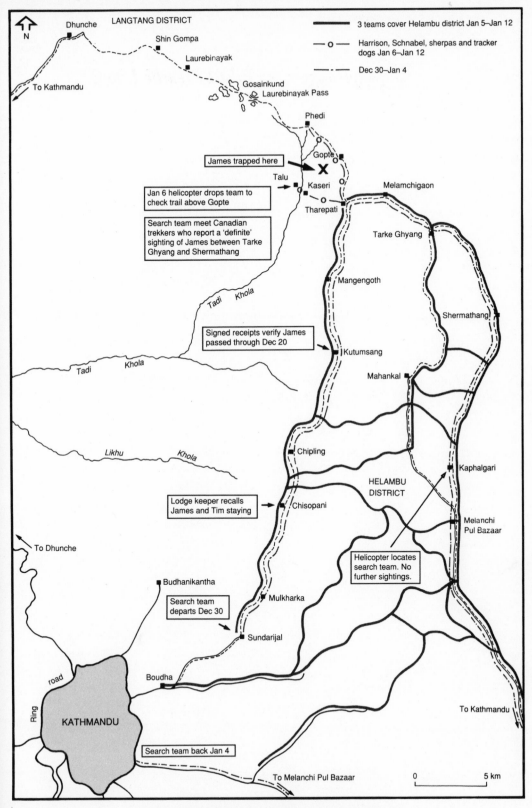

Search operations December 30–January 12

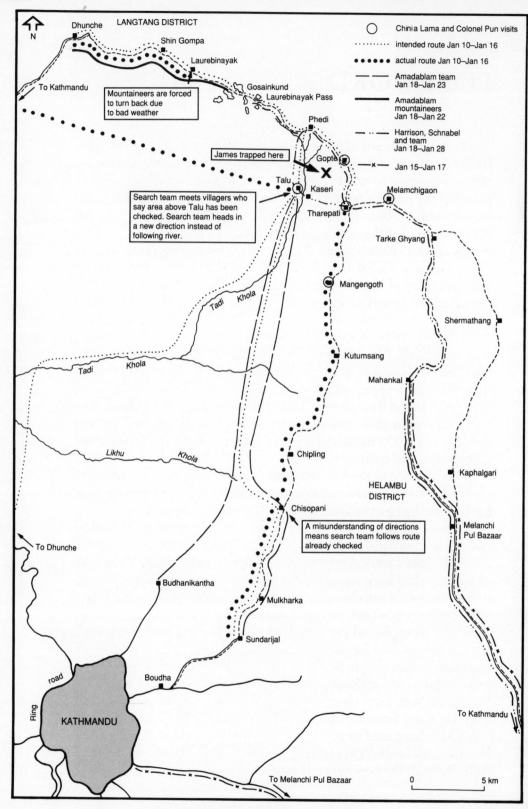

N

LANGTANG DISTRICT

○ Chinia Lama and Colonel Pun visits
‧‧‧‧‧ intended route Jan 10–Jan 16
●●●●● actual route Jan 10–Jan 16
– – – Amadablam team
Jan 18–Jan 23
—— Amadablam mountaineers
Jan 18–Jan 22
–‧–‧– Harrison, Schnabel
and team
Jan 18–Jan 28
–×–×– Jan 15–Jan 17

Dhunche
Shin Gompa
Laurebinayak

To Kathmandu

Gosainkund
Laurebinayak Pass

Mountaineers are forced
to turn back due
to bad weather

Phedi

Gopte

James trapped here   ✗

Talu   Kaseri
Melamchigaon

Search team meets villagers who
say area above Talu has been
checked. Search team heads in
a new direction instead of
following river.

Tharepati

Tarke Ghyang

Mangengoth

Tadi   Khola

Shermathang

Tadi   Khola

Kutumsang

Mahankal

Likhu   Khola

Chipling

HELAMBU
DISTRICT

Kaphalgari

Chisopani

A misunderstanding of directions
means search team follows route
already checked

Melanchi
Pul Bazaar

To Dhunche

Budhanikantha

Mulkharka

Sundarijal

Boudha

Ring   road

KATHMANDU

To Kathmandu

To Melanchi Pul Bazaar

0   5 km

Search operations January 10–January 28

FOREWORD

The first I ever heard of James Scott was via a barrage of phone calls from newspaper and radio stations eager to add an experienced mountaineer's opinion to what had the aura of a media frenzy. I was well aware of the media's weakness for beating up a story and getting the facts wrong. I'd been out of touch with current news at the time but they told me that the young Brisbane man had been found alive after having spent 43 days trapped in an ice cave with nothing to eat but two chocolate bars. I tried to explain that, if he had been trapped for 43 days, mention of the chocolate was as irrelevant as saying he'd had chocolate for dessert at his last meal. When told that the altitude he'd been found at was around 3500 metres, I tried to explain that it was unlikely to have been an ice cave he was trapped in: a rock overhang was more likely. Nevertheless, if it was true that he had been holed up for 43 days, it was a most remarkable story of courage and determination. With the snippets of information that I could filter out from all the hype, I found it surprising that someone who had the will and ability to survive in such conditions for so long could not find his way down to one of the numerous villages scattered along the flanks of the range which had trapped him.

In the absence of the full details of James's story, I could only marvel at his sister Joanne's perseverance with searching for so long after her brother had gone missing in such hopeless conditions.

It was a couple of weeks before I began to make sense of some classically bad journalism that had left many people sceptical about the truth of James's story. Only when I'd been given a reliable indication of where he had been trapped did I begin to understand how a strong, fit and obviously sensible person could get himself into such a seemingly unlikely position. In retrospect, it is all too easy to be critical, especially when not all the facts are known. Having read James's full story, I can see that he did nothing to deserve the criticism he's had. Everyone makes simple mistakes and we can learn as much from our own mistakes and those of our fellows as we can from our successes. We can do both from the story in this book but, on balance, we shall learn far more from its successes. What initially happened to James could have happened to any of the thousands of trekkers who venture into the high foothills every year. Few of them, I believe, would have come through the experience as unscathed as James.

James went missing in midwinter. He'd made a last-minute change of plan to go over a high pass with trekking acquaintance and fellow Australian, Mark Fulton, because that route offered the pair more exciting walking. Even though they had minimal equipment, it was a risk worth taking. Anyone with an adventurous spirit would have done the same. Taking calculated risks has always been an important element in the development of healthy human society. Unfortunately, as often happens around Christmas-time, the first heavy snowfall of winter came suddenly, just as James and Mark set out on the final leg of crossing the pass. With the route ahead obscured by blizzard conditions, James decided to turn back but Mark was determined to persevere. James's decision was undoubtedly the safer one, given the information they had. Ironically, it was James who got into trouble, not Mark. Retracing a downward-heading path in such conditions and over such terrain is amongst the hardest of all route-finding problems. Even if you are experienced, it is notoriously difficult to find your way and overwhelmingly tempting to go down sooner than one should.

He was in an area of high elevation not far from permanent habitation. He was also fit and strong. So, without knowing the true difficulty of the terrain, it was reasonable to assume that he should have been able to walk out to safety. That he had not done so seemed to indicate that he'd fallen on the steep slope and then suffered hypothermia. This was not the case.

I've done a fair amount of walking and climbing in Nepal. Mostly my walking has been on the well-made trails used for centuries by local people. Occasionally I've ventured off regularly used paths and have become embroiled in epic struggles to regain a good path. Within its context, some of the most psychologically and physically difficult country I've experienced anywhere has been the steep, forested gorges of the high hills, the sort of country that James became trapped in. When deep snow lies over the tangled undergrowth that provides a deceptive cover to the steep, bouldery slopes, some of the most frustrating terrain imaginable is made truly murderous to negotiate. With inadequate, sodden clothing, an empty stomach, poor visibility and little idea of his exact location, James did well to find shelter near a clearing. If you have never experienced those conditions, it's easy to be scornful of the fact that he was trapped within a few hours' walk of a village. Knowing those conditions well and looking back to some of my early epics of being disoriented, I think James did incredibly well to survive long enough to be found alive. Had he kept going, I have little doubt that his limited experience of the conditions, the deep snow and the cold would almost certainly have caused him to succumb to frostbite and a fatal dose of hypothermia. That he avoided those perils and survived to become dry and relatively warm is testament to an unusual degree of discipline and commonsense.

Most experienced walkers, including myself, would have felt little hope of finding James alive after two weeks. But there was a small chance that, against the great natural difficulties, he was still alive. It was by refusing to discount this slightest chance and by doggedly wanting to know what had happened that kept James's sister Joanne persevering in the face of different but nearly as daunting difficulties as her brother's. Her refusal to give in to an inept and uncaring bureaucracy is an inspiring example to all who face the intransigence of self-important individuals who forget their job is to serve the public. That she succeeded in keeping a well-organised search going against many uncertainties and dead ends, until no stone had been left unturned, is a shining example that, as long as there is any hint of hope, you must never give up.

Most significant of all to me, and what lifts the tale beyond the remarkable story of survival and dogged persistence that it is, is that throughout James's narrative there is a constant if not growing sensitivity and warmth to his surroundings. As a captive of nature with its total disregard for his suffering and the overwhelming feeling of insignificance forced on him by his surroundings, he became neither egocentric nor angry about his plight. Rather, he became aware of something greater than himself. He was able to appreciate the beauty of life on a scale few of us, under the burden of our human conditions, ever have the privilege of feeling.

Tim Macartney-Snape

Tim Macartney-Snape is an Australian mountaineer with fifteen years' experience in the Himalayas, both as a trekker and a climber. He has climbed Mount Everest twice without supplementary oxygen. On the first occasion he established a new route on the mountain's north face with a small team of friends. The second ascent began at sea level, in the well-known 'Sea to Summit' expedition. He climbed from base camp to the summit alone and unassisted and is the only person to have completed the climb from sea level.

PROLOGUE

JAMES: *Phedi, 22 December 1991, dawn*

The room was still dark when I awoke. I immediately pulled the sleeping bag over my head, curling up as tightly as possible. It was the coldest I had felt since arriving in Nepal. There was no movement from Mark's end of the room. I tried to muster the courage to get out of my sleeping bag and see how the weather looked outside. I lay there, alternately contracting and relaxing muscles, trying to generate some warmth. Light was starting to filter through some of the cracks in the wall of the lodge and I eventually decided it was time to get moving.

I was not particularly surprised to find the ground outside and the roofs of the lodges covered by the lightest sprinkling of snow. This rekindled the anxiety I'd had yesterday. I looked down at the clouds swirling ominously at the bottom of the massive valley, the occasional one detaching itself from the mass to be whisked up by the icy wind towards me. Visibility would suddenly decrease as the cloud surrounded me, to be restored only when the gusts pushed the cloud higher up the mountain, until it eventually disappeared over the pass.

The lodge keeper emerged from his hut with a cheery greeting and surveyed the valley below. As he did, he asked if we wanted porridge for breakfast. I nodded absently and asked him, 'Do you think it is going to snow today?'

He paused before replying, 'No, it won't snow today.'

This was not the answer I wanted. I glanced again at the threatening clouds in the valley and at the snow under my feet. Already, I was looking for an excuse to return down the valley with the lodge keeper and his family. I found it very hard to believe that there would be no more snow.

'Are you sure it won't snow today?'

He looked at me this time and repeated firmly, 'It will not snow today.'

Something inside was telling me I shouldn't climb the pass that day. When I'd left Kathmandu with Tim some three days earlier, we had no intention of crossing the Laurebinayak Pass.

Tim and I had arrived in Nepal in mid-November. Both medical students, we had decided to complete a term of practical work at Bir Hospital in Kathmandu. Having gone to considerable lengths to

13

organise this, we arrived at the hospital to be told we would have to pay a fee for attendance. Neither of us had allowed for this extra expense. We tried another hospital, Patan, but, apart from allowing us to do a ward round, they had not been able to fit us in either. So we had gone trekking the Annapurna region. Upon returning to Kathmandu, still with some spare time before our flights to Bangkok on 28 December, we had decided to go on another trek.

After some discussion and investigation, we had settled upon the Helambu trek. The books describe it as a relatively easy trail that provides distant but spectacular views of the Himalayas. We would require little extra equipment as the path was reportedly well maintained and the altitudes low, the highest point being 3600 metres. In addition there were plenty of lodges where food and accommodation, although spartan, would be available. We were assured by the book and by other trekkers that we would not need a guide, something we were pleased about as the guide we had hired for our first trek, Krishna, had been a source of problems rather than assistance. We had left on 19 December.

The first evening had found us in the village of Chisopani. Here we had met a German couple who had strongly advised us to walk the Gosainkund trail. This branched off the Helambu trek at the village of Tharepati. Incorporating the Laurebinyak Pass (4600m) and glacial lakes, the Himalayas, they said, appeared so close, 'you felt you could reach out and touch them'. It didn't take much convincing for Tim and me to change our plans. I asked if the pass would be safe at this time of year and they said it would be fine as long as it didn't snow.

'If it snows you must turn back,' the woman had said.

We had set off the next morning and not gone far before meeting another Australian, Mark Fulton. Mark was trekking by himself and was quick to volunteer to join us.

On our previous trek, Tim had been having problems with a muscle in his thigh. It now seemed he had injured it again. I offered to go back with him, but he had been adamant that I should continue. We split up our gear, I gave Tim the best map and Mark and I continued on. At every village, I had asked about the safety of crossing the pass and the advice was always the same: we should have no problems. Mark and I had spent yesterday walking a trail that ran across the precipitious slopes of an immense mountain range. Below us now was an enormous valley and above were towering, barren crags of rocks.

I decided to rephrase my question to the Phedi lodge keeper. 'Do you think we will have any problems getting over the pass today?'

The lodge keeper replied, more confident than ever, 'You will have no troubles crossing the pass.'

Mark and I went inside the family's hut where porridge was steaming over a warm fire. We sipped the hot tea served to us. The lodge keeper explained it would take three hours to cross the pass and another hour to reach the huts on the other side of Gosainkund. Even then I was tempted to ask him to guide us over the pass. I suggested this to him but he was quick to remind me that he had to pack and leave with his family that day in order to reach Talu before the weather set in. As he had explained the evening before, he needed to allow ample time because of the children.

We packed hastily and, with rucksacks on our backs, sought final instructions from the lodge keeper. He pointed to a rocky trail worn through the clumps of vegetation scattered over the hillside. The plants were thick and prickly and, although no higher than our thighs, would have been quite an obstacle without the trail.

'You take that track leading up the pass,' he told us. I asked him where he was going and he pointed to another track, different from the one we had used to get here. This trail was narrower and less conspicuous.

'This trail leads to my village. With all the goods we have and the children it will be a full day's walk.'

I held out my gloved hand and watched a snowflake fall lightly upon the palm. The lodge keeper must have read my thoughts as he said, 'Don't worry. You will be okay.'

JAMES: *Phedi, 22 December 1991*

All the time, as we ascended the trail, I looked back over my shoulder. The two huts at Phedi were no longer in sight. We still had a creek to the left of us. Some parts of the creek, I noticed, were iced over. The clouds appeared darker than ever and rose quickly towards us.

We'd been walking for just over an hour when the first real flakes of snow started to fall. 'It looks like we're going to have a white Christmas,' I said.

Although I was worried, I asked Mark to take my picture. He handed me his camera to return the favour. I focused and pressed the shutter button. Nothing happened. The batteries had failed in the cold. I offered to use mine and send him copies but he removed the batteries and began rubbing them briskly to warm them. It took fifteen minutes to get the camera working. In that time, visibility decreased, the clouds surrounded us and the trail disappeared. When we got going again, a thick white blanket covered our route. We could no longer see the path and instead tried to follow gaps in the brambles that suggested the presence of a trail. Each time we found a path through we became excited. Repeatedly, our way was blocked by boulders or thick vegetation; at other times, we would find ourselves in the midst of a steep field of snow, unsure in which direction to head. We could only tell if we were ascending or descending. The Laurebinayak Pass was no longer in view.

As the snow fell more heavily and the clouds thickened, our visibility dropped to about ten metres. We crossed the creek. I felt that we should be heading more to the west which would keep us on the left side of the creek as we climbed. Mark disagreed, saying the map clearly showed the trail lay to the right of the creek, the side opposite to where we stood. I agreed, but we could still see no sign of a trail. Furthermore, there were several creeks racing down the mountainside. I felt the trail could be near any of them.

There was a ridge, easily climbable, just to the left of the creek. I thought the view from the top might help. Mark said he would keep close to the creek. I scrambled up the ridge. Losing sight of him for a short time didn't seem a problem. At the top, I found the ruins of some huts. Nearby was a continuous break in the vegetation that was easy to follow. It was about the width of the trail we had taken earlier that morning. I called excitedly into the whiteness. There was no reply. I called again and whistled several times. Still no answer. I headed back to the creek, shouting every few paces. I was sure that we were no more than a couple of hundred metres apart. Why did he not respond? Suddenly I felt very much alone. I was well aware of my insignificance compared to the power of this environment, aware that I had got myself into a situation over which I had little control.

It was a great relief to hear Mark shouting through the curtain of snow. I pushed towards his voice, through bramble and over rocks, losing sight of the ridge behind me. I found Mark on the right side of the creek, higher up than I had left him. The water had now completely frozen over. I crossed it carefully. At these temperatures I was sure wet feet would lead to frostbite.

I told him what I had found. He listened but insisted the trail had to be on the right-hand side of the creek as the map showed. I looked into the whiteness: 'But there is no trail here to follow,' I said.

Mark explained his plan. He decided that the trail lay further to the right of the creek than we had thought and proposed we continue in a north-east direction to ensure we crossed the trail. Yet the pass through the mountains lay to our north-west. If the map was accurate, this way made sense to me. However, I was not convinced of its accuracy and I felt confident that what I had already found on top of the ridge on the other side of the creek was the trail we were searching for. Mark still felt it would do no harm to walk a short distance north-east away from the creek so I conceded but my doubts grew as the slope grew steeper and the climbing became more difficult. I now had a headache which was getting steadily worse with the increase in altitude.

In exasperation, I pointed out that this was ridiculous. We were now a good distance from the creek (our only point of orientation); we had no idea which direction we were heading in and, with the snow increasing, we were putting ourselves into great danger. I said, 'The safest thing we can do is head back to Phedi and wait for the snow to clear so that we have some chance of finding a way over the pass.'

Mark disagreed. 'I want to keep looking for a few more hours. It's 10.30 now. If I haven't found the path by 1 p.m., I will turn back.'

We were at an altitude of almost 4600 metres in very rocky, difficult terrain. Neither of us had the equipment necessary to exist for long in the conditions. I knew the best thing would be for us to stick together but I disagreed so strongly with Mark's notion of blundering around on the snowy mountainside that I felt I had no option but to return alone to Phedi. The increasing intensity of my headache made me feel it would not be wise to ascend, particularly because we would need to move quickly. The only available precaution I could see was to exchange addresses in Kathmandu so that we could each check that the other returned safely. I was more concerned for Mark's safety than my own. I felt he was taking the riskier option. We swapped addresses and made a date for dinner on Christmas Day.

I turned my back on Mark and headed for the creek which I could use as a landmark to locate Phedi. I could not help but fear for Mark's safety and I hoped that he would have the good sense not to attempt any precarious climbs. At that altitude, with the equipment he had, I knew he would not last a single night especially if he was injured.

I reached the creek and climbed down beside it. The walking was difficult. The slopes of the creek banks rose and fell sharply, made slippery by the sleet and snow. I slipped and slid downwards, keeping the creek to my right and searching for any sign of the trail or the Phedi lodges. Suddenly, my feet were skidding and I crashed on the rocks. Fortunately, my rucksack broke my fall, but my water bottle fell and bounced down the cliffs towards the creek. I considered climbing down after it. The three- to four-metre drop, although not sheer, could still result in a nasty injury if I lost my footing. I looked at the bottle for a moment and wondered just how essential it was. I was walking by a creek, a ready source of water and, even if I returned to Tharepati the way we had come the previous day, there were creeks at regular intervals. I decided there was no real need to carry water. However, by leaving the bottle behind, I felt I was further losing control of my circumstances. Not being able to go and get it was frustrating and seemed an ominous sign. I felt the cold bite more deeply and thought, 'I've got to find some shelter quickly.'

The snow continued relentlessly. The rim of my straw hat bowed under its weight. I tried to keep dry by brushing the snow from my clothing before it could melt. I was wondering how much further I would have to walk to find Phedi when the creek fell away abruptly, cascading down to form a waterfall. I picked my way down next to it to a wooden bridge. It looked similar to the bridge we had crossed the previous day but I knew there were at least two, if not three, bridges near Phedi. Not only did they all look the same, but they were all at the bottom of waterfalls. I was on the eastern side of the creek. I believed Phedi was across the creek, on the western side. I also felt that the two huts were much higher than I was, perhaps on top of one of the steep banks in front of me. I crossed the bridge and looked for a trail. There was none to be seen.

'A bridge that leads nowhere,' I thought with annoyance. I was fairly sure the steep banks were part of the same hill we'd climbed to reach Phedi the day before but the heavy snow masked any path that might lead up it. I could see no further than five metres up the face and was reluctant to try climbing it. I crossed back over the bridge but there was no trail on that side either. By my calculations, any trail there would have led to Gopte. I didn't want to climb back up to the top of the waterfall that I'd picked my way so carefully down. In this weather, the climb would be challenging and dangerous.

For about thirty minutes I circled the area around the bridge, certain that Phedi was near, but I was unable to find the elusive trail in the white-out conditions. It was very frustrating. I could no longer prevent the snow melting on my jacket, trousers and gym shoes. They were getting sodden, deepening the cold. It was essential I get down lower. At least at a lower altitude, I might expect some cover from vegetation and, with any luck, I'd be able to get below the snowline.

Desperately I pulled out my map. It showed that the creek would join the Tadi Khola, which flowed between two villages, Talu and Kaseri. I knew the lodge keeper from Phedi, our last stop, was making for Talu. It *must* be possible to reach this village if I followed the creek.

It was about midday. I felt confident that, if I did not get to Talu that night, I would surely arrive some time next day. With new optimism I set off, bursting through the brambles and keeping west of the creek.

Although I had to watch my footing constantly, I found the descent easier now. With each step, I was more certain I had made the right choice in turning back. My headache disappeared at the lower altitude. The vegetation became thicker: the bramble bushes were replaced by tall, bamboo reeds which I could grasp to steady myself in steep places. Most of the time I slid down on my backside. Fir trees mixed with broad-leaved shrubs. The snow was still falling heavily but the change of vegetation gave me a sense of security. I was no longer exposed to the icy winds on the barren landscape now hundreds of metres above.

The creek roared as it gained speed over large boulders, racing down the steep mountain. It lay to my left, some 20 or 30 metres below in a deep ravine. As I followed each bend of the creek, I hoped to find the bridge that must surely join Kaseri and Talu. I was cold and wet and I kept thinking how nice it would be to change into a dry set of clothes, sit by a warm fire, and eat. Talu was not on the normal trekking routes, but I was sure I could persuade them to sell me some dhal bhat or maybe even some meat. But every turn of the creek was a disappointment. I kept telling myself, 'Just another kilometre. You'll get there.'

The ridge dropped to the level of the creek and I found myself in a gully. The water beside me became deafening. Around a sharp bend I found to my dismay the reason for the increased noise: the water disappeared over a cliff. I edged across the icy rocks and peered down. The drop would have been no more than fifteen metres but it was sheer and totally without foot- or handholds. The creek turned another corner only several hundred metres beyond the waterfall: did Talu lie just around that bend?

I decided it was too dangerous to climb down the waterfall, especially since I had no rock-climbing experience. I looked back up where I'd come: nothing to be gained by returning. There was no shelter for me up there and I doubted, anyway, if I could retrace my steps. On either side of me now were the steep banks of the creek. Perched on a rock in the middle of the white water, I took stock. The bank on my right, like the waterfall, would be impossible to climb: nothing but sheer rock and ice. The bank on my left, I convinced myself, could be no more than ten metres high and I searched it for useful ledges, vegetation and cracks. If I fell I would crash on the rocks below or even plunge into the creek to be swept over the waterfall. I did not wish to take any risks but I felt strong and fit. Talu could not be too far away, another day of walking at the most. Nervously, I started up the cliff.

Pushing my hands and feet deep into the cracks and crevices, I only looked upwards. At times the climbing was easy. At others I felt like going back. I took my time, digging out solid footholds and, when I came to the occasional bush rooted firmly into the cliff face, I rested, caught my breath and told myself I could overcome my fear of heights and make it. On one of these stops, I ate half of one of my chocolate bars for an extra boost of energy.

Halfway up the rock face, I realised that ten metres had been a gross underestimation. I looked down and saw that I was at least four times my own height above the creek and I still had almost the same distance to go. I was terrified.

Several times, when I felt the weight of my rucksack dragging me away from the side of the cliff, I contemplated tossing it down. Many times I slipped and would grasp any available crack or ledge, sometimes clinging on for fifteen minutes, wondering where to go next.

Finally, I scrambled over the edge. I gazed back down the cliff. Surely the worst of it must be over.

It was getting dark. In front of me was a large rock with an area, well sheltered from the wind and snow, that was reasonably dry underneath. I pulled off my clothes, lying my ski jacket out in the hope that it might dry a bit overnight. I towelled myself down, taking special care to dry between my fingers and toes, checking for any black patches. There were none. All the tissue appeared viable, despite being numb. I put my longjohns on and a couple of pairs of socks and pulled on my windcheater and, as my gloves were soaked through, used socks to cover both my hands.

My hands and feet were numb with cold and I desperately wanted to get a fire going. I searched every corner of my rucksack for the lighter, all the time wondering if the wood would be dry enough to burn. I shook out every piece of clothing but, to my astonishment, could not find it. The last time I had seen it was in the lodge at Chisopani, when Tim was still with me. We had used it so little that I had carelessly forgotten about it. I figured the lighter must be back in Kathmandu with Tim. I cursed silently, tidying the area before trying to rug myself up in my sleeping bag.

I tucked my hands tightly between my thighs. As the warmth returned, my fingers and toes began to burn. I was pleased, despite the pain, as I imagined the tissues in my hands and feet returning to life as the blood returned to vessels constricted with the cold. I nestled into my warm sleeping bag with the other half of my chocolate bar, this time sucking it slowly, savouring the sweetness as it melted. The snow was still falling heavily outside and a cold wind was blowing. I said a prayer for Mark's safety, a prayer for my family at home in Brisbane and my fiancée Gaye and, finally, one for myself. Tomorrow I would reach Talu. I drifted off to sleep, my last thought being of where Mark might be.

JAMES: *23 December 1991*

Cloud and mist shrouded the small ridge where I had camped. The view was distressing in the cold light of day. It had continued to snow heavily through the night. I scooped up a large handful of powdery snow to wash my hands. It was almost weightless. When I dropped the ball it disintegrated.

I removed my thermal underwear, dressed and packed up. Yesterday's sodden tracksuit pants, lying under the rock were semi-frozen and very heavy. I decided not to take them. I had an urge to defecate and purposely did so under the rock, near the tracksuit pants. I thought that leaving the pants and faeces would help tracker dogs trace me at least this far. I still rated my odds of finding Talu as good but the heavy snow overnight had surprised me and I knew that

21

reaching the village through this rugged terrain in deep snow would be difficult.

I thought back to the bridge that led nowhere. Should I have stayed and searched longer for Phedi? Should I have left a note on the bridge, saying which direction I was heading? I put on my ski jacket and gloves. Both had frozen on the outside, but were still warm. I told myself off for thinking negatively. I would surely be in Talu by nightfall, if not by lunchtime: it was only a couple of kilometres away.

The cliff I had climbed yesterday lay to the west; the creek and waterfall thundered below. To the east, I could hear a similar sound and I believed the ridge I was on could be followed past the waterfall. I set off through the snow, the sound of rushing water growing louder on either side. The snow was above my knees and the uneven ground made walking difficult. Before long, I came to the end of the ridge. A steep drop lay in front of me. At the bottom the two creeks from either side formed a raging torrent. There was no way down here. So I retraced my steps to the rock where I had camped. From there, I took the gentler slope to the east until I reached the creek at the bottom. It was pure chance that here the creek was at the base of a massive waterfall. I was thankful I had not been forced to find a way down the sides of this waterfall.

With renewed confidence I followed the creek downstream past the junction. Feeling smug about my progress, I continued on, expecting Talu to appear in front of me at any turn. The going was slow, as I had to jump from rock to rock. Where there were no stepping stones, I clambered along the banks by holding onto the vegetation. Occasionally, I would jump onto a rock covered in ice and my footing would go completely, leaving me thigh deep in icy waters. The effort this required kept a reasonable body temperature which prevented me suffering from the cold. No more than a kilometre from where the two creeks joined, I was dismayed to hear the familiar deafening roar again.

'Please, God, don't let it be like the other waterfalls,' I thought. I could only smile at the irony because, on our first trek, I had spent so much time admiring the waterfalls that Tim had grown tired of hearing me say 'Bloody excellent waterfall!' How circumstances change perceptions!

The waterfall was completely unnegotiable. I sat on a rock, starting to shiver, the water dripping off my trousers. I was determined not to be defeated: there had to be a way of getting around it to reach Talu. It occurred to me how stupid I had been in trying to follow a creek down. With a drop in altitude of nearly 2000 metres between Phedi and Talu there were bound to be waterfalls. If I could get away from the creek and follow a ridge that ran parallel to it, maybe I could avoid these sudden, steep drops.

The creek flowed south along the base of an enormous valley into which I had spent the previous day descending. I looked at the banks rising on either side and decided to try to climb the west bank first. In comparison with yesterday's cliffs, the climbing would be safe, although the extra snow would make it difficult. Scrambling up, using any vegetation for support, I climbed away from the creek before heading in a direction parallel to it. The slope became so steep it was becoming treacherous. I retraced my steps to the creek to try my luck on the opposite bank. This would be more difficult because of a sheer rock face against which the river flowed. I had no fear of slipping and injuring myself, for it was no more than two and a half metres high, just enough so that the top was out of reach.

I perched on a rock near the cliff face. Clawing with my fingers, I tried to get a grip that would allow me to scramble up the surface. No grip available, I decided to jump and grab for the top of the cliff. My hand fell short and I slid painfully down the rock face, up to my thighs in the icy waters of the stream. As quickly as I could, I scrambled out and tried again. On my fifth or sixth attempt I managed to get a hold and pulled myself up and over the edge.

Water had splashed everywhere. I was bitterly cold and savagely angry about the state I had got myself into. I could feel the water squelching in my shoes and all my clothes below the waist were completely soaked. My feet were icy cold and frostbite was now a very real danger. I knew from my medical training that the constriction of blood vessels in my feet due to the cold would allow no more than twelve hours before causing irreparable damage. I had to get to Talu as quickly as I could.

I climbed higher along the east bank before turning south again to follow the line of the creek. As on the west bank, the slope became too steep to be safe. I took out my map. Talu, I decided with some resentment, was an impossible destination.

It was around midday and I allowed myself the luxury of two more cubes of chocolate. Looking at the map, the contours that led up from the Tadi Khola towards Tharepati appeared well spaced, indicating an easier gradient. I thought about the effort needed to climb 1000 metres, the minimum to reach the trail that led from Gopte to Tharepati. The deep snow, and the valley wall being so steep, I was uncertain whether it would be possible to hike up such terrain. But the idea of continuing on to Talu, across country I knew to be extremely precipitous, was foolhardy. As long as I had two good arms and two good legs, I felt sure I would get out of this valley. It would be stupid to take any more risks. The most important thing was to set a safe goal and work hard to achieve it. I decided to change my course, directly up the eastern face of the valley, towards the top of the steep valley wall, where I should be able to see the trail we had followed a couple of days earlier. I would be able to follow this track to the safe haven of Tharepati.

I have never exerted myself as physically as I did that afternoon. The steepness of the slope, combined with the weight of my rucksack and the knee-deep snow was exhausting. The ground beneath the snow was a thick mixture of vines and brambles which entangled my legs. Every step was a huge effort.

I wondered how far I would have to walk to reach Tharepati. I figured it was possible to get there by nightfall and that was my goal, for I was certain that I would not last another night in these conditions. The mist and cloud brought visibility down to less than about 100 metres. Again and again, I would set my sights on the most distant tree visible and trudge as quickly as I could to it, in the hope that the ground would start to level off and that Tharepati or the trail would come into view. But all I would find before me was more uphill walking and another tree to aim for. This went on all afternoon. Then, as snow started to drift down again and visibility diminished to nothing, I could not even aim for a tree! I might pass within 50 metres of Tharepati and never know it.

I ate two more cubes of chocolate as I assessed the situation. Things seemed very grim. I had no option but to find shelter. I had not seen much in the way of suitable cover, certainly no rocks as grand as I had found the previous night. After struggling for a further fifteen minutes, I came to a small ledge that barely provided a metre of shelter from the snow.

'This will have to do,' I thought. I threw off all my wet clothes, drying myself down fastidiously, taking extra care with my feet and between my toes. There were still no black patches, but my feet had gone a disturbing shade of blue. When I was certain they were dry, I put one pair of dry socks over them and got into my thermal longjohns. I was relieved to find that the rucksack had proven waterproof and the contents were still dry. I had one last dry pair of trousers and one windcheater. All the clothes I had worn that day were soaked through. I spread them out as much as I could, but there was little room under the tiny ledge. I got into my sleeping bag and zipped it up, still feeling incredibly cold. My hands were blue and it was difficult to control my fingers. My teeth chattered incessantly and this would be the first of many nights that I would feel the cold more than I could ever have imagined. It was not the superficial cold that most people can relate to, but a deep, chilling cold that feels as if it's killing the very life within. The cold was like pain. Just as it seemed as bad as it could possibly get, it got worse and the suffering increased. I was sure it would be impossible to be as cold as I was and still survive the night.

I would have been at an altitude of at least 3500 metres, on the eastern wall of an enormous, heavily forested valley. Here I was, hidden under a tiny rock ledge. What chance was there of my body ever being discovered? This insignificant shelter in such an expansive valley could well hide my body forever.

In psychiatry we had studied the factors that exacerbated grief felt by close family members after the death of a relative. One of the most significant factors in making a loss hard to accept is the failure to discover the body. I knew that, if I did not survive the night, this was most probably what would happen. My overriding concern, more than my own death, was the suffering that my family and Gaye would go through. I really had no fear for myself: all my anxiety lay in the grief those back home would have to endure. The guilt that I would cause this grief was a terrible burden. I wanted to write to let them know what had happened.

How does one write a letter to summarise adequately all the emotions I was feeling and say a final goodbye? These words, if they ever got them, would be the last they would remember me by. I shivered in my sleeping bag and, curled up in a ball, I read the three pages I'd written to Gaye whilst at Phedi. Then, I had been warm, dinner was on its way and I had less than four weeks before joining her. The scrawl I had written read like that of an excited child telling a story. I felt as if I'd aged in the meantime. I began where I'd left off.

> I'm continuing this letter two days later and things have gone horribly wrong. I intend to write a letter to you first and then my family, I suspect my death is imminent, probably tonight.

As I wrote this last sentence, I was surprised by my lack of emotion. The idea of death fascinated me. It wasn't the end at all, but just the beginning. Of this I was certain. Imagine the things I would learn when I died, probably just a few hours from now!

I gave a brief synopsis of the circumstances under which Mark and I split up, hoping he had made it over safely.

In two short pages, I had described how I came to be under this tiny ledge. It was time I spoke from my heart. This was a more difficult task. Writing a factual account is far simpler than putting emotions onto paper.

> I am cold but, apart from this, I am not suffering. Everywhere is beautiful with a lot of snow. No doubt it will be deeper tomorrow. The only unfortunate thing about where I am is that I doubt I will ever be found. I do hope I live tonight and keep climbing tomorrow morning.
> Gaye, I love you fanatically and my only regret about dying is that I will cause you and my family so much grief. I am so glad that I met you and the happiness I experienced whilst with you in the short time we had together has no comparison. I am very sorry I won't be marrying you.
> I LOVE YOU I LOVE YOU I LOVE YOU!
> Please don't grieve too long but go and live your life to the fullest and enjoy it. Always remember me and I will watch down on you from Heaven and take care of you. I hope that one day this letter is found and you get to read it.
> I love you with all my heart and all my mind for eternity,
> James xxxooo.

'Please, God, let this letter be found early in spring so that Gaye can get on with her life,' I thought as I addressed an envelope to her parents' home in Cairns, Australia.

Night was fast approaching and, despite the numbness in my fingers, I decided to get on with the letter to my family. This was much harder to write. Our family had never been openly affectionate and, although we were all aware of the strong bonds between us, they were rarely expressed physically or verbally. I reflected on how little I'd seen my family over the past six years since I had left high school. In a way, I had taken them for granted. There would always be time to spend with my family later on, I had thought, justifying the hours I'd spent with friends studying, training, travelling or just socialising. Now time had run out and I couldn't even say my farewell to their faces. The cold sent me into spasms, making it difficult to write.

> Dear Mum and Dad, Joanne, Robbie, John and Calum,
> It may be many years before you get this letter, I doubt I will be found for some time. I have gotten horribly lost in a blizzard, the details of which you can read in my letter to Gaye.

I felt this was a little abrupt but, if I wasted time retelling the facts, I would have no time to write about my personal feelings.

This is my second night out facing the elements and, I suspect, my last. At no time have I suffered although now I'm a little cold.

I am bracing death in a fairly serene manner. I have a lot of faith in God. He has looked after me very well up to now and I'm sure He will continue to do so after I die.

Mum, thank you for being the kindest and most wonderful person I know. I love you very much. I know you will take my death harder than anyone but, believe me, I am not afraid and I will see you in Heaven. I have tried to get myself out of this predicament with the utmost effort, something that I've tried to apply to everything I've done over the past few years. This is something I learnt from you. Thank you for everything and I'll love you always.

Dad, I know my passing will also be a great disappointment for you. I'm sorry, I should have taken more care of myself. My dearest father, you are the man I have the most respect for. Please believe me when I say you were a great Dad and I have an enormous amount of love for you.

Joanne and Calum, I'm sorry we haven't seen more of each other over the past couple of years. I love you very much Joanne, and I know, Calum, that you will do everything to keep her happy. Please have a family to give Mum and Dad grandchildren to look forward to. Take care, make good of your lives and I'll see you both in Heaven.

Robbie, I love you more than you'll ever understand. We grew up together, did everything together and I have the fondest memories of you. Please enjoy life, Rob. That is the most important thing. I am not sad that I'm dying because I was doing something I enjoyed. I am sad, though, for all the unhappiness I'll cause back home. Rob, you are the most generous person I know which is a good quality, keep that in yourself.

Dear John, you will be the only male in our family left and therefore have a great responsibility. Make a good name for yourself. Try hard at everything you do, treat people well, act honestly and you can't go wrong. You are a good man, John, with many talents, please use them. I love you John. Always remember this and remember good things of me.

I am cold, so I'll try and wrap up in my sleeping bag. I hope this letter gets to you all,

Bye for now,
All my Love
James.

In the dark, I set about addressing an envelope to my family in Brisbane and then I scrawled in large handwriting, 'IN THE EVENT THAT MY BODY IS FOUND PLEASE POST THESE TWO LETTERS, ONE TO MY FAMILY, THE OTHER TO MY FIANCÉE'.

Task completed, I packed the envelopes carefully in the brown, plastic folder in my rucksack. As I went to close my rucksack, I took out the last four cubes of chocolate. 'There is no way I am going to die with food in my pocket,' I thought, as I began to feel pangs of hunger for the first time since becoming lost. I ate the chocolate, cube by cube, trying to imagine the little bit of warmth that the energy would provide. All too quickly the last cube melted. My food was completely gone.

Lying back, I recounted every incident that had led me to this situation, stuck under a tiny ledge in dense forest, thousands of kilometres from everyone I loved. The irony of it all astounded me. When I had turned my back on Mark, unable to convince him to join me in what should have been the safe passage back to Kathmandu, I had held grave fears for his safety. My only worry was the few days I might have to spend holed in at Phedi. Now, I had walked and climbed through twenty kilometres of the most inhospitable terrain I'd ever encountered, and things were getting worse. These things happen to other people: they don't happen to me!

It seemed the result of such an extraordinary set of coincidences. The elective work at the Kathmandu hospital had fallen through, allowing us to go trekking instead. Tim and I had become lost on the very first day of our trek and had to lodge at Chisopani instead of Borlang Bhanjyang, where we met that German couple who persuaded me to take on this new trek. I had met up with Mark the next day so, instead of heading home with Tim, I continued trekking. To hammer the nail in the coffin, the weather had changed swiftly and dramatically (even the locals had predicted no snow for days), leaving us lost and exposed, totally unprepared for those conditions at an altitudes of 4400 metres. If it had snowed earlier that morning, I would have gone down the mountain with the lodge keeper; if later, we would have been over the pass.

I could not help but conclude that I was supposed to die and, as the wind shrieked up the valley, the cold penetrating still further into my body, I prepared myself. I prayed for all those back home, I said yet another prayer for Mark and I prayed that if there was any way I could get out of this situation, please Lord let it happen.

I tried to think what I could do for myself. I was wrapped in my sleeping bag, inadequate for the temperatures to which I was now exposed. I was dry, socks were on my hands and feet, yet I still felt that my body was losing its warmth, its energy, that my very life was slowly slipping away.

I recalled from hypothermia lectures that the majority of body heat is lost through the head. In the dark, I burrowed through my rucksack and took out dry cotton shorts and T-shirts, which I wrapped around my head.

There was little else I could do but even this small initiative had some bearing upon my survival that night. It might have been that covering my head prevented hypothermia, allowing me to think more clearly. I cannot say. I do know, however, that from that point on, I had an attitudinal change which would determine the way I behaved over the many days to come.

'I am going to make it,' I told myself. I went from a feeling of complete powerlessness to one where I was master of my own fate. Despite the worsening cold during the night, I held on to the belief that I would be able to continue walking up to Tharepati in the morning.

It was a night that will always be etched on my memory. Sleep did not come, only suffering. I thought of all the karate training I had done, the times when I'd been knocked to the dojo floor and forced to keep fighting.

'It is these times that one's spirit is forged,' my instructor would explain to me. He was right. Every time I'd overcome a challenge in martial arts, I was stronger and more confident than before. I decided to make the most of the suffering that night. I knew no one would ever understand what it was like. People back home would never have felt the pain I now felt. When I got back to karate, my spirit would be forged stronger than ever. I would have a new attitude to my training, having surpassed limits of cold and pain that I did not believe I could bear.

I believe it was this attitude of trying to capitalise on this terrible situation that played a major role in my survival that night. Along with this, I had an enormous will to live and see those I loved once again.

JAMES: *24 December 1991*

A very difficult decision faced me as my surroundings grew lighter. Although visibility was limited by the cloud that still hung in the valley, I was pleased to know that, somewhere up above all the clouds, a sun was rising.

I felt tired and every muscle in my body ached. The constant shivering throughout the night had made me feel very sore. I didn't feel as cold now. I was quite comfortable, which made my decision more difficult. I was wearing my last set of warm, dry clothes and was trying to convince myself to change out of them. If I didn't arrive at a village today, I would surely need them tonight to stay alive.

Reluctantly, I picked up the karate pants I'd worn yesterday. They were stiff as a board. I was able to hold them by the waistband and, rather than flopping down, they stood out horizontally in front of me.

'Bloody hell,' I thought, imagining how uncomfortable these

29

clothes would be. My ski jacket was much the same. I shattered the ice off the clothing with my fist, venting a little anger with each blow. I changed into the pants first, shivering in the cold. Then I pulled on the jacket. I wanted to get moving quickly now. Hard walking would be one way of generating heat. The frozen socks sharpened the burning in my feet. I was pleased that sensation had returned. Still no black patches to be seen there.

My shoes presented more of a problem. They were Nikes – good quality leather running shoes but now as hard as rocks. I worked at them ferociously, bending the sides and the tongue back and forth until they were once again pliable enough to force over my feet. Still frozen solid, they were most uncomfortable to wear.

All the books advised that one must wear boots if snow is likely. My trekking boots had caused me so much discomfort on the first trek that I had swapped them for sandshoes. Had I been wearing my hiking boots and had they become as frozen as my sandshoes, it would have been impossible to get my feet inside them. In addition, reflecting upon the walking I had done the previous day and the continuing struggle through snow that lay ahead of me, I was grateful that I didn't have to lift the heavier weight of boots with every step.

My rucksack packed, the hood of my ski jacket pulled over my head and my straw hat, now looking a little worse for wear, placed atop that, I set off into the snow only to come up against what would be the first of several shocks that day. I sank deeply. The tops of my thighs disappeared into the clean, white powder. I grunted and strained up the steep slope, sometimes hauling myself up by any available plant. As before, I aimed for a particular tree and struggled towards it. The going was far slower now and much effort produced little headway. It was, therefore, fortunate that the second surprise of the day occurred relatively early.

The vegetation had thinned, the slope steepened and, above me, through the wisps of cloud and mist, I could make out massive cliff faces, the tops of which were not visible. I battled to get a closer look and, as these enormous obstacles loomed in front of me, I couldn't help but think, 'I really don't deserve this.' They were patently unnegotiable. I dismissed the notion of climbing them without a second thought. Climbing the cliff two days ago had been a horrendous struggle, yet, by comparison, it was just an ant hill. I couldn't help but feel disheartened.

I would head for Talu after all, I decided, trying not to brood on the six hours I'd fought to get here. I walked along the base of the cliffs. I believed I was heading due south, parallel to the river now running far below me. I was trying not to lose altitude. I cursed the thick clouds which brought more snow. If it would only clear, I could get a bearing on exactly where I was and possibly even see a village.

Despite my resolution to remain high on the valley wall, I found myself heading gradually downwards. The snow was so deep in places that I had no option but to go down towards the river. I have to keep away from those creeks at the bottom of the valley, I reminded myself. Coping with more waterfalls and cliffs was out of the question. I barely had enough strength to make my way across the steep slopes up here, let alone scale the precipitous drops I'd been encountering near the river. The snow in some of the gullies that crossed the side of the valley was waist deep in places. In other areas, the vegetation – stubby, broad-leafed foliage interspersed with clumps of matted bamboo grass and vines – was too thick to penetrate.

I passed a small cave, its entrance less than a metre across. Large cat-like footprints broke the smooth snow in front of the entrance. The animal seemed to have entered and left several times that morning and I wondered if it was there now. Reluctant to find out, I moved from the area as quickly as I could, alert in case of a sudden attack.

A couple of hours after I'd encountered the cliffs I felt exhausted. Lack of sleep, combined with the strenuous effort needed to wade through the snow had sapped my strength. Cold and tired, I no longer had the energy even when the snow was only thigh deep, let alone when I sank to my waist.

The ice had now melted on my clothes and I felt completely sodden. I began shivering again. Not even the arduous walking was enough to keep me warm now. My teeth chattered uncontrollably and I felt as I had the previous night – that life itself was slowly slipping away. My feet were numb again which worried me greatly. I felt I was lucky not to have been frostbitten yet, but I knew that my luck was fading fast.

I was now so cold and wet I knew I was in great danger of dying from hypothermia. The memory of the torture I'd endured the previous night forced me to seek shelter. As the snow continued to fall, I knew that I could not go on in these conditions for much longer. I slid down the steep slope, making my way around an enormous boulder, at least the size of a house. When I got past this rock, I noticed how it jutted out, its overhang providing a sizeable area underneath clear of snow. That in itself was not so unusual. I had seen many rocks and caves that provided as much shelter, as well as better protection from the wind. My attention was grabbed by what lay beneath the overhang.

31

There were remnants of a campfire: large pieces of charred wood and long dead coals. The old fire had been made on the edge of the protected flat ledge, an area of around three metres deep and five metres long that was presently clear of snow. There were also two handles there, handmade and obviously once parts of an axe or a similar tool.

The other attraction was a large clearing to one side, some thirty metres across the slope of the valley wall and fifty metres down. This was in contrast with the rest of the valley, which was heavily forested. Just beyond the rock was a steep, formidable gully.

I could not give up yet. I have to get to Talu, I told myself, for I doubted I could survive another night exposed to the elements. But, as I climbed down into the gully, the snow was around my waist. I made little headway and tried walking downwards, hoping to find a way up the other side. The vegetation on the other side had become thick and impenetrable.

The gully ran steeply down the valley and I continued down, looking for a good opportunity to climb out. None presented itself and I was becoming increasingly concerned as I could now hear the river roaring below me. Although the water was at least a kilometre away, the slope was steepening and the side of the valley seemed to be falling away to nothing.

Bitterly cold, hungry and exhausted, I began to reassess my situation. I was very quickly getting myself into territory from which I could not return. I no longer had the strength to get out of this gully in which the snow appeared to deepen the further down I went. I knew that my only hope, in the short term, was to get dry and warm as soon as possible. It was very probable that I might perish because of the cold. Above all else, it seemed essential that my body be found one day so that those at home, whom I loved so dearly, could continue with their lives knowing what had happened to me.

This was the attraction of the enormous rock that I'd passed. The dead campfire suggested that, if people had been there before, they might return. This would ensure my body was found. Furthermore, if Mark had made it over the pass, he would tell Tim of the circumstances under which we had separated. Chances were a helicopter would be sent up to collect me from Phedi, and when I wasn't there, they might search the valley from the air. With the large, clear area next to the rock, I could wade out into the snow and signal the chopper. 'That's if you live long enough,' I reminded myself grimly.

Angrily, I reflected how my priorities had again changed so quickly. Only several hours earlier, I was expecting to struggle up to Tharepati, to a warm fire and food. Now my ambition was to get into an area where there was a chance that my family and Gaye would eventually know what had happened to me.

I scrambled back up the very steep gradients I had skidded down and, slowly but surely, I made headway. Eventually, through all the cloud and the snow, I could see my rock. As I clambered out of the gully onto the ledge beneath it, I quickly set to stripping down and undertaking the same obsessive towelling routine that had kept me dry on the previous nights. Emptying my rucksack onto the sheltered floor, I put on dry clothes. I laid out the sodden garments and the soaked towel. Completely drenched, the ski jacket, trousers, gloves and sandshoes were of no use to me. The multiple pairs of thick woollen socks that might have warmed my numb feet seemed to taunt me as I desperately tried to wring them dry. I was now wearing a T-shirt and sloppy-jo, thermal longjohns, my pair of thick, cotton, Nepali trousers and two pairs of socks, one for my hands and one for my feet. I picked up the remaining T-shirts and light shorts and wrapped them around my head. This would at least prevent some loss of body heat. All that remained now was the reading and writing material, toilet paper, medical kit and an extra sleeping bag cover, filled with various medications. None of this would help protect me. Even with my sleeping bag, I knew that what remained of my equipment was inadequate for the temperatures prevailing that day, not to mention what they would drop to overnight.

Rocks and pebbles lay scattered across the bone-dry surface of the ledge where I now sat. At the innermost part of the ledge, there was a sharp wall of rock and only enough height to sit up. Less than a metre from this back wall, the roof rose steeply and I could stand erect for the most part, with no fear of bumping my head. From there, the height of the roof soared up until it no longer provided shelter. The ledge had only one wall where the rock and floor joined. The other three sides were open. I was surprised that so much space was free of snow, considering how open it was.

The view was hampered by the heavy snow. I could just make out some large fir trees standing straight and tall ten metres away from the rock, down in the gully that had blocked my passage. I wondered if these trees were providing extra shelter. An icy wind shook the trees but where I lay, close to the back wall, there was no wind.

I picked up one of the tool handles, surprised by its lightness. I took to digging at the soil to break up the hard floor and make a softer bed. After only several blows the handle snapped, the old timber having rotted away. It had probably been a long time since another person had visited this site. I continued digging away at the dirt, using the broken handle. Once I had got through the top layer, I took out my hairbrush to sweep away the pebbles and rocks. Working on my hands and knees with my sleeping bag pulled down around my waist, I was shivering continuously. It was difficult to concentrate. I felt apathetic and lay down upon my crude bed. Pressure on my back told me I'd missed some rocks and pebbles and I made a half-hearted attempt to clear them but some were embedded too firmly to be removed. As I lay back a second time, I accepted wearily that what I'd done was adequate. I got pen and paper out to continue writing to Gaye. It was important that she and my family would know I'd tried my hardest to extricate myself from this situation. It was with some comfort that I realised there was a far greater opportunity my body would be found here than on the tiny ledge way up the valley where I'd sheltered last night.

> I'm very hungry and very cold, too exhausted to care. I hope that God is kind enough to take my life tonight so that I may stop suffering.
> I'm not worried about dying, but I am furious at myself that I could do this to you and to my family. I had great plans for us and now they are all shattered. I know it will be harder for you than for me; you must live with the loss forever. Still, as I wrote yesterday, live your life to the fullest. Remember me kindly, but don't give up anything because of me.

I think my greatest fear at this point was that Gaye would wait in Australia for me to come back into her life. I knew that for her to get any satisfaction out of the many years she had remaining, she would need to get on and lead a life of her own. I said a silent prayer that she would accept someone else into her life as soon as possible to help the pain of her loss diminish.

I thought of the money that we'd saved in preparation for buying a car the next year and I made it clear that all that was mine was now hers. My hands were growing cold from being out of the sleeping bag and I wanted to end the letter quickly.

> It is so hard knowing that I'll die either on Christmas Eve or Christmas Day and that you will have news of my disappearance at a time when you should be enjoying yourself. I am praying for you, Gaye, that you will have a happy life. I am sorry this trip has brought you so much unhappiness and, needless to say, I wish that I had never left your arms. I will love you forever Gaye, my darling. Take care and enjoy life,
> all my love,
> James.

I could not bring myself to write to my family. I knew it was a self-ish attitude, but Gaye was young. She could get on with her life. My mother and father would be crushed by my death and it was easier for me to block out thoughts of home than to write to them some more. I felt I had said my goodbyes the previous night and I could not face the pain of repeating them.

My mouth was parched. I had not drunk water since the morning before and, although I'd eaten snow whilst walking, it had obviously not provided enough water to meet my body's requirements. The thought of having to get up to collect snow to eat seemed too much. I could feel the icy cold prickling against the skin of my face, the only part of my body that was still exposed. I knew how essential it was to keep up my fluid intake and, taking the socks off my hands, I forced myself out of the bag, over to the edge of the ledge. I filled the sleeping bag cover with snow, packing it in tightly and hurried back to my sleeping bag. I greedily munched handfuls of snow, using only one hand at a time, keeping the other hand tucked firmly between my thighs. I marvelled at the flakes as they drifted downwards. This was the first opportunity that I'd had to watch the snow falling. The larger flakes danced downwards, moving gracefully with the breeze. The hard, sleet-like pellets plummeted heavily in a straight course, directly into the snow-covered ground. The snow itself had no taste, but it felt good to be eating something. I had to swap hands every few minutes, as my fingers became painfully cold. I steadily gorged most of the snow from the sleeping bag cover and, feeling full in the stomach, a strange sensation started to overwhelm me.

There was a core of coldness in the pit of my abdomen that seemed to spread out slowly to the rest of my body. Before long, I was shivering and shaking uncontrollably, finding it painful even to breathe. I felt nauseous and, as tiredness overcame me, I thought to myself, 'You've really done it now.' I realised, as consciousness slowly slipped away, that I was paying for my greed.

When I awoke, it took a while for everything to become clear but, once I had logically thought it through, I realised what a fool I'd been to eat such a large quantity of snow when I would have already been struggling to maintain a viable body temperature. I needed to urinate. Since it could be several days before the snowfall abated and a helicopter was sent up or I walked out, I thought I should designate an area for disposal of waste. I chose a site to the left of my covered area where I could urinate over the ledge into the gully below where the smell was not likely to reach my living area. Snow was easily collected from the opposite side, to the right, and I wanted to keep my living quarters as hygienic as possible. Straight out from the back wall, I could collect snow for washing my hands.

I was no longer shivering and the temperature was tolerable. I took Charles Dickens' *Great Expectations* from my rucksack and began to read. I could not help but wonder if I would survive another long night. I ate more snow, but slowly: one mouthful of snow per two pages of Dickens. I let it melt in my mouth and drank it as water. It would never be a great quantity but I knew that, if I continued in this fashion, it would be enough.

Darkness interrupted Dickens and the cold crept in, imperceptibly at first. I curled up more tightly and started the string of prayers that I would repeat continuously for many nights to come. These included prayers for Mark and Tim, as well as all those at home. The list seemed endless and, with no restrictions on my time, I was able to think back over many, many people that I had met or known during my short life. Most of all, however, I continued to pray for my family and Gaye, especially for their health and happiness. Gaye's father, Noel, had once said to me in his loud, confident manner, 'Look James, the only two things that are important in life are health and happiness.' How true those words seemed to me now and I dearly hoped that my family would continue to enjoy both.

As night went on, I huddled more closely, slowly losing control of my muscles as they contracted vigorously, causing me to shiver, chatter and shake uncontrollably. I willed myself to go to sleep and prayed to God that, if it was His intention for me to die, to please be merciful and take my life quickly rather than having me endure another long night.

JAMES: *25 December 1991*

That was not to be the case. Although not as painful as the night before, the cold still prevented sleep. Eventually, daylight arrived and the shivering eased.

The cloud was still thick and the snow deeper than ever. Branches bowed under the weight of snow. Beyond, I could see across the gully where the vegetation was thicker. Stumps and rocks jutted out from the white blanket that covered the ground. I wondered how deep the snow would be. About 100 metres away was a tall, straight fir tree, alone on a protruding knoll. Perhaps if I could get to that tree, I might be able to see Talu on a clear day. Today there was too much cloud and it was not long before the snow returned.

I started reading Dickens again. I was more optimistic now about my survival than I had been yesterday. I did not believe it would get any colder than it had been on the past two nights. My insides still ached from eating too much snow but I felt that death was no longer imminent. The pain of the cold was now replaced with hunger – cramping and nauseating. It took all my concentration to stop thinking of food and keep my mind on Dickens' words. As the day drifted on, my stomach became tighter and I found it harder to block out thoughts of food. It didn't help to know that my family would be getting ready for their Christmas dinner at that very moment. Word of my disappearance would probably not have reached Australia yet.

Christmas dinner had always been one of the highlights of the day for our family. My parents went to great pains to get a fresh turkey which Mum would then roast, full of spicy stuffing with heaps of golden potatoes, baked pumpkin and steamed greens. Slices of thinly carved fresh ham would sit on a platter, accompanied by a range of salads. Baskets of fruit and bowls of nuts would be added to the table which would be nearly sagging under the burden. Just when we felt we could eat no more, there was a flaming, brandy-soaked Christmas pudding with golden, whipped brandy butter melted over its fruity richness. No matter how full I felt after the first course, I could never resist the dessert.

Christmas Day 1991 was a stark contrast. I could not help but grin at the irony of the sleepless night I had just spent. As a child, there was never much sleep on Christmas Eve: I knew the presents would be waiting. Last night had been another Christmas Eve but there was no excitement, only suffering. Unable to push the images of Christmas dinner from my mind, I turned to my bag of snow. Cold and tasteless, it did nothing to take the edge off my hunger and seemed a poor substitute. I smiled at the thought that I'd come to Nepal to get a taste of Third World living. I was certainly beginning to appreciate what real hunger was, something millions around the world had to put up with every day of their lives.

I felt extremely lonely and isolated. I could do nothing to ease my pain. A cloud of depression hung heavily upon me and I tried hard to dispel it with thoughts of home. I remembered the letters I had picked up from the post office. I hadn't read them since leaving Kathmandu. Two of them were Christmas cards that might raise my spirits.

I read from my mother's letter first – two long, typed pages dated 1 December. The letter talked about all the things going on back home. How mundane its contents would have seemed to me under normal circumstances! But now every word mattered. Joanne had written about a weekend that she and Calum had spent at a National Park in Springbrook, a rainforest area south of Brisbane. Those two letters sharply reinforced a lesson I had learnt during my time in Nepal: how much of what I had and did at home I took for granted. Now, as I sat under my rocky outcrop, I felt the impact of that message more strongly than ever. Reading Joanne's letter reminded me how the four of us had always said we'd go on a camping trip. We had never got around to it. I wished now that we had all made the effort to find the time. Over the days to come, when my spirits sagged, I would imagine this camping trip, the meals, the hiking and each other's company. Just the thought of this trip was enough reason to keep living: a weekend with Gaye, Joanne and Calum.

By now, my thoughts had gone full cycle and I ended up thinking too much about the possible meals of the trip. To distract myself, I now read over the two Christmas cards. The one from Gaye's mother, Beverley, was full of ordinary things which I now found intriguing. She had finished the card with the words, 'Please take care, love Bev and Noel'. Reading those words made me feel I had let the Ryan family down very badly. It wasn't much to ask – to take care of myself – and I hadn't even done that.

Gaye's card contained a warm and loving message. She said how much she missed me, making me feel as though I'd let her down even more. The printed message read 'Have the Happiest Christmas'. I could not think of many people having an unhappier Christmas than mine.

I would read the letters and cards obsessively over the days to come. Knowing those back home loved me so much helped me through the suffering that was to follow. I decided to write again to Gaye.

> My dearest Gaye,
> Well, I have survived my third night and fourth day since getting lost. I am still kicking myself. I should be in Kathmandu or, better yet, in Cairns with you. This is no way to spend Christmas. I've managed to stay warm and dry, though I am absolutely famished. I'm located in an area which would be easily spotted by helicopter in the event that one was sent to look for me.

I thought about the last sentence. Should I leave it in the letter? How would my family feel if no helicopter was ever sent into the valley and, in years to come, they read the statement. 'But surely a helicopter will come,' I thought. It was just a case of Mark getting back and telling

Tim the conditions under which we separated and Tim notifying my parents and the embassy. They might give it a couple of days, just in case I was only running late or had become snowed in but, when I didn't appear for my flight on the 28th, they'd know that something was wrong. It would be a simple case of sending a helicopter up to Phedi and searching the valley below. With the clear space beside my rock, I could easily signal the helicopter. I had proven I could beat the cold and now it was just a matter of waiting it out. All I had to do was wait for the weather to clear and the snow to stop, so that a helicopter could fly up safely into the valley. And it couldn't keep snowing forever.

JOANNE: *25 December 1991*

Christmas 1991 had been a quiet and relaxed affair. It was the first Christmas that Calum, my husband, and I had spent at home for several years. Both veterinarians, we had arrived back in Brisbane in August, after two and a half years based in the United Kingdom.

It had been wonderful to return to our families, both of which were in Brisbane. The oldest of four children, I have a younger sister, Robbie, and two younger brothers, James and John. Christmas was celebrated at my parents' farm, a quiet haven on the outskirts of Brisbane. The high-set house catches cooling breezes, allowing some relief from the oppressive Queensland summer. My parents, Ken and Janet, are both academics at the University of Queensland.

It was rather a shame that James was away. It would have been nice to have the family together. Still, we knew he would be thoroughly enjoying himself. He had been looking forward to this trip immensely and he had a big year ahead in 1992. He had surprised us all by announcing his engagement to Gaye Ryan a few months earlier. An engagement party was planned for 24 January and a June wedding in Cairns, where Gaye's family live.

I suspect that James's enthusiasm for Nepal had been dampened by leaving Gaye. Certainly she had been a little concerned at his going – not surprisingly, given the only contact she had for him was Poste Restante Kathmandu. James and I had spoken about his proposed trip before he left. He had told me how, in a previous year, a medical student doing his elective in a Third World country had died of an illness which was never diagnosed. I had expressed amazement that knowing this, James still wanted to go. He replied, in jest, that at least if he died in Nepal, he'd die happy.

39

Four days after Christmas we received a message that would totally change our lives.

JAMES: *26 December 1991*

I had been so sure that I would be able to withstand the freezing night temperatures but, after last night, I was not so sure. As with every night, I lay shivering, tossing and turning in my sleeping bag. I was careful to prevent the top from opening, to keep as warm as possible. Although still cold, I knew now the temperatures were not likely to be life-threatening as long as I remained in the protected warmth of my sleeping bag. This had given me confidence about my chances of survival. But last night, as I turned, I heard the fabric rip as it caught on a sharp rock beneath me. When the dawn came and I poked my head outside, I found down feathers scattered across my ledge and blowing into the gully below. The tear had only been small, but my constant movement during the night had let an alarming amount of down escape. I knew it would be a long and fruitless task to try to collect them from the grime of the ledge floor. My only option was to tape up the tear with the elastoplast from my medical kit. I noticed a difference in the warmth the sleeping bag provided from that night on. With my other clothes still soaked, there was little else I could do to insulate myself from the night temperatures.

JAMES: *27 December 1991*

I would take considerable time to draw up enough courage to brave the morning temperatures, depending on the need to urinate and to get more snow to quench my thirst. Some mornings, the urgency to pass urine would be considerable, as I would have lain in bed awake for hours waiting for the opportunity to go. Last night, I could not hold off. I had unzipped my sleeping bag and sat upright. The cold in those first few seconds was unbelievable, piercing every bit of my body. This heightened the need to urinate and I stood quickly, crashing my head on the rocky roof. I swore with a vengeance, rubbing the painful lump quickly forming on my head. I stumbled towards my latrine, stepping on boots and rocks, but the numbness of my feet made it difficult to tell what lay beneath them. I walked as far as I dared, shivering violently and fumbling with the knot on the drawstring that held my trousers up. With great relief I let go but could hear it landing on the ledge rather than in the gully. I dared not walk closer to the edge in case

I fell into the snow below. I could not bring myself to wash my hands; the cold was now unbearable. Frightened of hitting my head again, I crawled back to my sleeping bag and covered myself quickly. The cold had left its mark and I continued to shiver, unable to regain any body warmth for almost an hour. I had learnt another lesson the hard way. I vowed never to leave my sleeping bag at night again.

JAMES: *28 December 1991*

Dear Gaye,

I can't believe that I'm still alive. I'm still in the same spot and I accept this is where I will remain until I am found. I'd be very surprised now if I am found alive. I'm not suffering in any way, although I am a little hungry. The snow has hardly stopped. Yesterday it did in the afternoon, but it is so deep now I can't go anywhere. It must be a little warmer today as it is more sleet than snow.

I want you to realise that, for the last seven days, I've had few regrets apart from the pain I will have caused you and my family. The time I had in Nepal was good fun and I did really enjoy the trekking. I was very unlucky and very careless and I'm paying for it now.

You know, Gaye, it breaks my heart to think that today I should be flying out to Thailand and, in three weeks, we would have been reunited. I have read what I have written to you and, of course, my sentiments remain the same.

Gaye, believe me, there is a Christian God and I know He is going to take care of me after I leave this life. Please continue to have faith in Him, to trust Him and to love Him. I know He exists. This knowledge has made me very comfortable. I have no fear of death and I can honestly say that the good Lord will take care of me.

I had reached the end of the page with these words and continued on a new sheet of paper. But, before the end of the first sentence, the ink refused to flow. I tried flicking it and scribbling ferociously on the paper. I rubbed it between my hands and tried blowing into the end of the ink barrel. But it made no difference. The pen was my only means of communication with those back home, the only way I had of letting them know what was happening. It was yet another thing that had gone wrong. Since separating from Mark six days earlier, no luck seemed to have come my way. 'I should have been able to make it to Talu,' I thought, 'but this bloody snow just keeps coming down.'

I couldn't see why the pen had stopped so suddenly. There was still ink in the barrel. I resigned myself to this new aspect of fate and carefully placed it to one side in the dirt, hoping it might work again later. Losing my pen was even more distressing than the hole in my sleeping bag.

41

I'd suffered unimaginable pain every night because of the cold but had established a routine during the days by which to obtain water, sleep and help pass the time. I could not believe the snow kept falling. The rocks and stumps that had been visible on Christmas Day were now completely covered. The snow in the gully had been waist deep when I had tried to cross it on Christmas Eve: I didn't like to think how deep it would be now. When I threw a rock into the gully, it sank immediately, the snow offering no more resistance than a pool of water.

As I reflected on all the events that had led to my being trapped in this valley, I still believed that the chain of circumstances was too much of a coincidence. I felt certain that, for some reason, I was destined to be here. I tried to console myself with the thought that maybe God had work for me to do in Heaven. Thoughts like these gave me great comfort. Although not a regular church-goer, I had always believed in God. It seemed strange in a way that, only when faced with death, did I really give a lot of thought to what lay ahead of me. It was something I had denied or ignored up until that time. As I watched the sleet deepen the snow further, I had come to terms with my fate. There was no denial, no bargaining, just a resignation that the most likely outcome was that I would die. I firmly believed that there was a life for me hereafter and I was surprised how easily I accepted all this. It didn't upset me in any way for, as I'd said in my letter, I had been doing something I enjoyed when disaster had struck and I took consolation in the fact that, as I reviewed the previous week, there was absolutely nothing that I would have changed, given what I knew at the time.

My only regret was for all the suffering that I would cause back home but I realised I had to stop dwelling on this or the guilt might drive me mad. I selfishly concentrated my thoughts towards my own future. I now had my own little world, entirely detached from those so far away in Australia, and it was this world in which I would have to survive.

Whenever I thought of home, I thought of happy times in the past, purposefully ignoring any bad times at home or any arguments I'd had with friends or family. My memories of home were all good. Everything that I associated with Australia was positive and these thoughts kept my spirits from sinking.

The nights were the worst. During the day, I could sleep, read or get up to gather snow to keep my mind occupied. Once darkness came and with it the extreme cold, I would lie awake on the uncomfortable, rocky surface, shivering uncontrollably and find my spirits flagging. It was hard to remain reconciled with my situation. Although death itself did not frighten me, the pain of cold and hunger during those long, dark nights seemed a terrible injustice.

At times, to distract myself from my woes, I would tear at my hair or pinch my skin to remind myself that the pain I felt could well be worse. It was little consolation.

During the day, a disciplined routine kept me occupied and helped me survive. I would wait for the first, feeble light of dawn. I never liked the familiar but ominous curtain of thick, grey clouds that engulfed the area each morning. I still had no real idea of my location in relation to the Laurebinayak Pass, Phedi or Talu; any of the landmarks that might help me understand exactly where I was. After six days in fog and cloud, I was not even certain of the altitude. I could hear the creek below me, echoing around the valley, but it was impossible to tell just how far below me it was.

Once out of my bed of a morning, I would walk the few paces to the edge of my ledge and watch with satisfaction as my urine melted the snow. This helped reinforce in my own mind that the snow could not last forever. If only it would stop falling . . .

From there, I would walk across the front of my ledge, pausing at the centre to rub my hands clean in the snow. It was not only that I was worried about the urine contaminating my hands. During the night, my sleeping bag would sometimes slip down and leave my head exposed and I would have to scrabble in the dry dirt to replace the bag. After four days, the socks on my hands and my feet were filthy. The smell alone would make me feel like gagging. In some ways it seemed futile to wash my hands, knowing that I would have to put the socks back on later. However, before collecting my snow to eat, I thought it essential that my hands were clean so that the water I drank would be uncontaminated.

Having washed my hands, I would go to the right-hand side of my shelter where the floor rose sharply and I could climb a little way up and sit with my legs resting downwards on the sloping rock below me. Within arm's reach was plenty of snow. I could sit comfortably for quite some time until the cold drove me back into my sleeping bag.

I would reach out and dig my hand deep into the powder, picking up massive lumps of snow and packing them into the waterproof cover of my sleeping bag. Whilst doing this, I would allow myself the pleasure of tasting an occasional, small ball of snow, to relieve my parched mouth. Several scoops easily filled the bag which I carried back to my bed. At dusk, I would carry out the same routine in reverse. By the end of the day, my supply of snow would have run low. The snowfall was heaviest in late afternoon. Occasionally, the monotonous roar of distant running water would be broken by a crack as a branch gave way under the weight of snow.

I took pleasure in watching the snow fall. During the time I sat collecting the snow, I felt freer and cleaner, sitting upright, enjoying the spectacle before me. I felt it was in my interest to stretch a little whilst out of my sleeping bag. My joints creaked and cracked like an old man's. My flexibility was diminishing daily as my muscles tightened with the cold. Each day, I would find it more difficult to stretch, with a noticeable loss in the range through which my joints could move. My fingers and thumbs were the worst. The joints always felt tight and I had an urge to crack my knuckles repeatedly. I wondered what damage this would be doing to the bones as they grated noisily against each other.

Whilst I was climbing the cliff on the very first day, I had used my fists to punch into the ice and soil, trying to make sturdy footholds. At some stage I had cut open my first knuckle. At the time, the wound was insignificant and I paid it little attention. Now, however, it had become infected and the surrounding area very red and sore. I used a needle from my medical kit to dig into the wound and squeezed it hard, watching the pus ooze out. I was worried infection might spread into the joint or, worse, into my blood stream. I dabbed mercurochrome onto the knuckle as a source of antisepsis.

Having collected my snow for the night and done my stretches, I would return to my sleeping bag and read until the light was too dim to make out the words. Then I would get up and use my latrine once more, hoping to avoid the need to go again during the night.

Most days, I had plenty of time to spare and much of this would be spent reading. I had conquered Charles Dickens by the end of Christmas Day and moved on to *Silence of the Lambs*, a book I had bought the day before we set off on our trek. I had seen the movie earlier that year and many of my friends had recommended the book as being even better. I read it hungrily, absorbing every word with rapt attention. I now began my Nepali guide books. I was still mesmerised by the description of the Jomsom trek which brought back so many good memories of the two-week trek Tim and I did before Christmas. I was also captivated by the description of the Gosainkund trek and, as I read of the mountain views and glacial lakes, I couldn't help but feel resentment that I hadn't seen it all for myself.

By what I guessed to be around midday, tiredness would overcome me. The cold would have relented a little and I would be comfortable enough to drift off to sleep. My sleep would be disrupted as I couldn't roll over without waking. My dreams were pleasant and very vivid. They centred around food. Often I was at home at a barbecue lunch where piles of meat, salad and dessert would be spread out on a table, begging me to help myself. Members of my family were always with me and there would be happy conversations taking place as I ate. It was remarkable how clear these images were: the details of the house, the words that were said. It seemed as if I was actually there. When I awoke, it was hard to believe I was still trapped under this rock. Indeed, the dreams seemed so real that I would wake to find saliva had dribbled out of my mouth and left a spot on the sleeping bag.

When I realised where I was, I would initially feel colder and hungrier than ever. Then, as the minutes passed, I would slowly resign myself to the reality of the situation and desperately try to block out the pain. As I pushed from my mind all thoughts of what I knew would be going on back home, I was left with a feeling of indescribable hollowness.

Today, 28 December, had particular significance. Tim and I were due to fly out to Bangkok. Logically, today would be the last possible day that he could ignore my failure to return to Kathmandu. I had spent a lot of time thinking of Tim during the previous few nights. I considered the shocking position I had left him in. There was no doubt that Tim would contact my parents at some stage but he would be holding off for as long as possible. There was no way that he would want to pass on such tragic news or concern my parents unnecessarily over the Christmas season. If Mark had not made it across the pass, Tim would know something was wrong. If Mark had accurately reported the conditions under which we separated, Tim would have again acted promptly. There was another possible scenario: Mark had been so blasé when we'd split up that he might have told Tim I should have no problems getting back. He might have felt that, if he had made it, surely I would also. Perhaps he had dismissed my late return, suggesting that I had become snowed in temporarily. This would put Tim in a spot. He would not know how urgent my predicament was. No matter, the fact that I was not in Kathmandu today would force Tim to do something.

Another problem, as I saw it, was that I had now been in these horrendous conditions for close to a week. I knew that when people have been missing for a short time in bad weather conditions back in Australia, a large search is usually mounted and scaled down in a relatively short time if nothing is found. Knowing the conditions in which I went missing, I suspected that, apart from sending a helicopter to check the huts at Phedi, no search would take place above the snow-line. Six days had now elapsed since I was last seen. People would not believe I could survive these conditions.

I felt that as soon as the weather cleared, a helicopter would be despatched to check the huts. This would be my only opportunity to be rescued. By my calculations, it would have to fly up the valley to reach Phedi and, as it passed me, I would have a chance to signal it from the clear area next to my rock. Whether the helicopter would spot me or not was questionable. But with the depth of the snow precluding any chance of trekking out, I felt this was my only chance of rescue. It was this hope that I was clinging to now.

My mind turned back to our flight with Thai Air to Kathmandu. After six days without food, in my imagination 'airline food' was transformed from on-board snack to gourmet feast. What I would do for a glass of wine, a can of Coke, a jug of orange juice . . . The cravings started again. Tim and I had spent the last two weeks of our stay in Kathmandu pining for take-away fast food. In Nepal, I had especially missed Kentucky Fried Chicken. This was not something I ate often, but, when I did, I thoroughly enjoyed it. We had planned to use any spare hours in Bangkok finding the nearest Kentucky Fried Chicken outlet. I started to think of the menu. I fantasised about being rescued right now and getting on a plane immediately to Bangkok and going direct to Kentucky Fried Chicken. I imagined what I would select from the menu. I started with the dinner box (three pieces of chicken and chips), but I knew that would not even take the edge off my appetite. I would move on to their bacon and cheese, chicken fillet burger – two! Then, half a dozen chicken nuggets and a couple of cans of Coke help wash it all down . . . And then I had a sudden sad thought: I'd never tried those chocolate mousses that sat invitingly in the fridges. I'd have to have at least one of those.

The cramping in my stomach was becoming unbelievable and I was gritting my teeth and giving myself a headache. Having tormented myself with the thought of all this food, I was now paying for letting my imagination run riot. Once again, I worked to block out the thoughts of food and wondered if I'd ever see Tim again.

JOANNE: *29 December 1991*

To: Professor Scott
c/- W.D. Hooper
From: Tim Hooper
Date: 29.12.91

Dear Professor Scott,

I do not wish to alarm you unnecessarily but I feel I should inform you that James may be in some difficulty. He has not returned on time from a trek in the Langtang National Park area of Nepal. I expected him to be back in Kathmandu by the 25th and we were both due to fly to Bangkok on the 28th. The most likely reason he is late is that he has been snowed in as, apparently, there have been heavy falls in the area.

I have been in contact with the Australian embassy since the 27th. They have James's details and are checking with police along the trek route to try to establish where he last registered. (There are checkpoints every day or so along the trail.) If James doesn't show up today it is likely that I and an Embassy official will set off to look for him tomorrow.

The details of the trek we were on are as follows: On the 19th James and I both left Kathmandu to trek on the Helambu circuit for several days. After two days I strained a thigh muscle and was forced to turn back. James continued on with an Australian we had met. The two of them walked to the base of a pass (Laurebinayak Pass) and attempted to cross it on the 22nd. Around 11 a.m. it apparently began to snow heavily when they were halfway up the pass. James turned back and the other Australian, Mark Fulton, continued on. I have since spoken to him. He walked over the pass and returned to Kathmandu by bus on the 24th. The last information I have is, therefore, that James was walking back to a village called Gopte on the 22nd. As this is now a week ago the embassy here is cabling Foreign Affairs in Australia today.

I'm afraid this is all I can tell you at the moment. The name of the embassy official I am dealing with is Graeme Fay. I am checking this centre daily for faxes. I have spoken to my father to get your phone number and will call you as soon as possible or if I have any further news.

Yours sincerely,
Tim Hooper

So went the fax that Dr Hooper read to my parents over the phone, the first indication we had that James could be in trouble. It was a tremendous shock.

If we had not been so sure that James was able to look after himself, we could have had some warning of a hitch in his plans. But James was a clever, confident, outgoing person who had a black belt in karate and an amazing ability to land on his feet. He had travelled extensively. In fact, even when they later heard about James's lateness back from a trek, many of his friends just shrugged and said 'He'll be right'.

Somehow, James had an air of invulnerability and many did not even entertain the notion that something bad could happen to him. Gaye was not so certain.

Gaye was expecting James to call her on the 27th December. She had received a letter from James before Christmas. He had completed a trek around the Annapurna region. The rest of his time in Nepal would be spent working in a hospital.

But James had not called her on the 27th. She had waited all day on the 28th (the day James was supposed to be heading off to Thailand) and still no call. On the 29th, she could stand the suspense no longer. She telephoned my parents at lunchtime, saying that James had not called her and asking if they had heard from him. Dad made light of the situation, laughingly saying, 'What, Gaye? Do you think he's got lost?'

Mum also spoke to Gaye. No, they had not heard anything either, but they were not concerned. After all, it probably wasn't that easy to find a telephone in Nepal. Calls were also very expensive. Perhaps he was getting settled in Thailand and would then call. Perhaps James had tried and Gaye had not been home. There were many possible, logical explanations. Mum told Gaye not to worry. A matter of hours later they received the information in the fax.

About an hour after they first heard, Dad called and told me what he knew. James had not been seen since the 22nd, exactly seven days ago. When he separated from this other fellow, Mark, he was a matter of three or four days out of Kathmandu at the most.

'So, who is Mark?' I asked.

'Just another trekker they met up with on the trail,' Dad replied.

'Why did James not go back with Tim?'

'I'm damned if I know.'

'Where is Mark now?'

'He's left for Thailand. He flew out on the 27th. They are not sure where he is.'

A search party had been organised to leave first thing tomorrow. Tim and Graeme Fay were going with them as far as a town called Sundarijal. There were a number of huts at a village called Gopte and they felt it was possible James was sheltering in one of them waiting until the weather improved. It would take them at least three days to get to Gopte. The only contact with Kathmandu was through army or police radios. If there was any news, a runner would be despatched immediately to one of these radioposts. The earliest that we could expect to hear anything was Thursday.

'Thursday!' I could not believe we would have to wait so long.

The search party would comprise an experienced mountaineer by the name of Harrison, a number of sherpas and tracker dogs. They had some photos of James that Tim had taken. The plan was that they would walk up to Gopte and would talk to everyone they met in the hope that someone had spotted James. The embassy would notify all hospitals and clinics as well.

'What gear did James have? Can he light a fire? Has he got extra food?'

It seemed that James had not been carrying much equipment. He was not, as far as Tim knew, carrying any food and he did not have fire-lighting equipment. Tim thought he probably had a map. When questioned about his footwear, Tim said he had only been wearing sandshoes.

'What on earth is he thinking of?' I exclaimed to Dad, 'Trekking through snow in sneakers! Why didn't they have a guide? Why did he separate from Mark? I don't understand!' Dad obviously couldn't answer any of my questions.

There was a chance that James was making his way back to Kathmandu and would arrive even as the party was searching for him.

'There's nothing we can do except wait,' Dad told me. 'Your mother and I have to send some money to Nepal to cover the search costs. I have told them not to worry about money, to spend whatever is necessary. We have to go into Foreign Affairs in the city tomorrow to send an initial sum.'

I put the phone down in a daze. This was the sort of thing that happened to other people. Not to us. I felt sick with anxiety. I realised that, although it was possible that James was sheltering in a hut at this Gopte place, something far worse might have happened. It must be freezing up there. I thought back to the peaceful, happy Christmas we had just celebrated. There we had been, complaining about the heat as we enjoyed a turkey dinner while James might have been lying dead at the bottom of a cliff for three days. What if he had fallen and broken a leg? He could be waiting on a ledge for someone to find him and here it was a whole week later and a search team hadn't even left yet! I closed my eyes and tried to think positively. What could I do to help? Who did I know that might be of use? I had a friend who worked for Foreign Affairs in Canberra. Perhaps he could suggest something.

I rang straight away, but when it came to explaining the problem, I could not hold back the tears and Calum had to take over. When I recovered, my friend told me there was a person who was assigned to help in situations such as these, a Consular Duty Officer. He would ask this person to call me.

Very shortly, the Consular Duty Officer rang. He said that he was aware James was missing: he had received a cable from Kathmandu that afternoon. He went on to say we should organise communications. One person should be selected to whom Canberra would talk: more than one person would cause confusion. He advised me we would not need to contact Nepal direct and should not do so. All news from Nepal would be cabled to Canberra and immediately passed on. I asked him if someone should think about going to Nepal. He said that there would be nothing achieved by a family member going; things were under control and would be handled by the embassy. Dad would be the person they communicated with.

I wracked my brain for any other contacts or for anything else that I could do but could think of nothing. I tried to convince myself to look on the bright side. James was probably sitting at Gopte, waiting for the weather to clear. After all, Mark had managed to climb through new territory and cross the pass. By turning back, James appeared to have made a wiser decision. If Mark had made it, then so should he. We would probably hear that he had nonchalantly wandered into Kathmandu overnight. As I tried to reassure myself, I could not keep my mind from turning to the possibility that something was terribly wrong.

The week that followed was extremely difficult. It seemed there was nothing we could do except sit and wait. Kathmandu time was five hours behind our own. That meant that in Australia we might wake at 7 a.m. and would have to wait until at least midday before it was even light enough in Nepal to start searching. Offices closed at 10 p.m. here. It would make for some very late nights. During that week, Calum and I would arrive home and spend three or four hours on the phone, speaking to my parents, Gaye, Canberra and Nepal. Midnight would come and we would not have had dinner or changed out of our work clothes.

My parents chose not to tell many people. The last thing they needed was solicitous friends ringing to offer sympathy or help. The most important thing was being able to receive calls from Kathmandu as quickly as possible. There was nothing that anyone could do, so why cause others so much grief and worry? I did not agree completely. I had no problem telling anyone who they thought might be of use to us, but I could also understand why my parents opted not to. We just kept hoping that by Thursday the nightmare would be over.

I was working all that week except for New Year's Day and was glad of the diversion. I would have gone crazy sitting at home. People I told about James were often optimistic. Some had been to Nepal themselves and commented on how surprisingly populated the routes along these treks were. It sounded as if there were lots of huts and local people and it was not unheard of for them to care for trekkers who were unwell. Perhaps James was sitting warm and fed in a hut waiting for a rescue team, or for the weather to clear.

My parents had to organise funding in Kathmandu. A bank account would be opened in Nepal and money cabled through by Foreign Affairs. On Monday 30 December, they sent the first $1000. The only reason searching had already begun was because Tim Hooper in Kathmandu had personally guaranteed the costs would be met. Gaye was in frequent contact from Cairns. Her father, Noel, was ringing the embassy in Kathmandu daily. We later learnt that Graeme Fay had asked for permission from Foreign Affairs to communicate directly with the family, but it had been refused. The department was adamant that all communications be done by cable from Kathmandu to Canberra and then Canberra would contact Dad. Graeme had his knuckles rapped for even receiving phone calls. We felt it was vital we kept in direct touch with Nepal. After all, it was there that things were happening. We had to impress upon them how concerned we were and how they had to do all that they could. We had been repeatedly assured that as soon as there was any news, regardless of the time of day or night, Canberra would let us know immediately.

Trying to get through to Kathmandu was frustrating beyond belief. It seemed at least every second time one dialled, there would be a recorded voice announcing, 'The number you have tried is disconnected. Please try again,' or 'We are unable to place your call due to congestion on the lines. Try again in a few minutes.' Dad would get particularly exasperated, slamming the phone down and swearing. When we did manage to get through, the call would often be answered by someone speaking Nepali. We would try, time and time again, to convey a message to them. They would respond in rapid-fire Nepali. Then it might be 'One moment', and you would be left hanging on the end of the line interminably if they simply didn't cut you off.

Gaye was due to return to Brisbane from Cairns on Friday 3 January, but she and her parents decided to fly down on New Year's Day. Gaye had taken the news very badly. She had been to the doctor to get medication to help her sleep at night. She had been worried about James from the moment that he left for Nepal. When he failed

51

to phone her on Friday 27 December, she was not surprised. She had told her mother on the morning of that day that James would not be phoning. In fact on the night of Sunday 22, the day James was last seen, Gaye dreamt James had died.

I was able to immerse myself in work during the day but nights were very long. We would all feel better each morning. We would feel optimistic that James would be okay. But at 2 a.m., unable to sleep, we would agonise over James's possible fate.

I can't exactly recall when I decided that I would go to Nepal but I knew by New Year's Eve that, if no news had come by Thursday, I was going. Calum and I talked it over and he was completely supportive. It was not a decision made lightly. In nearly seven years, Calum and I had only been apart two nights. The thought of being so far away indefinitely was frightening. There was no way that he could come with me. We had financial commitments and one of us had to keep earning. As it was, I would have to borrow the airfare from my parents. I had never travelled alone and I had never been to Asia.

I'm afraid I have not been one to take a back seat and let other people handle things. I believe that, if you want something done properly, you often have to do it yourself. I did not like putting all our trust in people we did not know. I did not like the lack of control we had over the situation. I also knew if James's body was later found, or if nothing was ever found, I would forever wonder if I might have made a difference by going. I could not allow myself to carry a question like that for the rest of my life. I knew I would go if I had to, but I kept praying that it would not be necessary.

When I brought the topic up with my parents, they told me to sit tight: 'There's no point in you racing off to Nepal.'

JOANNE: *31 December 1991*

It was a horrible New Year's Eve. It had previously been arranged that the whole family go to a restaurant for dinner. Dad phoned me at work to say that he and Mum were going. After all, they could do nothing at home. I said I would rather not. I felt that someone should be by the phone at all times. It poured with rain that night and I can remember watching a television programme in which an old man was dying. It made me cry for over an hour.

Andrew Ross, a close friend of James, had visited my parents at the farm during the day, with $1000 collected from friends towards the search. He had planned to spend New Year's Eve at the north coast, but his enthusiasm had quickly waned and he had found a lift home.

JOANNE: *1 January 1992*

If New Year's Eve was bad, New Year's Day was worse. Calum and I joined the Ryans and my family out at the farm. Dad had asked that we refrain from discussing James.

'It upsets me too much,' he explained with tears in his eyes. My parents looked awful. They were not sleeping at night. Mum said she lay awake wondering what on earth had happened. I was appalled to see how badly affected they were. Neither of them seemed capable of performing even simple tasks. They would forget where they had put things and, when asked a question, would often seem vague. Dad went to drive somewhere and could not remember how to get on to a road he'd travelled nearly every day for a decade! I silently cursed Foreign Affairs for their rigid policy that all communication be through one family member. My father had every right to hear all news first hand, but he was not necessarily going to be able to interpret and recall the information that was passed on. I did not see why they could not also communicate through me. I was upset, but certainly functioning better than my parents.

In addition to the grief and concern we felt for James, there was also an element of anger, anger at James going to Nepal in the first place. He might just as easily have done his practical work in a Western country, or even locally. Anger at his decision to go on this last trek. He had said he would stay in the hospital until he left for Thailand. Anger for his attempting such a trek without a guide. I resented James for subjecting my parents and Gaye to this terrible ordeal that could so easily have been avoided.

By the same token, this did help a little to assuage the grief we felt. If (God forbid) James had perished, we knew that it was because he had been doing what he wanted to do. It was nobody's fault that he was in Nepal or had gone on that trek. In that week, I often thought of the words he had uttered to me before he left for Nepal, 'At least if I die there I will be happy.'

We made light conversation all day on that first day of 1992, even discussing James and Gaye's upcoming engagement party and plans for the wedding. We were seated around the lunch table, when Dad proposed a toast.

'Let's drink to James and his safe return.' We all raised our glasses.

I talked alone with Gaye. She had applied for a new passport. She said she had walked into the post office with tears streaming down her face and hadn't even cared. I told her that I was going to Kathmandu and asked if she wanted to come. She said that she would love to, but her parents were extremely concerned for her well-being over there. She was only just recovering from a severe bout of glandular fever and the trip was going to be extremely stressful. It was also to a Third World country where one was likely to get sick. She did not have the money to go and felt her parents would prefer not to support a journey to Nepal for her.

We all went for a walk after lunch. As we wandered past familiar landmarks, Dad took to reminiscing about James. 'This was where James first drove the tractor' and 'This was where James used to help me with the cattle.' Everything he said was in the past tense, as if James were already gone.

We took solace in the fact that it was now Wednesday and kept re-assuring each other that good news would be through within the next twenty-four hours.

JAMES: *1 January 1992*

Water trickled steadily over the edge of the rocky roof above me and fell into the gully. With the temperatures now above freezing, my spirits had also risen. It was coming to the end of the first day of sunshine and it had been glorious to bathe in gentle, warming rays. I could not fathom why a helicopter had not yet been sent to Phedi.

When I peered out of my sleeping bag, I was surprised to find the cloud had left, giving me a clear view. I sat up. The cold remained as sharp as ever, but I could now see where I was in the valley. Rays of sunlight lit the caps of the mountains opposite, craggy peaks white with snow. As the sun was rising from behind me, the mountain where I was trapped cast its shadow on the opposite wall.

What had surprised me was the vastness of the valley. I could clearly see the Laurebinayak Pass from where I was sitting. It was to the north-west, perhaps twenty kilometres away. I estimated where Phedi would lie, some distance down the mountains towards me. The range opposite was possibly as much as three kilometres away and, as I looked up at the soaring peaks, I imagined they were probably very similar to what was now above me. I recalled the cliff walls which had blocked my path upwards on Christmas Eve. As I surveyed some of the sheer cliffs opposite, it crossed my mind just how close I might have been to plummeting a great height in the white-out conditions that day.

The range of mountains opposite me continued to the south. I could not see where it ended but, directly across from my shelter, the mountains were at their highest and seemed to fall away gradually from that point. Despite their massiveness, I could see, jutting up beyond, peaks of yet another mountain range. I was a mere dot in the midst of this magnificent landscape.

I figured that the creek flowed at least 500 metres below me. I wondered whether it would be significantly warmer lower down but decided there was no way a helicopter could ever spot me on the valley floor. I had done the right thing in remaining near the clearing.

I could see no signs of civilisation. Even knowing the approximate location of the two huts at Phedi did not help. I searched for the end of the forest, for a place where intensive farming had cleared the vegetation, but could see none.

I had been missing for eleven days. Would anyone believe I might have survived so long? It was likely that the only real hope they would hold of finding me alive was if I had been sheltering at Phedi. Today was the first day of clear weather. I felt optimistic that a chopper would be sent up. All I had to do was to wave my sleeping bag and ensure they saw me. The determining factor would be if, having found the huts at Phedi empty, the searchers then scoured the walls of the valley. They may well feel this would be pointless. I weighed up the odds of everything going to plan. Not wishing to get my hopes up unrealistically, I put my chances of getting rescued at around five per cent. This didn't worry me, as I recalled only nine days earlier I had been so sure I would die that night. I had given myself no chance of surviving then. Now, I had managed to stay alive and got myself into the best possible position to get rescued. My days had not been spent just idly reading books and sleeping. I had also tried to get a fire going. I tried a variety of methods of rubbing wood together, none of which worked. I had then taken dry rocks and hit them hard against each other, trying to get them to act as a flint but there were no sparks. I was discouraged and had given up several days ago. Today, I decided it was more essential than ever to light a fire, not only for the warmth but because the smoke would be especially visible on such a clear day. My efforts were to no avail.

After several hours of daylight, I noticed that the shadow on the opposite wall had crept downwards and the tops of the tall fir trees in front of my shelter were in the sunlight. To my delight, small birds appeared. They flitted from tree to tree, occasionally landing on the bamboo grass quite close to me. They were beautiful. Until now, everything had appeared so dead I'd decided I was the only living creature on the hillside, the only one left to cope with the coldness and the hunger. The presence of these tiny birds strengthened my resolution that survival was possible in this area.

I felt an opportunity had been presented to me to gather food. For the past week or so, my hunger had driven me to sample all accessible vegetation. This included the bamboo grass, the leaves of the fir trees that had been blown my way and the lichens and moss that grew upon the rock. All were fibrous and bitter to eat. The mosses left a grittiness from the soil. The thin needles from the fir trees had a pungent, acrid taste that sent me racing to rinse my mouth. Bamboo grass was tasteless but fibrous. I could eat it but it was not satisfying. In fact, although not being too unpleasant, if anything, it aggravated my hunger. There was one little bush, a weedy sickly looking shrub that sat with me on my ledge, close to my latrine, and which had broad leaves with jagged edges. These leaves had a spiciness which, although once again doing nothing to satisfy my ravenous appetite, provided a sensation for my mouth which was on the whole quite pleasant. The problem was, as I chewed the leaves to a pulp, an overwhelming sickly flavour would develop and I would end up having to spit it out. I learned that I could get a spicy sensation by chewing on these leaves for a short time and spitting them out or swallowing them before the other taste pervaded. I was wary about eating them more than very sparingly.

I made an excursion into the clear patch to the right of my rock. The snow was incredibly deep, but I felt that there might be some form of food under the thick, icy blanket. I dug away, wearing my frozen ski gloves, until I hit rock and soil. Here were small bushes that had been covered and flattened by the snow. I tried one of the brown leaves. The taste brought to mind rotting vegetables. Even in my famished state, I could not stomach it. I imagined the bushes would produce wild berries in spring. My imagination ran wild with thoughts of the plentiful food supply that would follow winter. If only I could find enough calories to live through the winter.

I watched the small birds hopping gracefully from branch to branch, quite close to me. Although the thought of raw bird was not exactly delectable, I was desperate and here was an accessible source of protein. I slipped from my sleeping bag and gathered some rocks. Whenever a bird came close, I tried to hit it, but always missed. Often the birds would take off as I raised my arm. My shoulder ached. It was the first active movement of my upper limbs after nine or ten cold days and the jarring left my elbow and shoulder sore. But this was not the main reason I stopped: as I watched the way they moved so daintily, I could not help but feel that they had more right to be here than I did. I was an alien in this environment, not a natural predator. They had given me great joy with their beauty and movement and I was trying to destroy them. It seemed so wrong. I sat down and nibbled away at the snow, enjoying the show the birds put on for me. I would leave them be, I decided. In a short time, the cold drove me back to my sleeping bag.

More hours passed as I read, keeping one ear strained for the sound of an approaching helicopter, and I became aware of direct sunlight upon my ledge. I got out and sat in the sun for the first time in many days. I could look at the sun directly. It did not have the power of the Australian sun, but the warmth boosted my morale. I had the idea of concentrating the light from the sun through some glass onto a piece of paper to get a fire going. I looked through the medicine containers in my extra sleeping bag cover. I had two bottles of medication, both made of dark glass. When I looked at the sun through this glass, I realised that it would absorb the light rather than concentrate it.

I could, however, use the sunlight for my advantage in another way. I gathered the frozen clothes scattered across my ledge and laid them out flat in the sun. They had refused to thaw even slightly since I had found my rock and were all still as stiff as boards. Perhaps the direct sun would defrost them.

I lay out in the sun in my sleeping bag and read. I was going through Charles Dickens for the second time and enjoying it as much as the first. There were a lot of subtleties I had missed and I had a deeper perception of the story and its characters now.

The sunlight eventually reached the back wall of my rock, enabling me to lie in my usual bed and bask in warmth. I noticed the change in light and warmth as the sun moved behind the fir trees in front of me. It was quite remarkable the difference direct sunlight made. I read on, wondering if a helicopter would be sent up that day.

Towards the end of the day I dozed off and awoke at dusk to see the flaming, orange sun setting behind the mountains opposite. It was quite light for a long time after the sun had gone. Having that added warmth had been glorious. Unfortunately the night seemed even colder. The absence of cloud cover during the night meant colder temperatures.

JAMES: *2 January 1992*

Today was much the same. I woke with high expectations of seeing a helicopter pass by but, as the hours dragged on, my hopes waned. The environment had altered remarkably in these two short days. The mountain opposite me had shed much of its snowy cover, baring barren rock. Because the western face of the valley was exposed to the sun for the whole day, the snow melted much more rapidly. As for my side, the direct sun would not strike the snow until late. This meant the snowfall that imprisoned me was only slowly disappearing. Once again, I felt it was unjust. I had used logic to select which side of the valley I should climb. I had chosen the side where I knew villages would lie towards the top. Having struggled so fiercely, only to have my path obstructed and then to have become trapped under this rock seemed unfair. Now, to have to sit in an area which was shadowed for at least half the day and watch the face opposite quickly clear in the sunshine, whilst my immediate surroundings changed little, was crushing. As I mulled over how nice it would have been to be on the opposite side, it would have been an irrational choice at the time. I resigned myself, yet again, to the fact that it was fate that had left me stranded.

With the melting snow, the creek roared louder than ever. Occasionally I would be stunned by the sound of a thundering avalanche, tonnes of snow crashing towards the valley floor. The water that drizzled over the edge of my rock indicated the snow around me was thawing very slowly. I willed it to hurry. As I watched the sun's golden glow at the end of the second clear day, I realised that no search was being conducted for me. I decided it was entirely up to me to get out. Obviously something had gone wrong in communications between Tim and my parents. Had they given me up for dead and decided a search was impractical? Common sense would suggest I was unlikely to be alive. Nonetheless, I couldn't help but feel a little neglected that they had not even tried to check the huts at Phedi. I sat for a while trying to communicate telepathically with my father telling him that I was still alive and begging him to come and get me. I soon abandoned this as a waste of energy and concentrated on formulating a logical escape plan.

A few more days of sunshine and I would attempt to leave on foot. My clothes were no longer frozen but had not dried enough to be of any use. The cold, cold air that accompanied nightfall brought on the string of prayers that I'd said every night. Now I prayed harder than ever that all would be well at home and that God would be good enough to bless me with more of the fine weather I'd come to enjoy so much. I still held no fears for death for I knew that God was on my side. But the prayers and thoughts of everyone back home and how they would be suffering made me more determined than ever to escape from this prison.

JOANNE: *2 January 1992*

Thursday 2 January came and went and still there was no word of James. Gaye and her parents spent the day hunting down maps and books on the area where James was missing. I raced home from work feeling very positive, sure we would hear that James was now safe and about to come home. Calum was home before me. I burst through the door.

'Any news?' Calum shook his head.

I telephoned my parents. Every time they answered I would hear the note of hope in their voice and the disappointment when they realised the call was not from Nepal.

'There's no point getting negative,' said Mum. 'Thursday was the very earliest we could expect to hear anything. Maybe conditions are worse than they thought. Maybe the runner has not been able to get through.'

This made good sense. Calum and I discussed all the possibilities and decided that there were plenty of logical reasons why word had not come through. We would probably hear something Friday morning.

By 10 a.m. we had not heard. I could not stand it any longer and rang the Consular Duty Officer in Canberra. If I had to go to Nepal I had better start finding out what I was required to do and if Foreign Affairs would be able to help me with visas and so on. I was very taken aback by the reception I got.

'Hello,' I began, 'It's Joanne Robertson speaking. I am James Scott's sister.'

'Tch,' came the response, clearly exasperated. 'What do you want now? I've just had a very long session with Gaye Ryan. We told you we would contact you if there was any news.'

I was furious. I could not believe the lack of professionalism being shown. As a close family member of the missing person, surely I was at least entitled to a degree of tolerance if not to empathy and compassion!

'I beg your pardon,' I said, 'but I am not ringing to see if there is any news and I had no idea that you had been talking to Gaye. I am ringing because I intend to go to Nepal, despite your advice not to, and I was wondering if you could give me any information about visas. I am terribly sorry if you find talking to us such a stressful thing, but we are under a little bit of a strain ourselves you know.' I could not help the sarcasm.

He did not apologise. He repeated the stand of Foreign Affairs that there was nothing to be achieved by a family member going to Nepal but, if my mind was made up, the best person to contact would be Linda Griffith, the Honorary Royal Nepali Consul-General in Brisbane.

Dr Griffith was exceptionally helpful. She was most sympathetic when she heard what had happened. She had lived in Nepal for several years and said she could have a visa for me by the afternoon. She also had a number of contacts in Kathmandu that might prove useful.

'They usually find the people that go missing though, don't they?' I asked. 'It's just not possible for someone to vanish into thin air.'

Dr Griffith was silent for a moment. 'Sometimes nothing is ever found,' she said, 'but it is absolutely essential that someone go to Nepal.' I dropped my passport off and then I decided to call by and see my parents.

Dad told me a letter had arrived from James, written before he went on the trek. I picked it up and looked at the familiar scrawl but could not bring myself to read it.

'Dad,' I began, feeling nervous about broaching the subject of my trip to Nepal. 'I've put my passport in for a visa for Nepal and just had all my shots. The next flight out is Tuesday. If there's no word by then, I'll be on it.' He did not object. I guess he too had started to realise it was imperative that someone go.

I arrived home that night to hear there was still no news. Gaye had rung Kathmandu to try to find out what was happening. It seemed that contact with the search party had been lost.

'How the bloody hell can that happen?' I said to Calum. 'For God's sake! Why don't they have walkie-talkies? What sort of a search party is it that they can't even organise a message back?' We could not believe it. James's life was depending on these people finding him and it seemed they had got lost themselves! I was sick of ineptitude. I phoned the embassy in Kathmandu. It was just after 10 p.m. our time which meant there should still be someone in the embassy office.

I got a connection fairly promptly. A couple of far-away peals were audible from the other end, although almost hidden in a harsh static. This, like rubbing salt into a wound, echoed the tremendous differences geographically as well as technically between Australia and the Third World. Then the phone was answered by a Nepali woman.

'I am calling from Australia. Put Graeme Fay on.' The dreaded 'One moment' echoed faintly down the line. This time, however, it was just a short break before a woman came on the phone.

'Who am I speaking with?' I demanded.

'This is Auli Uotila. I am the Deputy Head of Mission here.'

'My name is Joanne Robertson. I am ringing from Australia about James Scott. What's going on over there?'

'Joanne, we have sent up a helicopter this afternoon to try to locate the search party. Tim and Graeme went up in the helicopter. It has just returned. We have yet to hear what they have found. Ring back in fifteen minutes.'

'Right. Fifteen minutes.'

My anger had faded for the moment. That fifteen minutes seemed to take forever. The television was on but we did not take in a word of it. I looked at my watch every thirty seconds. When the fifteen minutes was eventually up, I forced myself to wait another five minutes before I rang, just to give them plenty of time. Nervously, I dialled the number. Auli answered.

'Joanne, the search party was found near Kaphalgari. That's well down in the Helambu area. They met with a group of Canadians at Tharepati who have given a highly probable sighting of James down below the snowline heading back to Kathmandu.

'What?' I squealed into the phone, 'You mean he's been spotted?'

'The Canadian party were unanimous that a lone trekker they spotted was James. This trekker was down below the snowline in a well populated area and heading back to Kathmandu. They saw him on 30 December which should mean he'll be back in Kathmandu at any time. The search party also found someone else who saw him as well.'

'This is wonderful news,' I said. 'So you're pretty sure it's James?'

'Yes. We feel there is at least a 95 per cent chance it's him and that he's out of the danger area.'

'That's just marvellous. I assume that you will be cabling all the details to Canberra immediately?'

'Yes,' replied Auli.

'Okay, we'll hear the details from them, then. Keep us posted!' I hung up with a real feeling of euphoria. Although not as good as actually having found him, it was a hell of a lot better than having found a body. I wasted no time in ringing my parents.

Dad asked me a string of questions I could not answer. The names Auli had mentioned meant nothing to me. 'The best thing to do is sit tight until Canberra phones you. Kathmandu is sending a cable immediately, so you should hear soon,' I told Dad. I remember being disappointed at his response. This was the first positive piece of information we had received but Dad did not sound convinced or overly happy. Maybe it seemed too good to be true to him.

I then rang Gaye's flat. Her father, Noel, answered, and I told him the good news. Again, he wanted questions answered and I assured him that we would know the details once the cable came through from Canberra.

It was nearly 11 p.m. I sat cross-legged by the phone waiting for Dad to ring back. The phone finally sounded at midnight. Dad had heard nothing from Canberra. We decided to wait another half-hour. Thirty minutes later, there was still no word. Dad rang Canberra himself. He was told that there had been no helicopter flight and no one knew anything about a sighting of James. Dad told them that we had been in contact with Kathmandu and knew there was one and that a cable had been sent. Foreign Affairs assured him that there was no cable. We could not understand why there was no information through. I, however, felt a lot better. James had been seen! He was below the snow line! I slept a lot better that night. Things were going to be fine.

We learned the next morning that Canberra had in fact received a cable the night before (which we later found had been marked 'immediate precedence' in Kathmandu). Dad asked them why they had not let us know immediately. He was told that someone had felt it could wait until the morning and had filed it in a 'non-urgent' category. Strange that they could consider a definite sighting not urgent and so much for their assurances that we would be alerted to any news as soon as they knew themselves . . .

JOANNE: *4 January 1992*

On Saturday afternoon we went out to see my parents. They had a number of maps with them and, for the first time, I had a chance to study the area. The information in the cable had left a number of questions unanswered. The town where the Canadians had seen James was not marked on our maps. We still did not understand why the search parties had not got a message through earlier. Where had James been between 22 and 30 December? We wrote out a list of questions and I phoned Graeme Fay at the embassy in Kathmandu.

Graeme patiently answered all my queries. James had been spotted by a large party of Canadian trekkers the search party had met at Tharepati on New Year's Eve. I checked our map. It was the village before Gopte. At Tharepati, one could take three possible directions: first, south towards Kathmandu following the western leg of the Helambu trek (which is how both James and, subsequently, the search party had arrived at Tharepati). Secondly, one could head north-west up to cross the Laurebinayak Pass (this was the route that James and Mark had taken from Tharepati). The final route was to the south-east to the eastern leg of the Helambu trek that followed another route to Kathmandu.

The Canadians had arrived at Tharepati from this last direction. They had told the search party they had passed a lone trekker the day before, halfway between the villages of Shermathang and Tarke Ghyang. They looked at the photos the searchers had of James and all agreed it was him they had seen.

'Did James talk to them?' I asked Graeme.

He said that no conversation had taken place. The Canadians told the search party that this person had seemed in some distress. He was walking resolutely with his head down. One of them described him as 'desperate'. The person was, however, walking strongly with no obvious injury. As the Canadians had seemed so certain that it was James, the entire search party had headed off along the route that the Canadians had just travelled.

This would later cause us tremendous concern. The search party was a matter of hours away from Gopte when they met the Canadians. Surely it would have made more sense for the party to split up, so that at least someone went up to Gopte to see if James was sheltering in the hut there, in case it was not James they had seen? When I put this to Graeme he said that the way the Canadians described James had made the searchers feel they should find him as soon as possible. The leader of the party, Carl Harrison, when later asked the same thing, was far more blunt: 'If he was above Gopte, he'd be dead. It was more important to try to find him alive.'

I asked Graeme about the other sighting. Graeme replied that the search party, as they followed the trail the Canadians had come along, encountered a lodge keeper who had also seen a solo trekker. Here, there was some confusion. The lodge owner was not so certain he had seen James. He reported seeing the hiker about twenty minutes' walk from where the Canadians passed him. The lodge keeper saw this trekker mid-morning. The Canadians claimed to have seen James after lunch. If they had both seen the same person what had he been doing for all that time, when it should have taken him less than thirty minutes to cover the distance?

'But there must be lots of solo trekkers on the paths,' I said. Graeme denied that this was so. Being the coldest time of year, there were not many trekkers and few travelled solo.

It seemed odd that James might have chosen to descend via a different route from the one that he would have followed with Mark on the way up. Wouldn't it have made more sense to return along a familiar route? Graeme explained that there was a road partially along the track that the Canadians reported seeing James on. It could be that James had seen this on his map and headed for Melamchi Pul Bazaar where there was a bus service to Kathmandu. This would make sense, as James would be wanting to return as quickly as possible.

'Have any of the bus drivers seen James?' I asked. Graeme said that the search party had spoken with all the bus drivers they had encountered and none of them could recall seeing anyone fitting James's description.

'We are going to have a meeting to decide what to do next,' Graeme told me. 'I suggest you ring back in an hour or so.'

We studied the maps in the light of what we had learnt from Graeme. One thing that struck us was the enormous number of minor trails in the Helambu area. One of the maps also showed lots of dwellings. James could be in any of these. They all had to be searched.

I guess, in retrospect, I should have started to accept then that the Canadians' so-called definite sighting was anything but that. If it was James, why had he not stopped and spoken with the Canadians? He would have to know that we would be searching for him! Why had he not left messages with everyone he met, telling them who he was, or asking for help if he needed it? Why had other people not seen him? James's bright red hair made him stand out. But, from Graeme and Carl's comments, it seemed that this sighting was the only real chance of finding James alive and we were clinging strongly to that.

We phoned Kathmandu again after an hour. We were able to speak with Carl Harrison as well as Graeme. It had now been decided that the search team would split into two groups. The first would comprise six men who would head off into the Helambu area. They would split up into three groups of two and would scour every path and speak to every person. They would take with them two copies of a reward poster to distribute. A reward of 20,000 rupees would be offered for finding James alive and 10,000 rupees for finding his body. This search party would leave first thing on Sunday and would not return for at least five days. The sums of money being offered were not large. To find James alive would only earn the person just over A$600. We were assured that, in Nepal, this was a significant sum of money, more than a year's wages for most. We also wanted to know why there should be a reward for finding a body. It seemed that for a local person to admit to seeing a Westerner's body could cause them trouble. Without a reward, locals were more likely to ignore a corpse.

A second team would go back up to Gopte and search between there and the pass. They would take a tracker dog and be flown up by helicopter. Leaving on Monday they would also take at least five days to complete their search. All hospitals would be checked again and a missing person poster printed in English distributed around Kathmandu.

This all seemed to make sense. Dad talked to Carl for a while longer. He told Carl that he refused to accept that a person could just vanish off the face of the earth, that James had to be somewhere. Carl agreed but indicated that the terrain could be very hostile. It was possible to get lost very easily. Once a trekker had turned up in Kathmandu after being missing for twenty-three days. He had been wandering in forest just north of Kathmandu, totally disoriented.

We only had the sighting by the Canadians as an indication that he could be below Gopte. We still did not know why he and Mark had separated. It was important we try to speak to Mark. Gaye had also received a letter from James where he mentioned a man called Krishna with whom he was to be having dinner the night before he and Tim headed off. Gaye wanted someone to speak to Krishna as well.

The search party that had been out the previous week had cost about US$250 daily. The one positive aspect to searching for James in Nepal was that wages were reasonably cheap. Employing a mountaineer of Carl's standing was more expensive, but still inexpensive compared with what wages would be in a Western country. For the services of the sherpas, we were being charged from US$10 to $30 daily per sherpa, depending on their skill and the conditions they were searching under. Carl was charging us US$100 per day. The use of the helicopter was the largest outlay. It would cost around US$800 per hour. I wondered what would happen to people who could not manage to fund a search.

Early in the week, my parents had faxed over all details of James's travel insurance. None of this searching would be covered by James's policy unless he were found injured or a body located. In either of these situations, the cost of the particular search that had led to the discovery and the evacuation of the injured person or the body would be met. If it took a hundred searches to find the injured person or the body, ninety-nine would not be covered. In a country like Australia, the government will fund a certain amount but of course, in a place like Nepal, with people starving on the streets, the government could not possibly justify expenditure on tourists who go missing.

We were extremely fortunate. We were able to say, 'Money is not important. Even if it costs us a million dollars, in ten years' time it will not matter what it cost, it will only matter that we know that everything was done.' My parents had several assets: two houses and some land. If it came to it, they would sell them to cover costs. In the meantime, we were very touched by the generosity of friends, and the Ryans were pledging support too.

JAMES: *4 January 1992*

I watched the shadow on the opposite wall sink towards the valley floor as the sun began to climb. Across there the mountains were now largely free of snow. The morning trickle of water over the roof of my rock had not yet started, but I knew the monotonous dripping would begin in a few hours. I had been allowed another small delight. The dripping water had frozen during the nights, forming icicles of various shapes and sizes. Some clung firmly to the rock while others seemed so precarious I waited for them to fall. It was beautiful to watch their shapes change as the day warmed and the dripping started.

This was the fourth clear day. The fir trees were almost free of snow now. The stumps and rocks which had disappeared after the heavy snowfall now poked through, reaffirming that the depth was slowly but surely diminishing.

I eventually forced myself to get on my with my daily routine. Lazily stretching before unzipping my sleeping bag, I rose and stepped over to my latrine. In due course I found myself sitting on the right side of my ledge, gathering snow. Daily temperatures now rose enough to melt the snow. As the night temperatures dropped below zero, the snowmelt refroze. It had lost its powdery quality and was now ice-like and more compact.

I drove my hand into the bank of snow, grabbing large chunks to eat. It was now difficult to push through. If I were to walk through now I would not sink as far as I'd done when it was powdery. It was a beautiful, clear day and the clothes on the ground were almost dry. My sandshoes were now certainly wearable, although still damp. I decided to venture away from my rock.

It was not just escape that was on my mind. About thirty metres across the steep gully to my left were trees that appeared to have fruit upon them. I noticed them when the weather cleared. The trees were squat, with a wide canopy of broad leaves and I could see conical shapes at the tips of the branches. Desperate hunger convinced me these thickenings, whether buds or fruit, might be edible. Beyond was the knoll with the lone fir tree where I believed I would get a good view and see how to reach Talu or another village.

My socks were now dry so I had no fear about getting the pair that I was wearing wet. Their ingrained grime repelled me and I would be happy to change when I returned. I pulled my shoes on, and stepped out into the ice. I sank to just above my knees. I climbed steeply down into the gully. I picked my way carefully among the rocks, stumps and fallen trees. In places my foot plunged through the ice into a deep hole. I struggled on, working steadily towards the 'fruit' tree, with my sleeping bag cover ready to be filled.

It was a battle to reach the tree. As I got closer, I saw that the bunches were not fruit, but only buds. Still, I thought these could be edible. Breathing heavily, I snapped a branch off roughly. I broke off a bud, bit into it deeply and spat it out in distaste. The bitterness convinced me it was poisonous. Annoyed, I fought my way up the opposite wall of the gully.

I was surprised at how much strength and fitness I had lost in such a short time. It was just on two weeks since I'd become lost and, although I was noticeably thinner, I really hadn't expected it to affect my vitality as much as it had.

I had to stop and rest every few steps. When I finally stood next to the tall fir tree twenty minutes later, I felt that I had really achieved something. I looked out over the valley with great expectations, hoping to see Talu or, at the very least, some cleared farmland. Fog and mist covered the southern end of the valley towards Talu. I could see clearly for at least ten kilometres but there was nothing but rocks and trees and cliffs and snow. My heart sank as I looked at the distance and the terrain that I would have to negotiate to reach civilisation and I knew that, as long as the snow remained, I would not escape.

I stumbled back, my sleeping bag cover empty. The return journey was slightly easier as I was able to follow my own tracks. Once under my rock, I removed my sandshoes, socks and sodden trousers. After towelling down, I put on my dry clothes and examined my feet for the first time in two weeks. They still had a worrying hint of blue to them but there were no black patches. The skin was beginning to peel away in places but there was new growth underneath so I knew this was not ulcerative. What worried me most was the lack of feeling. I touched my toes lightly and felt nothing. Using the tips of my fingers, I gently touched my legs, starting at my knees and working down to my toes to find where the feeling was dulled. The backs of my heels, the arches and soles of my feet and all of my toes were numb to light touch. I looked in my medical kit. The only sharp object was a pair of scissors. Testing for pain, I pressed the point of the scissors over the same area. I could feel pain all the way down both legs but, in the same area where sensation to light touch was lost, so was the feeling of pain. I wasn't quite sure what to make of this. Were my feet frostbitten? The pulse on the arches of my feet and the inside of my legs was still strong. 'The large vessels can't have been damaged,' I thought. I pressed more firmly now with my thumb into the arch of my foot. I could feel the dullest hint of pressure but that was not what I was looking for now. I took my thumb away and watched to see how long it would take for the colour to return. It remained white for as long as I watched. I tested over the inside of my foot with the scissors, pressing more firmly. I could not accept that I had lost all sensation in my feet. I was sure, if I pressed hard enough, I would eventually feel something. I pushed the scissors harder into my foot and watched the skin break and the blade of the scissors pierce the flesh. With the tip of the scissors penetrating perhaps half a centimetre, blood finally oozed to the surface. I still felt no pain. I was both shocked and curious: shocked because I believed it suggested a poor prognosis for my feet, and curious as to the exact cause of the numbness. Obviously, I had reached an area where blood was still flowing yet for some reason the nerves weren't working properly.

It also occurred to me the danger I had now put myself in. I had so far avoided frostbite and subsequent gangrene. By breaking the skin in an area not well supplied by blood, I had greatly increased the risk of infection. I was still troubled by the abscess on my knuckle. The last thing I wanted was an infection in my foot. I dabbed mercurochrome into the cut.

I scrambled around my ledge, gathering up the warm socks which, until today, had been sodden. I laid out to dry the thin, old grey socks that had offered so little protection and happily replaced them with two pairs of thick, woollen ones. It made no difference to the feeling in my feet but I felt it important to thaw them as soon as possible.

It had been a disappointing morning and now I had grave fears about my feet. Even if I could get out of this, would they require amputating? I felt strongly that, without my feet, I really didn't want to escape. The pessimism was difficult to deal with. I had tried so hard to rise above the situation. Careful analysis of the events that morning and the condition of my body showed that I had no chance of escaping while the snow remained. I knew that I could not expect to live without food for more than seventy days. I recalled the IRA hunger striker, Bobby Sands, who had survived almost this long. If he could do it, so could I. After all, I had been solidly built to begin with; I was fairly inactive and the surrounding temperatures would lower my metabolic rate and decrease my energy requirements. Even if I couldn't walk when the time came, I could still crawl out on my hands and knees. I recalculated the odds and decided the chances of surviving were one in a million. Yet I had to remain optimistic. I had to have a goal. I could live through these awful conditions only if I had hope. Seventy days would be my new goal. I knew it would be difficult but sincerely believed it was not impossible.

To occupy myself, I returned to my reading. I had finished Charles Dickens for the second time and was now well into my second reading of *Silence of the Lambs*. The first time I had lapped the words up with excitement. Reading it for the second time disturbed me greatly. The only people with whom I now had any contact were the characters in the novels – in this case, a tale of two psychotic killers. I finished the book and set it down beside me, sick to my stomach. I vowed not to read it again and was tempted to throw the book into the gully but, watching the sun set over this peaceful white landscape and hearing the birds' evening call, I felt the book would be a pollutant.

I carried out my usual routine of gathering snow, swallowing quite a lot as I sat there admiring the mountains before moving to the other side to use my latrine. I was now able to wear my ski jacket that had finally dried and it brought me considerable warmth. The clean pair of socks on my hands were a welcome relief after the pungent pair I had been wearing for almost two weeks. I said my long string of prayers and, after many hours of thinking about home and food and family, I drifted off to sleep.

I awoke during the night, sore on the side where I had been lying, but as I rolled over the extra warmth that I now felt was wonderful.

This was the first night in a long time that I hadn't spent shivering. Instead, for a few hours, I had enjoyed the peace of wonderful dreams about my family and Gaye.

JOANNE: *5 January 1992*

Sunday was a very long day.

In the morning, Dad offered to come to Nepal with me. I felt a surge of relief. I'd not had a moment to think about it but deep down I was very worried about having to go alone. My relief did not last. I recalled how distraught he and Mum were. They were not really functioning well. Also, Kathmandu was, by all accounts, a filthy place. What if he got sick? It would only serve to double the pressure on me. Mum was very against the idea. It wasn't easy, but we persuaded him it would not be for the best.

Dad had also been thinking overnight about the proposed search plan. He was angry that we had funded a search already that had come within several hours' walk of Gopte, yet had not sent anyone to the village, and now they wanted to charge us for a helicopter to drop a search party off there. It was an indication of the frustration we were all feeling that he rang the embassy to double-check about the need for this second flight.

'I don't want to go financing any junkets,' were his words. We felt that we were being messed around. We were thousands of kilometres away with someone we loved seemingly vanished. We had been notified of James's disappearance not through any official channels but by a fax from Tim to his father, who had then contacted my father. Tim had not seen James for nearly a week before he heard there was a problem and the last person to have seem James was someone he hardly knew. And this person, Mark, had never spoken to anyone official and was now apparently uncontactable in Thailand!

After some discussion, Dad agreed to the use of the helicopter. It would save the search team several days of walking, which might mean we would hear something sooner.

I got home from work quite late in the evening feeling depressed and exhausted. The reality of having to get on a plane to Nepal to search for my brother, or perhaps his body, was starting to sink in. I would leave in less than thirty-six hours. I voiced my concerns at going alone.

'The only other person I can think of who I could even ask is Andrew,' I told Calum. Andrew Ross was a long-time friend of James. I thought about it. I knew that, not only for my sake but also for

Calum and my parents' peace of mind, it would be much better to have a companion. I called Andrew.

'Andrew, this is Joanne. Look, I know this is a terrible imposition and I'm not giving you any notice. Please don't feel obligated to say yes. It's just that I'm going to Nepal on Tuesday by myself and I'm really scared. Is there any way that you could possibly come with me?'

Andrew did not hesitate. 'Okay.'

I could not believe my ears for a moment. Then, I nearly wept with relief. I did not know it, but Gaye and Beverley had had a similar thought and had already approached Andrew, offering to pay his fare if he would go with me. That had given him some time to make arrangements at work. Calum was much happier that I would have some company. Also, Andrew was just a little further removed to help make decisions.

JOANNE: *6 January 1992*

The next day was a blur of activity. Beverley gave us some money the Ryan family had collected. Mum and Dad also had to send another $5000 to Kathmandu. From there, we went to the university where we dropped off a photo of James and Gaye at the photography department. We asked them for 250 copies in black and white, a large task which they did without flinching, cropping and enlarging James's image. We also made an extra 200 photocopies of the picture we had faxed to Nepal for use in the missing person posters. I wanted to ensure that I had plenty to give to people I met. We collected Andrew who was feeling very sore from his hepatitis A injection. Neither of us had sufficient time to be immunised against cholera or typhoid.

We got travellers' cheques and plenty of American dollars. We were quite prepared to bribe people in Kathmandu to get help. I asked Andrew if he had ever bribed anyone before. He hadn't; that made two of us.

It was time to drop Andrew home and do some last minute shopping. Before I knew it, it was 5 p.m. and we were heading back to my place. As the pace slackened, I thought of something I had to know before I left. I asked my parents what they wanted me to do if we recovered a body.

'Let the embassy and travel insurance people organise that. Just get yourself on a plane home.' I did not mention it but I knew there was a chance that the body would have to be identified before it left Nepal.

'You just be very careful over there, Joanne,' my father told me.

'Don't you go going up in any helicopters and don't do any trekking. I don't want you to leave Kathmandu. If anything happens to you over there it will be the end of your mother and me. You know that, don't you?'

I looked out the window of the car, my vision blurred from tears. I felt overwhelmed at the responsibility I was assuming. Everything had happened so quickly. A week ago I barely knew where Nepal was and now I was on my way there. My parents and Gaye would be relying on me to ensure everything was done. What if I failed? I blinked the tears away and pulled myself together. 'I'll be careful.'

At home I rang Linda Griffith to see if I could come over for some letters of introduction. I had not been home long when I got a call from Gaye. Some distressing information had come to light. In Kathmandu, as the search party had been getting ready to board the helicopter for Gopte, Ingo Schnabel (the leader of the search party's dog squad) had received a note from a German trekker called Mateus who had been travelling alone in the area where the Canadians had supposedly spotted James. It now seemed highly likely that it had been this German the Canadians had seen.

'So why doesn't someone ask the Canadians?' I asked Gaye.

'No one knows where they are.'

Again, this just seemed incredible. An entire search party had spoken to this group of Canadians and, as a result, had made a major change in plans, and no one had thought to ask for a means of contacting them.

'What about the German?' I asked Gaye.

'He's left the country.'

'Shit!' The only way we would ever know for sure if the Canadians had seen James or had seen this German was by asking one or both of them and, just like Mark Fulton, they were uncontactable.

I did not have time to brood on this for long. Calum arrived and we went to Dr Griffith's place. She has an amazing house full of art and crafts, I guessed from Nepal. She reviewed each of her contacts with me. They included a number of influential businessmen and a general from the army. She was also able to give me the name of the head of the Trekking Agents Association of Nepal. She told me a little about Kathmandu. Women were not always regarded with the highest esteem. It would help if I made a concerted effort to present myself as well as I could. In addition, she suggested that, in view of my veterinary degree, I call myself 'Doctor Robertson' which would command more respect. She was also very honest about the chances of finding James. It was now 6 January. James had last been seen fifteen days ago. She described how treacherous the terrain was and the dangers that lone trekkers could face. She said she knew of a man who went to Nepal looking for his son. He had stayed six weeks, spent $100,000 and found nothing. She conceded there was a chance that James was injured somewhere and being cared for but that in such cases the villagers were pretty prompt about getting word out.

'I guess it's a case of having to know what happened,' I told her. 'Even if it's to find a body. We can't spend the rest of our lives not knowing.'

As soon as we arrived home, I decided to telephone Graeme. 'What the bloody hell are you people doing over there?' were my words to Graeme. I asked him about the note that Ingo had received and reiterated our disbelief that the entire search party had followed what now seemed to be a totally wrong lead. I also indicated I could not understand why the Canadians had not been found.

'Kathmandu can't be such an enormous place, for goodness sake!'

I told him that Andrew and I would be arriving on Wednesday.

I had a few other calls to make that evening. I rang Kimberley, my half-sister in Edmonton, Canada. I knew she had been seeing a psychic who had made a number of correct predictions. I had toyed with the idea of asking her to consult him and now decided we had nothing to lose. She would have to fly to Toronto to speak with him face to face, but immediately agreed to do so. I rang some close friends and asked them to make sure Calum was okay for me.

It was past midnight before we went to bed. I was feeling very negative and depressed. I burst into tears. They were tears of grief for my brother, a young man with so much to live for who had quite possibly met his death under such unnecessary circumstances on an icy mountainside. And tears of anguish and fear, anguish at the impending separation from my husband and fear at what I might find once I got to Kathmandu.

JOANNE: 7 January 1992

The morning of Tuesday 7 January was fine and warm. I think it only really struck me as Calum was getting ready to go to work that I was actually going to go to Nepal. Calum was marvellous. Not once did he object to my leaving. When the moment came to say goodbye, I dissolved into tears. We held each other for a long time and Calum asked me to be careful and to come home as soon as I could. I nodded, we kissed and he went.

In the plane I watched the runway blur as we took off. Finally I really felt I was doing something constructive. I resolved that, no matter what, I would leave no stone unturned.

The flight to Bangkok was uneventful. I read about Nepal and studied maps of the area and descriptions of the Helambu and Gosainkund trek. Once I started reading, I could see why James had selected this particular trek. The descriptions of villages, mountain passes and the glacial lakes sounded wonderful. As I read a description of the trek James was on, a few questions came to mind. Our information was that James and Mark had separated about two hours above Gopte and that above Gopte there was virtually no shelter. However, one of the books mentioned a place called Phedi. Here, about four hours' walk beyond Gopte and two hours from the pass, there were supposedly a couple of huts for trekkers. Could it be that James and Mark had stayed at Phedi on the night of the 21st and not Gopte?

There was also mention of two different paths from near the pass back down to Tharepati: one that went via Gopte (presumably the one that James and Mark had used on the way up) and another much more rugged trail that bypassed Gopte. Could James have tried to take this other path back to Tharepati? I really hoped he hadn't as, by all accounts, this path was extremely dangerous and almost certainly fatal in bad weather. Several books also mentioned a cave at Gopte. I made a note to ensure that it had been searched, in case James had sought shelter there.

There were also the possibilities that James had changed his mind about turning back and decided to try to cross the pass and catch up with Fulton or that he had lost the trail and headed south-west to reach a village called Talu. Marked on the map was a river called the Tadi Khola that crossed the trail James and Mark would have been on and then ran towards Talu. If James had lost the trail it would make sense to try to follow a river that led to a village. On any of these he could have fallen, reached shelter injured or be lost and trying to find a village.

As I read more about Nepal's geography and trekking, I started to appreciate the type of landscape we were talking about. The Himalayas have many peaks over 8000 metres in height. That sort of altitude is almost incomprehensible to an Australian, where Mt Kosciusko is the highest peak at just over 2200 metres. Mount Blanc in Europe peaks at just over 4800 metres. The pass James was attempting took him to a height of 4600 metres. What on earth was he doing up there in sand-shoes? One of the first symptoms of altitude sickness was confusion. Could this have made James make irrational choices?

From Bangkok airport we caught a taxi to the Central Plaza Hotel. We went to the desk and I felt a wave of nauseous anxiety as we waited to see if there were any messages. If James's body had been found in the course of the day's searching, this was when we would find out. But, no. We went to our room and headed for bed.

It seemed my eyes had only just closed when the jangling of the telephone startled me. Andrew and I sat up in our beds and looked at each other: I could feel my heart pounding:

'What time is it?'

'Midnight,' Andrew replied.

'I'm too scared to answer, Andrew. Will you do it please?'

Andrew reached for the receiver. I watched his face as he spoke.

'I see,' said Andrew. He shook his head and, covering the mouthpiece with his hand, said 'It's nothing. Don't worry.'

I realised I had been holding my breath. I let it out and started to breathe slowly and deeply to slow my racing heart. It was just hotel reception wanting to let us know that Thai Air had arranged for us to be taken to the airport and that they would be paying our hotel bill. I still don't know why the reception thought they had to wake us for that.

The hotel breakfast was a huge buffet. We joked about how James would have loved it. 'When we find him, we'll have to come back this way so we can have breakfast here again!' we laughed.

JAMES: *7 January 1992*

'What on earth is that?' I thought, as the screaming echoed across the valley again. I couldn't imagine what in the world would make such a noise. It had an insane, human quality about it. But even the patients I had seen in the lock-up wards of the psychiatric institutions didn't sound this terrifying. It sounded like someone in unimaginable agony, high-pitched like a child or a baby.

The screams were coming from the hillside above me and I could hear the cracking of wood. I scanned the bushes and before long a large, black animal appeared. My immediate thoughts were positive.

'It's a buffalo or a cow!' raced through my mind, for I couldn't think of any other animal of this size that might be found in the region. I grew excited. I'd seen the villagers riding the buffaloes and cows around the trails and I thought, 'Maybe I can ride out on the back of this animal.' It seemed to have little difficulty in moving through the bushes in the snow. A second fate was for it to be butchered. The meat would be enough to keep me going for the rest of the winter . . .

But then, as it screamed again, logic prevailed: no cow would ever sound like that.

I was out of my sleeping bag by now and burrowing into my rucksack. I searched for my scissors, keeping one eye on the animal, maybe one and a quarter metres tall, pushing through the shrubs and occasionally rolling over. I grasped my scissors as it emerged from the bushes. Its head was not as large as a cow's, but its forearms and shoulders were immense. It roared again. 'My God! It's a bear!'

Strangely enough, I felt little or no fear. After all, I had faced death many times already. The only difference was that this risk was another living creature which was in many ways easier to deal with. As the bear snorted and screamed and waddled around in the snow just thirty metres away, I considered what to do.

One in a million were the odds I had given myself of surviving. Less than thirty metres away from me was a winter's supply of food. What were my chances of killing it? As I looked at those forearms and shoulders again, I couldn't really give myself favourable odds, especially given the scrawniness to which my own body had shrunk. Was one in a thousand too optimistic? I really couldn't lose. If the bear was able to kill me, all this suffering would be over; if I was able to kill it, my chances of getting through winter would be far greater.

'Come here!' I yelled at it and whistled loudly. Its ears pricked. It screamed in reply. I repeated the whistling, waiting to see what it would do. The bear stormed back and forth angrily, not coming any closer, but pacing as if undecided. We eyed each other off for a good couple of minutes, my body tense for the battle. But the bear began to move away and, although it continued to scream, it seemed to have lost interest.

I continued to whistle, for in those short, tense minutes, I had already decided what part of its stocky neck I was going to carve into with my scissors. I imagined how I would skin the beast and freeze the meat.

But the bear had no argument with me, and had walked away from the challenge. I was sweating profusely. I began to shake as the tension eased.

Some time later I looked at the whole situation logically and considered just how little chance I would have had of killing that bear.

More likely, I would have ended up seriously maimed, with more wounds to tend to and no benefit from the fight. I was surprised at my foolhardiness. I resumed my daily routine, excited to have seen a bear in the wild. It was a shame I hadn't managed to photograph it. I knew how excited my mother would have been if she knew what I'd seen. She loved wildlife and would have really appreciated seeing the bear in its natural environment. It made me sad that I couldn't share this dramatic morning with her. Nevertheless, my overall feeling was relief.

At night, the dark silence was again pierced by those horrible screams. Sometimes they would be no more than a faint echo. At other times I could hear the bear pushing through the bushes nearby. I didn't whistle for it now or shout out a challenge. I lay quietly in my sleeping bag, my head completely covered, clutching my scissors. I kept seeing images of the flayed victims described in *Silence of the Lambs* and imagined a horrible death. Despite my warm ski jacket, I shivered as cold chills of fear crept over me.

JOANNE: *8 January 1992*

One of the first things to strike us about Kathmandu was the light. It was a hazy, almost yellow light, the sort you might get by using filters on a camera. But this was due to air pollution. Kathmandu lies in a valley and the smog produced by vehicles, fires and industry often hangs over the city, depending on the conditions. I was under the impression that one could see the Himalayas from Kathmandu. Over the next six weeks, I glimpsed the mountains on only three days.

We were disconcerted to find nobody from the embassy waiting for us at the airport. We had two men from the customs desk hovering in the background, every so often furtively asking, 'Australian dollars? Thai baht?' Andrew was getting very annoyed, just daring them to so much as lay a hand on the luggage.

We decided the best thing to do was wait outside the building. Fortunately we were still in a cordoned-off area and were not overwhelmed by the eager drivers with their cries of 'Taxi sir? Taxi ma'am?' I was delighted to see a gaily-painted elephant eating hay nearby, while its handler tried to drum up passengers. After a while, we went back inside the building, wondering what to do next.

I nodded to a woman about my age who was standing near us. She wore a white scarf which, I was to learn, was something commonly worn and used as a welcoming gift by Buddhists. She said hello and we got talking. She was actually an American, living in Nepal to study

Buddhism. When I told her about James, she said that she'd seen posters about him around Kathmandu and suggested that I should go and see a Buddhist lama, specifically a Rinpoche Lama. She explained that sometimes the Rinpoche Lamas know things that others don't, that they are 'enlightened'. I said I would be prepared to see a lama (it wouldn't do any harm), but asked where I was likely to find one who could speak English.

'You're in luck,' she said. 'Chokyi Nyima Rinpoche is fluent in English and is at Boudha, not far from Kathmandu. You should go and see him. The morning would be best. You should take a gift. A white scarf is fine, some fruit, biscuits, or even a little money.' She then asked why we were waiting. I explained and said we had no Nepali money and were trying to decide what to do. She had quick word with her Nepali friend who went promptly over to one of the small tourist counters. He returned and told us we could use the phone there for free. I dialled the embassy number.

Graeme Fay had the wrong flight details and was expecting us later that evening. He was apologetic and said he'd come straight away. Andrew and I were not to be mollified, however.

Twenty minutes later a white Mercedes pulled up. A very tall, red-haired man with a beard got out. This was Graeme Fay. He would only have been in his early twenties. Despite our annoyance, we were both rather pleased to see him and the Mercedes. As we slipped into its plush interior, I thought maybe all was not lost.

After preliminary introductions, Graeme said that he assumed we would want to go straight back to the embassy so that we could be fully briefed on what had happened to date.

That first drive from the airport to the embassy is one Andrew and I will always remember. Driving down to the airport entrance, one passes clusters of ramshackle mudbrick houses, usually two storeys high, with flat roofs. From the buildings and fences hang material and clothes of all descriptions. Some of the items were carpet that had been dyed, and the rest was the washing. It amazed me that people would go to the trouble of doing their laundry and hang it up alongside dusty, dirty roads. Here and there people gathered around springs: women squatting doing their laundry, or men washing themselves. There seemed to be people and dogs everywhere. Piles of garbage were heaped along the streets. a torn banner proudly announced 'Nepal welcome turist'. My heart sank.

The roads were full of pot-holes and had no lines painted. Huge, old buses, full to capacity, belching clouds of black, diesel fumes, lurched and creaked by; rusty, dusty private cars careered in and out of the traffic and dozens of three-wheeled, motorised devices (known as autorickshaws, a term that conveys a far greater sense of the romantic than the vehicles deserve) puttered along, oblivious of the traffic built up behind.

Nobody willingly gave way to anyone else. Andrew and I exchanged more than one horrified glance as the driver of our vehicle dodged between pedestrians and other vehicles. When suicidal drivers careered out of side streets, mindless of any traffic on the main road he went on unflinchingly with one hand pressed firmly on the horn. As if matters were not complicated enough, people on push-bikes weaved merrily through the general traffic flow and domestic animals of various species wandered from one side of the street to the other at will.

There seemed to be a large number of people doing nothing, sitting on the paths in front of shops and standing aimlessly by the roadside. We passed some women hunched beneath heavy loads of wood. Children ran around playing games; some wore shirts and jumpers but nothing from the waist down.

The overall impressions from that first drive through the streets of Kathmandu were ones of filth and poverty. Even as we came into more populous areas, things seemed to get worse, with the same decrepit buildings, grotty shop-fronts and rubbish piles merely appearing in greater numbers.

As I looked out the window of the Mercedes, I felt very tired. How on earth were we ever going to achieve anything in a place like this?

Graeme said that they had managed to track down the Canadians.

'Where are they?' I asked eagerly.

'They are staying at the Kathmandu Guest House. I went and saw them last night. It was really quite amazing that we found them. A friend of Tim was talking to some people, and they put him onto them. They are actually French Canadians.'

'Was it James they saw?'

Graeme shook his head. 'No, I really don't think so.'

'I'm going to see them myself,' I announced. 'When do they leave?'

'They're flying out on Friday.'

A white brick fence with golden ornamentation over a black gate told us we were at the Australian Embassy. Moments later we were seated at a table in the embassy conference room. Auli joined us. The ambassador was back in Australia on leave. I don't know whether it was anxiety or tiredness, but I felt the room was very chilly and wore my anorak throughout the meeting.

Graeme ran through everything and told us where we stood. No word was expected from either search party for at least another twenty-four hours. The Helambu people planned to go along three main trails and return along three lesser known trails. They were unlikely to be back before the weekend. He was hoping to get some word from the Gopte party via radio in the next few days.

In the meantime, it had been decided to advertise on Radio Nepali three times daily, just before the news. Radio was a major source of entertainment in remote areas. The fact that there was a reward for finding James dead or alive should get local people out and looking as well.

Graeme went on to say he had spoken to the Canadians. Their story had changed considerably from the one reported by Carl Harrison who was leading the search party. Graeme had asked them if they felt they gave the impression that it had been James they had seen. They said yes, they had, but now they were not so sure. One woman was now claiming she spoke with the trekker they had seen and he had said to her that he was from Germany.

I must admit, having listened first-hand to Graeme and Auli's side of the story, I felt better about the way things had been handled. They explained what had happened in a clear and organised fashion. Neither Andrew nor I were happy about the delay in getting a party above Gopte but that had been Carl Harrison's decision.

'All right,' I said, 'I would like to meet some trekking guides. Looking at the maps, I think there are still a few possibilities we need to cover. I want as many opinions as possible. I also want to speak to these Canadians myself. I have some extra photos of James which might clarify if it was him or not. It's pretty important: if it was not James, we can be fairly sure he never made it back to Tharepati. If it was, then we have a lot more area to cover.'

Graeme suggested we get in touch with a Mr Ravi Chandra Hamal, the head of Amadablam, a company that catered more for Australian trekkers than the other agencies in Nepal.

I asked for more information about Mateus, the German trekker who had written to Ingo Schnabel, but Graeme and Auli knew nothing more about him. They assumed he was a friend of Ingo and thought he had returned to Germany. It seemed that Ingo would have to provide us with more information about him.

I wanted to phone my parents to let them know we had arrived safely. I was told that I would not be able to use the fax and telephone facilities at the embassy for contacting Australia.

'What do you mean?' I asked. 'I expect to pay.'

'I'm sorry but we can't authorise it.'

'Why not?' I asked.

'We have no way of monitoring the length of calls,' replied Auli. 'You are welcome to make the call from my private phone though, and I have some friends who have an architectural business just up the road who would be happy for you to use their fax and phone. They are the same people who helped us do the posters.'

I accepted Auli's offer gratefully, although I was still a little confused as to why I was not allowed to use the official phone and fax. The embassy had a large sum of our money in a trust that only they had access to – so it wasn't as if I could run off without paying them!

It was explained that a large number of Australian tourists passed through and the embassy could not allow them all phone access. I asked how many Australians had disappeared in Nepal. James was the first. Surely exceptional cases meant exceptions could be made? Whether they agreed with the policy or not, the decision to allow me to use their facilities could not be taken by either Graeme or Auli but was one I would have to take up with the ambassador who was away on holiday.

The embassy had organised our accommodation at a discount. Hotel Kathmandu was not really as grand as the name might have one believe. It was set back from the road, a four-storey building of red brick with a fairly impressive gateway and a purple and gold sign. The drive was cobbled and made my teeth rattle. There was always a door-man on duty, dressed in red and gold and proudly sporting immense silver swords. The brass handles on the glass doors were polished religiously every morning. The floors appeared to be marble and the place always had a strong smell of kerosene to it.

Our room was one of many along a red-carpeted hallway. It was a modest affair: two beds separated by a night stand and two benches for suitcases. In front of a window overlooking the driveway were some chairs and a table. There was a bathtub with a shower, sink and flush toilet: not glamorous stuff, but certainly fairly clean and would meet our needs. On the night stand was an outdated blue telephone. We dropped our luggage off and left to find Tim in Thamel.

Graeme was good enough to give us a lift. We parked near the Downtown Guest House. The roads had become very narrow and the pedestrian traffic denser, with a large number of Westerners mingling with the local people. I stepped out of the car and was immediately surrounded by people selling things. A group of men were peddling small, carved string instruments. Children held out bracelets, carved elephants and miniature chess sets.

I ignored them and followed Graeme into a dingy hallway between two shops. Bicycles cluttered the corridor. We climbed the dark staircase up the three floors to Tim's room.

Tim opened the door before we had a chance to knock. It was the first time that we had met. He looked unwell and had dark rings under his eyes. According to Andrew, he had lost a lot of weight. Obviously he was under a tremendous strain. I felt very sorry for him. What an awful position he had been thrust into, having to communicate with a distraught family, authorise the spending of money that wasn't his and no doubt feeling sick with anxiety himself! We all returned to the Hotel Kathmandu to decide what to do next.

Like Graeme, Tim felt certain that the Canadians were wrong about sighting James.

'Well, I still want to talk to them myself,' I persisted. 'Apart from the photos, I can't believe they could convince Carl to turn his entire search party around and suddenly change their minds. It's pretty important that we resolve once and for all if it could have been or if it definitely was not James. It makes a huge difference in the area that we need to cover.' Tim agreed and we headed back into Thamel to find the Kathmandu Guest House.

This involved our first taxi ride in Nepal. It was something of a comedown after the Mercedes to find ourselves in an old, rusty four-door car. A blanket covered the back seat, no doubt, hiding torn upholstery. One could tell which cars were taxis by their black number plates. The real trick was to get the driver to put the meter on. Tim was to educate us in the fine art of bargaining. After the driver refused to put the meter on, Tim asked, 'How much?'

The driver replied, '150 rupees.'

Tim laughed, shook his head and made to walk away. The driver called out, 'Okay, okay. How much?'

'Fifty rupees,' Tim replied.

It was the driver's turn to laugh. '100,' he offered.

I think they finally agreed at about 80 rupees. Andrew and I were quite impressed. Later we learnt that if the meter had been on it would have been about 15 rupees!

The Kathmandu Guest House is something of an institution in Nepal. If you ask directions for anywhere in Thamel, it will be given to you in terms of distance or walking time from the Kathmandu Guest House. It is very central for shops and restaurants and usually nearly fully booked. Trekkers meet, discuss their journeys and make plans for future expeditions. As we walked from the paved courtyard into the warm reception area, I was disappointed we had not chosen to stay there. An open fire blazed and people sat in chairs scattered around the room sipping tea and coffee. Everyone was very casually dressed (as was the norm for Kathmandu), many wearing the beautiful, brightly coloured jumpers so characteristic of Nepal.

Tim could not see any of the Canadians in the lounge, so we made straight for their rooms. The door was opened by a woman with short hair and glasses. There were only two women from the group in the room. I told them my name and that I was the sister of the Australian trekker missing in the Helambu/Gosainkund area. I asked for a name and contact address which the second woman, Nicole, gave me. I couldn't help looking at her eyes. They were a striking brown and one had a white mark across the pupil. I asked if I could see the rest of their party, but they were not sure where they all were. I asked them to tell me what had happened.

They said that they had been doing the Helambu trek, quite a large party with all their sherpas and porters. Nicole, the woman with the unusual eyes, said that they had seen a solo trekker walking quickly with his head down. He had seemed upset. When they had met him they were strung out along the trail. Nicole was at the rear of the party. I asked them what the trekker was wearing. Both agreed he was wearing a blue cap or beanie and that he had only a very small rucksack. He had light hair, they told me.

'Red hair?' I queried.

'No, light.'

I asked them if any conversation had taken place. The short-haired woman said they might have nodded, but Nicole claimed to have spoken with him.

'I think I asked him where he came from,' she told me.

'Did he answer you?' I asked.

'I think he said he came from Germany.' She shrugged. 'Maybe it was Germany, maybe it was Australia.' I managed to contain the rage I could feel welling inside. She obviously did not particularly care which it was.

They went on to say that they had later met the search party at Tharepati. The searchers had told them they were looking for a solo Australian trekker and showed the Canadians some photos.

'So why did you tell the search party that you were sure it was my brother? My brother did not have a blue hat and he would not have said he was from Germany.'

The short-haired woman said that the trekker they had seen looked exactly like the person in the photo. Nicole said that she had expressed some doubts at the time but, because everybody else had seemed so sure, she had not made an issue out of it.

At this point, another member of the Canadian party came into the room. He agreed that the photo the search party had shown them was very like the trekker they had seen.

'When we told the search party that we had seen the man they were looking for, they were very happy.' He smiled fondly at the memory. I wanted to punch him. 'They wished us a Happy New Year and immediately went along the way we had come.'

I could contain myself no longer. 'Do you realise that, on the basis of what you said, the entire search party turned and went in a completely different direction? And now you say you are not sure. Do you realise that what you told the search party might have cost my brother his life?'

To my amazement, they all shrugged and looked relatively unconcerned. I was not going to be able to shame them into admitting they had made a mistake.

I asked them to confirm that it was 30 December that they had seen the trekker. They were adamant that this was the case. I pulled out some of the photographs I had brought with me. Nicole shook her head. 'This was not the person we saw.'

The other two mulled over the pictures.

'I am not so sure,' said the other woman. 'I think it could be him.'

Tim and Andrew were over in a corner of the room shaking their heads. The Canadians had a brief discussion in French. The man said to me, 'If you think you know who the other trekker is, why don't you show us a photo of him? Then, perhaps, we will know whether it was him or your brother.'

'How am I supposed to get a photo of this other trekker?' I said. 'I don't know him.'

'There will be a photograph with his trekking permit,' the man replied. We left. I could not bring myself to thank the Canadians for their time or even to say goodnight.

Tim said that their story had changed even from last night when he and Graeme had spoken to them.

'What do you think?' I asked Tim and Andrew, 'Any chance it was James?' Both Andrew and Tim said they were now sure it had not been James. I was not convinced.

'They obviously saw someone and that person must look like James's photograph.'

'For goodness sake, Joanne,' Andrew said, 'the person they saw was wearing a blue hat. James didn't have a blue hat. James wouldn't have said he was from Germany and James would have spoken to them. The only reason that those two are saying they aren't sure is because they are too embarrassed to admit they made a mistake. They are covering their tracks. It's outrageous that Nicole did not speak up and say she wasn't sure. We know from the note Ingo had that there was a German trekker in the area at the time. It was him they saw.'

I still harboured some doubts. The only way to be sure whether it was James or Mateus was to find Mateus. I would try to find his trekking permit as soon as possible.

Mr Ravi Chandra Hamal was the head man in Amadablam trekking. Graeme brought him to our room at 8 p.m. With him was his head guide. They had only just returned from a trek in the region of Langtang National Park, north-west of where James had been.

Mr Ravi thought the chances of finding James alive were very slim. He never allowed trekking groups anywhere near the Gosainkund trail in winter. He said that it invariably snowed there and was very dangerous. There was a high probability that James had slipped and fallen to his death above Gopte. I asked him what he felt the chances were if James had made it down past Gopte into the Helambu area. He conceded that James would have a chance below the snowline, but there was a possibility of being attacked in the Helambu area. There had been several murders for robbery in the area and lone trekkers were particularly at risk. Apparently, a Nepali-speaking Peace Corps worker had been murdered this way and her body had been found in a cave years later. Some bodies are never found.

'And if someone is attacked,' he said, 'the whole village will never speak about it.'

I mentioned the possibility of exploring the area south-west of Gopte, towards Talu. Mr Ravi shook his head. 'That area is very, very dangerous. It is unexplored.' He seemed to think that it would have been almost impossible for James or anyone else to get down that way.

He agreed it might be worth sending some people up to Dhunche at the end of the Gosainkund trail beyond the pass. They could make their way from Dhunche through Gosainkund across the pass and down to Gopte, in case James had tried to cross the pass.

When asked about the possibility that James had been injured or sick and was being cared for in a village somewhere, he said that, if that was the case, word would have probably leaked out by now.

'One thing you could do,' he suggested, 'is to broadcast on television.' I was surprised. I could see the value of television broadcast in Kathmandu, but would it help in the area where we really needed word to be out? Mr Ravi assured me that television existed even in remote areas, often powered by generator.

Another point raised that night was the possibility that James had intentionally disappeared and did not want to be found. I became angry at the very suggestion. I pointed out that he was engaged to be married and had only one year left before becoming a doctor. 'He knows we would be beside ourselves. James would never do that.'

Over the coming weeks I would be called upon frequently to defend James. It seemed that a number of people decide to opt out of society whilst trekking in Nepal. One American elected to join a Buddhist monastery in a tiny village. He had 'disappeared' for two years. Occasionally trekkers will meet a man or woman in a village and decide to settle down for a while. It was put to me on more than one occasion that James might have decided to 'elope' with a Nepali woman.

I felt pretty low by the time Mr Ravi left, two hours later. There had been a lot of negatives that day and not much to raise our hopes. Andrew was sceptical that James might have been attacked. Having studied karate with James, Andrew was confident that, even with an injury, he would be able to defend himself against several Nepali.

We decided to organise a television broadcast. I felt it was important extra search parties go out. I wanted one to go from Dhunche, across the pass, and another to make its way up through the south-west, following rivers and checking villages in case James had made it down the Tadi Khola. We would let American Express know all of James travellers' cheque numbers and I would try to track down the solo German trekker in the hope of establishing once and for all if it were he or James the Canadians had seen. We also had to get a physical description of Mark Fulton cabled to our embassy in Thailand. They would ask the police to look out for him. Tim could not recall any particular features, so the description was pretty vague. I asked Tim what were the chances Mark had hurt James in some way. Tim thought any foul play highly unlikely; after all, Mark had come to see Tim almost as soon as he arrived back in Kathmandu. I also asked Tim about Krishna, the guide they had used on their first trek, and how James had planned to have dinner with him before they left. Tim said he had tried to find Krishna twice with no success. He felt that Krishna was not going to be able to shed any light on the matter.

JOANNE: *9 January 1992*

Morning found me feeling I had not rested at all. My mind was churning over the day's tasks and the decisions to be made. I crept out of bed at 6.30 a.m. It was still very dark. I sat in a chair by the window, as far from Andrew's bed as possible, and switched on the lamp. I took out a writing pad and started what would be the first of many faxes home. Having been at the receiving end of phone calls from Kathmandu, I realised how difficult it was to absorb information. The long-distance connection was often bad – with that horrible pause between you speaking and the other person hearing and the names were so foreign to the ear. Add to this the emotional stress of every call and it meant that facts were often quickly forgotten. I decided the solution was to fax hard copy they could refer to again and again. I wrote for a good hour, expressing my despair at the filth and poverty in Kathmandu and wrote down all the numbers where we could possibly be contacted.

At around 9 a.m. the embassy's white Mercedes bounced over the cobblestones to collect us at the front door. It was cold and a swirling mist created quite a ghostly atmosphere. Cars and cyclists would suddenly loom in front of us and vanish in the haze.

Graeme was at his desk, a blow heater warming the room. In no time at all, dainty cups balanced on saucers and full of steaming, sweet Nepali tea arrived. Our first task was to write an advertisement to be broadcast on television. We decided to broadcast twice daily for two days and see the response. We would also provide a black and white photo of James to display during the broadcast. We arranged to continue the radio bulletins for a further two days and to place an advertisement in *Gorkapatra*, the Nepali language newspaper, on Saturday.

After some discussion, I decided we should use a helicopter to drop two searchers at Dhunche the next day. They could cover between Dhunche and the Laurebinayak Pass on foot, in case James had changed his mind and decided to cross the pass after all. Andrew did not think this was likely. 'There's no way that James would change his mind about something like that,' Andrew told me. 'He's too pig-headed. Once he made a decision he would stick to it.'

I had other reasons. While the helicopter was in the area, I wanted them to find the search party above Gopte and see how things were progressing. I asked Graeme if he would mind going on the flight as well.

'I promised my parents I would not go up in any helicopter,' I explained, 'but I would really like you to take some photographs of the area. I can't begin to imagine what it must be like. I know my parents would also like to see it.' Graeme agreed. He actually enjoyed helicopter trips.

I gave Graeme the description of Mark Fulton but it was so vague he said it was not worth sending. Instead he would talk to Thai Air to see if they had information about further flights that Mark might be taking or a contact address. The Australian Embassy in Thailand would be looking for Mark at their end. Tim was under the impression Mark would be returning to Australia somewhere around 18 January. We also knew that he had flown Thai Air between Kathmandu and Bangkok on 27 December. I made a mental note to ask my parents to ring our Thai Air contact in Brisbane as well. The more people working on it, the more quickly we might get an answer. We knew Mark's surname and the town where he lived. I suggested we should contact Mark's parents in case they knew of his whereabouts and Graeme agreed to ask Canberra to do that.

My next task was to send my fax home. Auli called Tom Crees and Maria Young at Blue Mountain Design Company which was only a short walk up the road from the embassy. They had printed all the 'missing' posters now displayed in Kathmandu and on the trekking trails.

Tom Crees is a most interesting person. Born in India of a Nepali mother and an English father, he had studied architecture and lived in Sydney for a number of years. His father owned a tea plantation in Darjeeling where Tom had grown up. Maria is a pretty, petite woman with startlingly blue eyes, short dark hair and an efficient manner. A teacher by training, she seems able to turn her hand to just about any-thing. The two of them would become my very close friends. They would provide unfailing support and be a great source of strength in the weeks to come.

They took us upstairs into their living area. A kitchen at the top of the stairs looked out onto a deck where a long table caught the warm, morning sun. Although I suspect it was unbearably hot in summer, it was beautiful in winter. They offered us some tea and we chatted for a while. They already knew much of the story. I checked that they had a way of keeping track of all the faxes and phone calls. I stressed that I did not want them to be out of pocket over this and that, if I could not pay fully, I would not feel right about using their facilities.

Having seen the fax on its way, we returned to the embassy. Our next port of call was the immigration office to try to track down a photo of Mateus. The Immigration and Trekking Permit office is in

Thamel. Several Nepali men were serving people at a counter. There seemed to be a queue, mainly tourists waiting for visa extensions or trekking permits. I looked around. A poster described a trekker who had been missing since March 1991. A wave of depression swept over me. I stood in the cold, grotty office and looked from the poster to the lines of people doing battle just to get a trekking permit. How were we ever going to get anywhere?

Eventually it was our turn. I had decided the best way to get people to help was to impress upon them the seriousness of my request. I had dressed that morning in culottes and a blouse, instead of jeans and sweatshirt, in the hope that I would be able to make myself appear different from the normal tourist. I caught the eye of the man who was to serve us and kept eye contact throughout our discussion.

'Good morning,' I said. 'My name is Dr Joanne Robertson, from Australia, and I am hoping that you can help me with something very important. My brother is missing in the mountains. I have come to Nepal to look for him.' I paused to ensure that he understood. 'Now, I think I have found someone who might know what has happened. Unfortunately, all I have is his name and nationality. I am hoping that you will be good enough to use your records of trekking permits to help me find him. It is very important.'

He studied me for a minute and then nodded and said, 'Go to room nineteen, through that corridor.'

We found room nineteen and knocked. A man with a cigarette hanging out of his mouth and frayed cuffs on his coat sleeves looked up.

I repeated what I had said to the man behind the counter. He looked a bit uncertain about it all and consulted another man before saying, 'What number is the trekking permit you need?'

'I don't know,' I replied. His eyed widened in surprise and he pushed a manilla folder in front of me. The manilla folder had a date on the front and, as I turned the cover, I saw it contained what had to be trekking permits. Each permit was a three-page document. It included, amongst other information, a contact address, home address, passport numbers and, best of all, a photograph of the trekker.

'What number do you need?' he asked again.

'I'm afraid I don't know. Is there a way we can find out? This is very important.' For a minute, I was sure that he would dismiss me and say it was impossible to help. He had already done more than he was supposed to by showing me some trekking permits. It would be far easier for him to not help me. I held eye contact with him. I saw a flicker of indecision and then he sighed.

'You come with me.'

We followed him into another cramped room – more tables and more men. I was glad of Andrew's company.

'Where was your brother trekking?' the official asked.

'Helambu and Gosainkund.'

He reached into a cupboard and produced a large ledger. 'You look,' he said and opened the book. Each page was headed by a date and divided into a number of columns. As I scanned the page, I realised that this was a record of all the permits issued for trekkers on a particular day for the Helambu area. Across the page there was a name, nationality, intended route, departure and returning dates and visa and trekking permit numbers. From this, I should be able to find the trekking permit number for Mateus. There were a number of difficulties, however. The names were in an untidy scrawl. I picked out an English name. What must have been meant to read 'Colin' was written 'Colm'. There seemed to be countless similar spelling errors, and even the numbers were barely legible.

Each page was headed by a date. The huge ledger before me ran from mid-November to the end of December. I did not know the date of Mateus's permit. We knew he had been on the eastern leg of the Helambu circuit on 30 December and the Helambu trek should take approximately a week. Although you could get a six-week permit, the chances were he would have only got one to cover that particular trek. I decided to start looking from 15 December. There was no point in looking later than the 28th, as he would not have been able to reach the search area in under a day.

The most efficient method was to go through the nationality column. Every time we found a trekker from Germany we would trace across the row to see the name. Nepal was a popular destination for Germans. This method was far from foolproof. We were assuming that Mateus was German, as opposed to just being German-speaking, and that they had correctly written his nationality in the ledger. As I picked up more and more errors, I realised the latter was far from a safe assumption. Still, we had no choice.

Our efforts were finally rewarded. We found a German trekker who had obtained a permit on 25 December to do the Helambu trek. His name looked like Mathial Weigott. I noted the trekking permit number and his Nepali visa number.

Back in the first office, the clerk started sifting through a pile of manilla folders on the floor. Evidently, the one we required was not there. He turned and opened a cupboard to reveal a jumble of similar folders. They looked as if they had been tossed into the cupboard from a distance! But luck was with us, and he quickly produced the relevant folder.

It did not take us long to find Mathial's permit. I quickly wrote down his passport number and his German address. We turned the page to look at the photograph. Andrew glanced at me and I could only shake my head. He looked nothing like James. His hair was much darker and his face long and narrow, suggesting he would be far thinner and taller than James. On the way out, Andrew tried to slip our helpful clerk some money as an extra thank you but he would not accept it.

'It's okay. No problem,' he said. I smiled my thanks.

I really felt we had achieved something. We had not allowed ourselves to be daunted, had managed to convince someone to help and had got the information we needed. I felt good as we stepped into the bright light of the street. 'So, what now?' said Andrew. We decided to go to the Hotel Yellow Pagoda, where I hoped to meet Anoop Rana, one of the contacts Linda had given me.

Despite the tragic reason for being there and the depressing filth, I could not help but feel attracted to the city as we made our way through the streets. There was an element of surprise at every turn: ancient buildings, intricate carvings, temples, fabulously coloured clothing and gleaming silver jewellery. The city had an air of mystery and vitality.

Anoop Rana appeared very much the businessman. Tall and good-looking, he was dressed in a well cut grey suit. He stood as we entered. I handed him the letter from Linda Griffith and, after ordering tea, he read it.

'This is very sad,' he said.

I explained that we had to be certain everything possible was being done. 'We have to find out what has happened. We cannot always be wondering.'

He nodded and told us he might be able to help by arranging a meeting. We waited while he made several calls.

'Is 4.30 convenient for you?' We nodded. In a remarkably short time, he had organised a meeting for us with 'some people who know the area'. These people included the president of the Nepali Mountaineering Association and the director and past-director of the Trekking Agents Association of Nepal. I got the impression they owned trekking companies as well. We thanked him and said we would be back at 4.30.

We taxied back to the Hotel Kathmandu, feeling quite smug having negotiated a fee of 100 rupees (we still didn't know about the 15 rupees at that stage). It was past 2 p.m. by the time we got to our room. We ordered some food and phoned Graeme at the embassy. There was no word from any of the search parties but I passed on what we knew about Mathial/Mateus. Andrew made his daily call to the Ryans and Beverley told him Gaye and my parents were sending us a fax. It should be waiting for us at Blue Mountain. We went to the front of the hotel and asked the doorman to hail us a taxi.

'Where to?' he asked.

'We want to go up to Blue Mountain Design Company and then back to Hotel Yellow Pagoda.'

He looked confused and said, 'Where?'

'Blue Mountain Design Company. Just past the Australian Embassy. Then Hotel Yellow Pagoda, please.'

'One moment, please.'

He seemed to be busying himself with our request, so I walked over to wait in the sun. Andrew joined me and we idly watched an Amadablam Trekking van pull up. A Nepali man in his late twenties hopped out of the vehicle. The doorman quickly collared the van driver and spoke to him with some urgency, pointing in our direction. The man from the van walked over to us with a smile. I noticed he was wearing a T-shirt from Surfers' Paradise.

'Excuse me,' he said, 'the doorman does not understand where you want to go.'

I explained what we wanted and he relayed it to the doorman who looked very relieved. 'Have you been to Australia?' I asked our translator, pointing to his shirt.

'Yes. Are you Australians?' He seemed very pleased and told us his name was Balaram. He had enjoyed quite a long holiday in Australia and asked why we were in Nepal. Briefly, I told him the story. He asked where James had been last seen. I told him it was about three hours above Gopte. He shook his head slowly.

'You know, it's a funny thing. I was leading a trek down from the Laurebinayak Pass once when it started to snow heavily. I knew we would not make it to Gopte, so I led my group down the trail to the south-west, near the Tadi Khola.'

I felt my heart skip a beat. 'You mean down towards Talu?' I asked.

'Yes. It is not easy to find, but it is certainly there.'

'I've heard that region is very rugged. Was your group equipped for mountaineering?'

'No, no,' he said. 'They were just normal trekkers. Once you find the trail, it's not so bad.'

'Balaram, this is very important. I have been told there is no way that someone could make it down from near Gopte to Talu, but you say there is a trail?' He nodded. 'We must have a meeting. I will need someone to search that area for me. Can you help?' He seemed pleased to be asked and quickly gave me a contact number. He came from a village in the area where James was missing. We jumped into our taxi and I reflected on our chance meeting. I had nearly been persuaded not to worry about searching the area to the south-west. It had sounded impassable but now I had met someone who knew there was a trail there – all because the doorman had not understood us.

We were a little early at Hotel Yellow Pagoda, so I had time to read what had come from Australia. It seemed they were already feeling better about the communications. No small wonder, either: my long fax had given them more information in one day than we had received in the previous ten. They were anxious to hear from the search parties as soon as they got in and were still unhappy about Harrison's decision to turn the entire party around at Tharepati on the first search. Gaye had received seven letters from James since Christmas, all written before the 19th. I thought how awful it must be for her to be receiving the letters and not know whether he was alive or dead. With every letter, she must wonder if there could be a clue. They still wanted us to track down Krishna and felt it of utmost importance that Mark Fulton be traced.

I folded the fax away as Tim joined us. It was now 4.30 p.m. so we knocked on Anoop Rana's door. He invited us in and ordered tea. Shortly, we were joined by the men Anoop had organised. It was a very useful meeting, albeit somewhat depressing. They listened patiently and looked at my maps and photographs as I explained the story. It quickly became apparent they felt there was virtually no hope that James was still alive. They were shocked that someone had attempted such a trek without proper supplies and equipment. They felt to search from Dhunche to the pass was worthwhile. There were huts at Gosainkund where James might be sheltering if he had crossed the pass. They said the area south-west of Gopte was very dangerous and searching it would be useless. They knew nothing about a trail in there. I said a silent prayer of thanks for our chance meeting with Balaram.

They asked if we had written to the police. I was under the impression that they had been notified but I had written no letter. Anoop was quickly on the phone again. As luck would have it, he knew the Special

Superintendent of Police. In no time at all, he was talking to the police at Dhunche. Yes, they were aware of the missing Australian trekker and they were looking in the Langtang National Park. The Superintendent would also ensure forces were mobilised at Sundarijal, Tarke Ghyang and Tharepati. This would be important if James had been attacked. The police would be more likely to get the truth than the search parties. I was to write a formal letter notifying the police of James's disappearance and requesting their help in the search. I wrote it while the others supervised and Anoop undertook to see it was delivered. We included a colour photograph of James. They all felt the reward would be a good incentive for the police.

It was well and truly dark by the time we left. Tim suggested we get something to eat and recommended a Thai restaurant where he had eaten several times with no ill effects. On the way I rang Auli at the embassy: still no word from the search parties. Graeme had organised the helicopter for tomorrow with two people from Amadablam to search from Dhunche to the pass.

The food was good. Tim took a long, dark hair from his meal before eating. He must have seen the look on our faces as he said, 'You can tell how long a person has been in Kathmandu by the way they react to hair in their food. If it's one or two days, you might send the food back. If it's four or five days, you complain. Over a week, you don't even comment.'

After dinner we went to Tom and Jerry's, a popular tourist bar. Tim introduced us to Jack who had met James and Tim on the Jomsom trek. He had spoken to Krishna and had a phone number and address for us. He agreed with Tim that Krishna knew nothing about James's trek. How could he when James and Tim had changed their plans after they left?

We left Tom and Jerry's at about 10 p.m. when everything seemed to close in Kathmandu. Our taxi looked like it might fall apart on the way back to the hotel. It had been another very long day but Andrew and I felt we had achieved a lot in a short time.

JOANNE: *10 January 1992*

'I'm going up in the helicopter,' Andrew announced. I looked up from writing the morning fax.

'I'm going up in the helicopter,' he repeated. 'I think it's important one of us sees what the area is like. You can't go: you promised your parents. So, I'll go.' Andrew was adamant. I could see his point but I was worried about his safety, not to mention his fear of flying. But he refused to budge. 'My mind is made up. Nothing will happen to me and I'll get some good photos.'

The two searchers from Amadablam were at the embassy when we arrived. They seemed to have remarkably little equipment but assured me it was all they needed. I took Graeme aside. I told him I wanted it made clear that, if they found James, they would get a substantial bonus.

There was a knock on the door and in walked Balaram. Apparently he had rung Graeme after our conversation. We sat down with a map and Balaram again explained about the path from the Gosainkund trail, south-west to Talu. The fact this trail existed meant there was a chance James had found it. We decided to arrange for another four men to work their way through the sector between Talu and Kathmandu along the branches of the Tadi Khola. There were a number of minor trails in this area that James might have followed to Kathmandu. There was also the possibility that he could not find a trail and was instead attempting to return via the river. If James had found a route down past Talu, he would be below the snowline and there were a number of villages where he could get food. We plotted two courses for the extra search teams and Balaram agreed to organise the parties to leave the next day. I was grateful and asked him to call me as soon as they returned – in about six days.

We then turned our attention to the two men going to Dhunche in the chopper. I stressed how important their mission was and gave them each a bundle of black and white photos of James and asked them to tell everyone they met about my brother. They also took some missing posters for display in lodges and villages.

In the hope that, after dropping the men at Dhunche, the helicopter could fly on to Gopte to trace the search party, I asked Andrew to do several things. I wanted to know if Ingo had a contact for Mateus/ Mathial that might help the efforts of the German Consulate. I also suggested that, if the party had had no success above Gopte, they should work their way down branches of the Tadi Khola from where it began above Talu and along the trail to Talu. With luck they would meet the search parties working up the river. This would give us good coverage of most of the area where James might be. There were six men in Helambu; two men going from Dhunche, across the pass to Gopte; Carl Harrison and company should have covered the area around Gopte and, if they could then cover between Gopte and Talu, four other men would search the area between Talu and Kathmandu.

While I had been planning all this, Auli had asked Andrew for a word outside. He returned, looking a little grim, which I dismissed as apprehension. Andrew later told me Auli had given him a body bag and instructed him in what to do if James's body had been found above Gopte. The army chopper crew were reluctant to handle bodies so it would be up to Andrew to put James's body into the bag.

Andrew, Graeme and the two Amadablam searchers left just after 10 a.m. The mist was still heavy and Graeme was concerned it would delay take-off. I wished them luck and watched the embassy vehicle drive off. I suddenly felt alone and scared. With all the organising we had done I had not had time to think about the possible outcome of the flight. There was a very real chance Graeme and Andrew would arrive at Gopte to find the search party had found James's body. I tried to quell my feelings. 'There's nothing you can do about it, so wait and see,' I told myself.

When Andrew and Graeme returned at about 1 p.m. my heart was pounding. I had tried to rehearse hearing, 'I'm afraid James is dead' in the hope I could hold myself together if it came to that, but my shaking hands and dry mouth indicated I was nowhere near prepared to accept bad news calmly. They shook their heads, 'There's no news at all.'

They had dropped the two men off at Dhunche and flown to Tharepati. Even there, the amount of snow on the ground prevented them landing. Higher up, at Gopte, it would be worse. A man had run out of a hut and waved, indicating the search party was still above Gopte. That meant that James was not at Gopte, dead or alive. The search party was obviously scouring the trail above Gopte for a body.

I asked Andrew, 'So, what's it like up there?'

He was appalled. 'It's worse than I ever imagined,' he said. 'I can't believe that people even mountaineer there, let alone go walking. James was crazy to be anywhere near there!' Tharepati was perched on top of a ridge with steep slopes. 'The trail beyond is unbelievably narrow and incredibly steep. I'm afraid there is a good chance that James has fallen.'

They had flown over the area to the south-west of Gopte and seen a few sparsely scattered huts. It looked like our best hopes for finding James alive rested in one of three possibilities. One was that he had made it down through Gopte and Tharepati into Helambu. The second that he had changed his mind, crossed the pass and was sheltering beyond. Third, he had headed south-west and was sheltering somewhere there.

96

Joanne Robertson explored every avenue that might help her find her brother. Thrangu Rinpoche, a Buddhist lama, told her where James would be and that she would meet him again. James was eventually found in the area he had indicated

Thousands of missing person posters, in English and Nepali, were distributed throughout Kathmandu and the villages in the region where James had last been seen. They were part of a campaign that included radio and television announcements

नयाँ सूचना

इनाम

निठ्ठो पत्ता लगाएमा : रू एक लाख

निठ्ठो नपाएमा : रू दश हजार

हराएको व्यक्ति : जेम्स स्कट

अष्ट्रेलियन नागरिक, 22 वर्षको अग्लो
रातो नेपाल गएको, निलो ज्याकेट लगाएको,
रातो ब्याग बोकेको व्यक्ति ग्रिति पौष ७गते
२०४८ देखि हराएमा छ।

हराएको ठाउँ : हेलम्बु, गोसाइकुण्ड
फेलापारे सम्पर्क राख्ने छन।

कुनै पनि आर्मि पोष्ट
हिमालय रिसर्च कुकुर केन्द्र
जि. के. श्रेष्ठ, अष्ट्रेलियन राजदूताबास, काठमाडौं
फोन : ४१३०७६

PLS CALL THE AUSTRALIAN EMB. KTM - 413076
अखनी गोप्य लखरसे लि.ज.पि.लि. ४१३५४४ मा खबर गरिदिन

*Two local sherpas, members of the rescue party led by Carl
Harrison, were first to reach James under his rock. One of them is
wearing James's straw hat which he found on the way up. The whole
party trekked through deep snow in the dark to find him after the
helicopter sighting. It was to have been the last flight in the search*

The rescue team had to carry James into the clearing and tie him into the harness. The helicopter could not winch him into the cabin so he had to dangle below while it flew down to Talu

It was not possible to say exactly how much weight James had lost in the forty-three days he spent on the mountainside. Seen here with Joanne, in Patan hospital only a few days after his rescue, it was estimated he had lost about one-third of his body weight. But the measurements did not show all the damage: his vision and balance have been permanently affected

Almost a year later, James, Gaye and Joanne returned to Nepal. They met up with the local sherpas who had helped with James's rescue and went back to where he had been trapped. The visit was part of a television documentary produced by Channel Nine in Australia. The first two sherpas to reach James on his last night were Jih Bahadur Tamang (left) and Karsingi Sherpa (right). Many of the local people still talk about James as a god because he managed to survive the conditions so much longer than anyone else had before. Gaye and Joanne joined them all under James's rock in happier times

Even when there was no snow and the climbers were in perfect health, reaching the rock where James sheltered was a strenuous and dangerous exercise

We returned to the hotel where I managed to phone a contact my parents had found through some friends in Australia, Dr Sharma. He told me he knew the head of Himalayan Adventures trekking and would arrange for me to meet with him the next day.

We ordered dinner from room service and settled into our armchairs with a drink. This was the first of several evenings when Andrew and I would have long conversations. Andrew knew James very well. He told me a story about when they were camping in the French Alps beside a mountain. James had studied the mountain for a while and announced he was going to climb it. Andrew had told him he was crazy but he didn't listen. He just got up and left. He returned hours later, exhausted but had made it to the top.

'Once James decides to do something, he does it.'

We talked about James and Gaye's engagement. Tim had told us how the one thing that made him so very sad about the whole episode was that, the longer they had been in Nepal, the more certain James had become of his love for Gaye. It seemed such a tragic waste. I still agonised over the notion that he could be trapped on an ice ledge somewhere, but Andrew was adamant: 'Joanne, if you could have seen that countryside you would know. If James has fallen he's died instantly. If James injured himself he would have died of hypothermia in hours. There is no way he would have suffered for a long time.'

'I just wish,' I responded, 'that if James is dead, he could somehow give us a sign. Just so that we know what has happened. I wish he could, somehow, get a message to us, so that we know we can stop worrying.'

It was quite late by the time we headed for bed. I lay awake for a while, concentrating on making my mind as blank as possible and willing James to try to get a message to me. I felt sure that, if he was dead, he would let me know. However, there was no message. Was I acting irrationally? All I knew was that I had to keep looking until I felt it was all right to stop. If that meant taking steps that I might have scorned a few weeks ago back home, then so be it.

JOANNE: *11 January 1992*

Saturday morning dawned cold with the usual curtain of mist. We had no commitments until after lunch when we were to meet Dr Sharma and Mr Tschering of Himalayan Adventures at the hotel. We could not hope to hear from the search parties until later on that morning at the earliest. Today was the perfect opportunity to go to Boudha and see

Chokyi Nyima, the Rinpoche Lama that the lady at the airport had mentioned. I wondered if I would be able to persuade Andrew to come. I was apprehensive and had no idea what it might entail but I knew that, if I did not go, I would always wonder if it would have made a difference.

Andrew blinked sleepily from his bed. 'So what's the plan for today?' he asked.

'Well,' I said, 'I thought it might be a good day to go to Boudha and see this lama.'

Despite his scepticism, he agreed to come with me and after breakfast we caught a taxi to Boudha.

The drive seemed to take a long time. I guess I had envisaged Boudha as a peaceful haven of stately white buildings and ordered gardens. I pictured wise lamas dressed in saffron robes, seated under majestic trees, casting pearls of wisdom to avid, sandalled students and perhaps soothing music from softly played woodwind instruments.

I was wrong.

Our driver pulled over to the side of a road lined with shops. We looked around anxiously. The girl at the airport had spoken about a large, white monastery. Nothing here fitted that description. My first thought was we weren't at Boudha at all.

'Boudha?' I asked the taxi driver.

'Yes, yes,' came the impatient reply. 'I wait one hour for you.'

'Temple?' I queried.

With a wave of his hand he pointed to an alley. 'You go there. I wait one hour.'

Andrew and I looked at each other. I could tell that Andrew thought this was all a really bad idea.

We emerged from the alleyway in front of what we guessed was the stupa. A white, dome-shaped structure with a brick tower loomed before us. The tower had a square base and rose in the shape of a pyramid. On the sides of the base were painted eyes that gazed almost accusingly outwards. Gaily coloured pieces of cloth flapped in the breeze at the top. These were prayer flags. A paved area lined with ancient buildings surrounded the stupa. The shops and houses were well preserved and very beautiful. They were two or three storeys high with intricate wood carvings around the doorways and windows. People walked casually through a group of beggars and reached into recesses in the wall to spin wooden prayer wheels.

Custom demanded that one walk around the stupa in a certain direction. Everyone else was walking to the left, clockwise around the structure, so we copied. I felt a tug on my coat and turned to see a young girl of no more than ten or twelve. A tattered shawl covered her head and the customary gold stud pierced her nose. In her arms was a well-bundled up baby. Mucus streamed from the baby's nose and its eyes were outlined with black kohl.

'Rupee?' she begged, fixing me with puppy-like brown eyes. 'Madam? Please, rupee?'

With difficulty, I shook my head and turned away. 'How the bloody hell are we ever going to find this lama?' I asked Andrew. I looked around for someone who might know the area, perhaps even speak English. A woman with long, dark hair was surrounded by a group of children. She spoke to them in Nepali and strode purposefully across the square. I don't know if it was her Western-style clothing or sureness of stride but I suspected she would speak English also.

'Excuse me!' I called as I set off after her. She stopped and turned towards me. 'We are trying to find Chokyi Nyima. Could you possibly tell us where to go?'

Much to my relief, she did not seem to consider this an odd request. 'Certainly. I'm going that way myself.' Her accent was English. Andrew and I fell into step beside her. The children immediately began to offer us unbeatable deals on shoe polishing, even though I was only wearing sandals.

'What brings you to Nepal?' she asked. When I told her the reason for wanting to see a Rinpoche, she nodded.

'I'm not a Buddhist myself,' she said, 'but many people believe the Rinpoche lamas can make predictions.'

We were about halfway around the stupa before we turned up a muddy track. There were more shops running up to large buildings in vibrant mustards and oranges. These were the Buddhist gompas, two or three storeys high and often enclosed by tall fences. People flocked up and down the trail and the inevitable dogs scrounged by the side of the path.

'That's the soup kitchen where I work.' Our guide pointed to a rough shack beside a stagnant pool. Some monks standing outside waved to her. A group of children sat beside the water, absorbed in a game.

We passed several gompas before coming to one that was predominantly white. Standing apart from the others each storey was capped by a red band with golden decorations. 'This is where you will find Chokyi Nyima,' she told us. We walked through the gates and up a flight of stairs. A young boy wearing robes approached us. Our

English friend spoke to him in Nepali and turned to us. 'He will show you where to go,' she said. 'I have to go back. Make sure you come and tell me how you get on.' With that she departed.

The boy led us into a hallway and up more stairs. We could hear the crashing of cymbals, a rhythmic chanting and resounding booming of a gong coming from one room. On the top floor the boy showed us a corridor. 'You go there,' he told us.

Somewhat apprehensively, we obeyed. We came upon two Nepali men waiting near a desk in a room with a marble floor. One held a Kata and I realised I had forgotten to bring a gift for the lama. They told us they were waiting to see Chokyi Nyima and bade us sit on an old sofa, next to a bedraggled, elderly dog. It had little hair left on its body, foul teeth, and one eye closed shut by accumulated pus. The other eye had the blue opacity of a cataract. Andrew grimaced and sat beside the beast. He put out a hand to pat it but recoiled as the dog spun with incredible speed and snapped at him. I suppressed a smile and decided I would stand. On the floor near the couch was a pool of either vomitus or faecal matter, no doubt from the dog.

An archway led to an adjacent room where another archway was covered with a heavy curtain. I guessed that the Rinpoche was in the room behind the curtain. Several pairs of shoes had been left beside it, suggesting he had people in with him.

A group of Westerners entered the waiting area. They all had either white scarves or bags of fruit. I wished that I had brought something. They were followed closely by an Asian group that seemed more familiar with the routine. They walked straight up to the curtain, kicked off their shoes and entered. I looked at Andrew. I really wanted to have some idea of what was going to happen behind the curtain before I went in. The two Nepali men and the group of Westerners also entered. A monk came and gestured that we should follow. As I was wondering how tactfully to find out what would be required of us, a lady approached from the direction of the stairway.

'Excuse me,' I said. 'Do you speak English?'

'Yes,' she replied.

'I want to see Chokyi Nyima,' I told her, 'but I am not sure what to do.'

'Oh, it's very simple. You take off your shoes and enter. You must prostrate yourself in front of him and he will speak.'

'But there are other people in with him now.'

'Yes. He is teaching.'

'Ah. But, I only want to ask him a question.'

'Then you ask after he has finished talking.'

'How long will that be?'

'Maybe two hours.'

I blanched. I had not bargained on everything being so formal and taking so long. We simply didn't have the time to wait. 'Is there a day when he does not teach, when I can just talk to him?'

She shrugged. 'Chokyi Nyima is very busy.'

'Okay. Thanks.'

She turned and, like the others, walked straight up to the curtain, removed her shoes and entered. I turned to Andrew. 'I'm not really sure about this,' I told him.

'Two hours is a long time,' he commented.

'We have to meet Dr Sharma at one.' I was looking for an excuse not to have to go in. 'And I haven't got a gift.' I looked towards the curtain for a moment and decided I really couldn't face it. 'Let's go,' I said.

I felt like a coward. I felt I had broken my promise to myself. The promise that I would leave no stone unturned.

We followed the trail back and came to the soup kitchen. I peered inside. A group of people were seated around a table. Obviously, I was interrupting a meeting of some kind. A woman in flowing black robes came over.

I explained why we were in Boudha and that the other lady had asked us to report back to her. I admitted sheepishly that we could not wait for two hours to see Chokyi Nyima and that we had also felt a bit hesitant about prostrating ourselves on the floor. She was very nice. She seemed concerned to hear about James and quickly dismissed our guilt at not waiting.

'Nonsense. Two hours is a long time. Why don't you go and see Thrangu Rinpoche in that gompa?' She nodded to a building opposite, painted in shades of burnt orange, saffron and lemon. The Rinpoche spoke some English and would be just as able to help us.

'My name's Lea, by the way. I'll take you up there.'

'But I have no gift.'

'Don't worry! Some rupees are fine.'

We followed her to the gompa and, as before, we were left in the care of a young man in maroon robes. He asked us to wait. We sat on a wooden bench and looked out a window that faced towards the stupa. Directly below was a field that was partially walled off. From our vantage point we could see pedestrians on the path we had just walked. A few head of cattle grazed in the field. I watched a woman walk from the path into the paddock. For a moment I wondered what she was doing. Then I realised, as she bunched her long skirt around her waist and crouched on her haunches. She was screened from the path by the crumbling brick wall but she had not spared a thought for the overlooking monastery. I turned away.

The youth came back and took us to a room that was once again partitioned by a curtain. We took off our shoes and he held the curtain open for us. Nervous, we entered. The Rinpoche was seated on an armchair, resplendent in saffron and maroon robes. Before him was a small table. Andrew and I both knelt down beside the table. I looked up at the lama. His age was indeterminate. He had very closely cropped hair and a kind face. His fingers were stained red from his prayer beads.

'I am hoping that you can help me,' I began. 'My brother went on a trek. He has not been seen since 22 December.' I drew out a map and spread it on the table. The lama remained silent. I wondered if this was a good thing or not. Had we breached some crucial rule of etiquette? Gamely, I persevered. I pointed to Gopte on the map.

'This is where he was last seen.'

The lama studied the map for a while, before finally speaking. 'Your brother was last seen here?' He indicated Gopte. I nodded. 'On 22 December?' I nodded again. 'That is a long time,' he said, thoughtfully. 'I will make a prayer for prediction.'

He rose from his chair and picked up a set of prayer beads. I kept my head bowed but Andrew watched and later told me that he ran the beads through his fingers and appeared to be talking to himself. After perhaps two minutes he leaned forward.

'I think you must look here.' He pointed to the area on the map to the south-west of Gopte, between Gopte and Talu. 'You will find your brother there.'

'Is he alive?' I questioned.

'You will meet your brother again.'

I felt absurdly happy at this. I grinned widely and felt tears prick my eyes.

'Thank you. Thank you so much.'

The Rinpoche seemed genuinely delighted to have made me so happy. He too smiled broadly. I picked up my map and awkwardly placed two hundred rupees on the table. I felt great. Even now, the search parties should be heading to look in the area the Rinpoche had indicated.

We went straight back to the soup kitchen. Lea was waiting for us. 'How did it go?' I told her what the lama had said. She was also overjoyed and gave me a hug. 'We will all pray for you,' she told me.

Andrew and I made our way back to where our driver was waiting. 'That's amazing, isn't it?' I said to Andrew. 'Perhaps he does know.'

'Well,' Andrew responded, 'I hope you're right. I'll tell you one thing though: if James is found alive there, I'll become a Buddhist!'

We got back to the hotel just after 11 a.m. and immediately phoned Graeme to see if there had been any word from the search parties. They had still not turned up.

Dr Sharma arrived after lunch with Mr Tschering, the owner of Himalayan Adventures trekking company. Mr Tschering said he thought he employed some sherpas from the area where we felt James might be found. Obviously, it would be to our advantage to hire local searchers. He said he would talk to his employees and let us know as soon as possible.

Andrew and I decided to find Tim and see if we could speak to Krishna. We headed into Thamel and found Tim at the Downtown Guest House. He took us along the narrow streets towards Durbar Square where he thought we could find Krishna.

The temples of Durbar Square are quite impressive. I wished I had made an effort to read more about the sights and buildings we encountered when we got there. It was obviously something of a meeting place. Many people sat in the square, sitting on walls and on the steps leading to the temples. There were piles of firewood for sale and the inevitable pedlars. Tim scanned the area but could not see Krishna. He approached a group of men standing on a cement platform nearby. 'Excuse me. I am looking for Krishna.'

'Ah, Krishna!' Several of the men nodded knowingly. With nothing more interesting to hand, a small crowd began to gather. It seemed they all knew Krishna and had an opinion as to his whereabouts. Their discourses on Krishna's probable location were regularly broken to spit. Distasteful though this habit was, I found it preferable to when people would block one nostril and blow a stream of mucus from the other onto the street, usually without breaking their stride.

They were telling Tim that Krishna had left Kathmandu to visit a sick relative when I suddenly saw him frown and roll his eyes in exasperation. 'For goodness' sake!' He pushed through the small crowd. 'That's Krishna over there.'

I followed his gaze to a line of men sitting on a wall. As we approached, Krishna recognised Tim. It quickly became clear that Krishna knew nothing that could help.

'It is very sad what has happened to James,' he told me, not even entertaining the notion that James could be alive. 'He was my friend. He had dinner at my house and bought candy for my children. I did not even know he was going trekking. I wish he had told me. If I had gone with him, I would not have let him try to cross the pass. It is very dangerous.' Krishna told me that he had seen posters as well as the television bulletin and heard the radio broadcast. It seemed that news of James's disappearance and the reward for finding him was spreading fast. Krishna had relatives in Kathmandu who were heading back to Dhunche the next day. He also said he had friends guiding treks into Helambu. I pulled out a number of black and white photographs of James. Quickly another crowd gathered around me. It seemed that the distribution of photos was something of a novelty and everyone wanted to see the photograph. I passed out several along with a bundle of the missing posters. There was a lot of conversing in Nepali and most people seemed to recognise the photos and posters. They all seemed very anxious to help.

Later in the evening, I thought about calling Calum. I had not spoken to him since leaving. It seemed like a long time ago now! I had deliberately refrained from dwelling on how much I was missing him and decided against phoning him now. I suspected it would upset me to hear his voice from so far away. The last thing Andrew needed was to have me teary and morose for the rest of the night.

JOANNE: *12 January 1992*

As we were wondering what the best course of action would be for the day, Sunday, Graeme called to say half of the Gopte search party was in. Carl Harrison would arrive in Kathmandu at about midday and we could meet him in the afternoon. This was a little surprising. After the helicopter flight on Friday we had assumed that they were still above Gopte. Obviously, they must have been on their way back down. It also appeared that they had found nothing. The news was disheartening. It was becoming obvious that, if James was still above Gopte, the best we could hope to find would be a body. The weather was likely to get worse before it got better. It may well be that the team could do no more before the spring thaw.

We breakfasted in the hotel restaurant for a change but the menu was identical to that in room service and the food no better. The view, however, was superior. A gardener was snipping at the brilliantly coloured marigolds. The sky was blue and the sun warm, a pleasant change to the usual mist. Right beside our window, a sparrow hopped delicately across the sill in search of crumbs. It was a very beautiful morning. It suddenly struck me how tragic it would be if James could never see a morning like this again. I felt tears well in my eyes and an almost overwhelming sadness.

Mr Tschering called as promised. He introduced us to two sherpas he employed from Trisuli Bazaar. It turned out that one of them also knew of the trail between the path to Gosainkund and Talu. I mentally chalked up another point for us versus popular opinion.

From the meeting, we went up to Blue Mountain. I had yet another update to fax home. I was still feeling depressed. I also felt I had to start preparing my parents for the worst. There was no point in sending fax after fax that might create false hope. The vast majority of the people I had met so far held no hope for James's survival. I wrote in this fax that we would meet with Carl that afternoon and would be sure to question him thoroughly about all that had happened so far. I added, 'If James did not find a way down to the south-west or did not change his mind and try to cross the pass there is no hope of finding him alive. We will have to consider the possibility that he may never be found or that he is buried under snow and carefully weigh the value of more searching above Gopte before the warmer weather begins. I will have to question Carl closely about this.'

I tacked on another paragraph to soften it. 'I am sorry this fax is so blunt but we have to accept that, as time goes by, the chances of finding James alive grow less and less. However, I refuse to give up all hope and we will continue to pursue every possibility no matter how remote.'

We returned to the Hotel Kathmandu and joined Tim in the coffee bar where we waited to hear from Carl Harrison. The hours passed and still we heard nothing. I eventually rang Graeme. He'd had not been contacted by Carl either.

Maria turned up a short time later. She had been out with some friends she thought we might like to meet, Dorrilyn and Prajan. Dorrilyn is an intensive care nurse from Australia; she had come to Nepal on an aid project and met Prajan. They had married and were now living in Kathmandu, just a short distance from Tom and Maria's. Jon and Anne-Maree Young joined us. Anne-Maree was a doctor who had trained in Brisbane and was here with her husband who was working as an engineer in Nepal. They all offered to help in any way they could. So, there were plenty of people to chat with while we waited. I probably appeared quite rude: I could not concentrate on the conversation. My eyes kept sliding to the entrance of the hotel, looking for

Carl or Graeme. It was 6 p.m. when they walked into the foyer. The others left quickly, leaving Andrew, Tim and me to talk with them.

My first impression was that Carl looked the part. Not overly tall, he was slim and appeared very fit. He had black hair that fell in curls to his shoulders, striking grey-blue eyes and a thick moustache. He spoke slowly and precisely with an American accent. It did not take long before I accepted that Carl knew what he was talking about. He was thorough and conscientious and explained unhurriedly what had been done on their last expedition. The party had been dropped by the helicopter at Tharepati. Graeme looked surprised.

'I thought it was Gopte,' he said.

'No,' said Carl. 'It was Tharepati.' They had borrowed some cooking equipment from the lodge keeper at Tharepati and had climbed up to Gopte where they had camped the night. From Gopte, they had walked upwards for four hours to Phedi. My ears pricked up at this. Carl was the first person to mention Phedi, despite my having read of it in some of the trekking guides. From what Tim and Mark had told us, James had been two to three hours out of Gopte. By travelling as far up as Phedi, Carl should have easily covered the area where Mark and James parted, possibly a bit beyond.

From Phedi they had searched down to Gopte. They had searched every hut and every cave, looked over the edge of every ridge and into every gully. Carl was confident that, if James had died between Phedi and Gopte, they would have found his body. He explained that footprints can be frozen into the snow. Also, he pointed out, food was scarce above the snowline. If there was a body it would be found by scavenging animals and their tracks would reveal where the body was.

I asked Carl about the high and dangerous trail I had read about that bypassed Gopte on the way to Tharepati. Carl said that, if James had been on that trail and fallen, he would have fallen onto the lower trail which runs below it and, again, they would have found his body.

The party had stayed three nights at Gopte, scouring the area between there and Phedi. Then they had gone back to Tharepati and taken a trail to Talu and Kaseri. There was no sign of James at either village.

This was a bitter disappointment. I had reasoned that, if James had headed south-west, he would have had to pass through either Talu or Kaseri. Carl told us that the lodge keeper from Phedi was at Talu and he did not recall either James or Mark passing in any direction. The lodge keeper from Gopte was now at Tharepati. He also had not seen

106

James or Mark. But both lodge keepers should have been at their lodges when Mark and James passed through. Had they forgotten or were they not telling the truth for some reason?

Carl said that, from their very first expedition, the one that had turned around at Tharepati on the basis of the Canadians' words, they had verified that James and Mark had been in Kutumsang on 20 December. They had found the signed receipts for both of them allowing their entry to the National Park. For all we knew, if Mark had not shown up in Kathmandu on Christmas Eve, the two of them could have vanished off the face of the Earth after Kutumsang. None of the lodge owners further along the trail could recall them. Yet they must have stayed somewhere . . .

The men from Helambu were also in. Carl had yet to speak to them but there was possibly something more to be learnt from the lodge keeper at Chisopani who remembered James passing through. Carl asked Tim to accompany him to a meeting with the Helambu searchers next morning. I looked hopefully at Tim.

'Don't get excited,' he told me. 'I'll bet the lodge keeper remembers me coming back down and is getting me confused with James.'

There were still a few things that bothered me. I could not help but wonder if Mark and James had stayed at Phedi instead of Gopte overnight on the 21st. Had we searched close enough to the pass? Why were the lodge keepers not being truthful about James and Mark having stayed? I knew my brother. He was outgoing and would have talked to them. He also had striking red hair. That was enough to draw attention. Could they have found James's body and robbed it? Had they offered to guide James back and attacked him? How could we get them to tell the truth?

These were the questions on my mind after everyone left. We would meet at the embassy after Carl spoke with the men from Helambu in the morning. He felt there were still two likely areas to search. One was above Phedi and over the pass. He said it would be easy to wander off the path once over the other side. The other was in the Shivapuri forest, just north of Kathmandu, in case James had followed the trail they had used on the way up but become lost in the forest. This was a long shot. It depended on whom the lodge keeper at Chisopani had seen on the way down.

While we waited for room service to bring up our dinner, the phone rang. It was Maria.

'Joanne, I don't know if you are interested in this or not . . .' she began. She told me about her friend, Lottie Weisse, who had a message for me from a psychic. 'I thought I should give you Lottie's number. It's really up to you whether you follow this up or not.'

I thanked her and hung up. Andrew shook his head in disgust. The excursion to see the lama had tried his scepticism of the supernatural.

Stubbornly, I dialled Lottie's number. She spoke English with a Swiss accent and seemed glad to hear from me.

'Yes, Joanne. I have a message for you from a psychic friend of mine.' Lottie's friend was Chinese and believed she was visited by the spirit of a female god. This was getting a little too mystical even for my new-found open-mindedness.

'Oh, yes,' I said. 'And what does she say?'

Lottie told me this lady had seen an image of James in a hut at Gosainkund and that he was in very great danger.

'My friend says you must get there very quickly. He needs you to be there. You must hire a helicopter.'

'I want to speak to your friend,' I told Lottie. She was not sure if her friend would agree.

'I will ask her and phone you back.'

It was not long before she called again. I found myself shivering as I answered the phone. Lottie's friend had agreed to call me in hour. It was after 10 p.m. and was going to be another late night. I tried to eat some dinner while I waited. Andrew was still fairly disparaging but I pointed out that no one had checked the huts at Gosainkund yet.

Eventually she called. She repeated what Lottie had told me: James was in a hut at Gosainkund and in very great danger.

'You must get there very quickly. He is being held against his will. You should hire a helicopter tomorrow and send up some people in authority. He is in great danger.'

'But we have men who left Dhunche on foot going to Gosainkund now,' I told her.

'I do not think they will help you,' she said. 'You must get to your brother quickly. He is waiting for you to help him.'

I thanked her and hung up. The call had left me feeling quite rattled. I was shaking and my teeth were chattering. Andrew tried to reason with me.

'Look, you've got two men who should get to Gosainkund in the next day or so. They will check all the huts. If James is there they'll find him.' I had to agree that what Andrew said made perfect sense. What was the point in chartering a helicopter when the men were nearly there on foot, anyway? As for James being 'held against his will', Andrew dismissed the idea that other people were involved.

'That could mean he is snowed in. There's no way James could be overpowered by even three or four Nepali.'

I accepted Andrew's opinion but lay awake for quite a while thinking over what she had said.

JOANNE: *13 January 1992*

Tim arrived by 9 a.m. to join Carl and the Helambu search team. Before they left I told Carl what the psychic had told me. He said it was extremely unlikely that anyone would stay in huts at Gosainkund at this time of year as it was so cold. I put it to him that James could be trapped there by the weather and he replied with a shrug, 'It's possible.' I would later learn Carl kept an open mind about most things. He would say those words to me many times over the ensuing weeks.

I had been up early, writing a fax to send home. Andrew and I went up to Blue Mountain to send it. Maria was eager to hear how I had fared with Lottie. I guess we must have looked pretty miserable because Tom stopped work to join us.

He suggested increasing the reward for finding James alive to A$3000 to get more people motivated. It was not much and, if we found James alive, it would be worth every penny. Tom said he would arrange for new posters, offering 100,000 rupees.

Tom also said he knew Colonel Pun, the leader of the Army helicopter unit. He phoned the colonel and arranged a meeting for that evening. Tom was quite excited by the time he finished.

'It looks very promising,' he said. 'Colonel Pun has to take training flights out every day. He has offered to conduct all those flights in the Gosainkund area.' This was far better than I had dared hope, and cheered us up.

Andrew and I walked to the embassy for our meeting with Carl and Ingo Schnabel. Ingo is the field officer of the Himalayan Rescue Dog-training Centre, a project for Sundarijal Bikas (Sundarijal development). As Tim had suspected, the lead from the Chisopani lodge keeper was nothing more than his recollection of him returning through Chisopani on the night of 20 December. Ingo agreed with Carl that they would have found a body if there was one to be found: 'Let me tell you – we found a lodge that was completely locked up but two crows were pecking on the roof. We wondered if there was a body inside, so we broke in. There was nothing.' He also explained that his dogs could smell bodies under deep snow. He was not happy about the lodge keeper from Phedi. Ingo explained that Talu was near a lot of forest where it would be quite easy to hide a body.

Obviously, they had been very thorough. I told them I wanted them to go back up as soon as possible to check the area from Dhunche to Phedi. The two men that had gone up by helicopter to search that area would only look on the trail. I asked Carl and Ingo to check off the trail as well. If Ingo and Carl had found nothing by the time they reached Phedi, I wanted them to go down along the trail between Phedi and Talu. They were to keep asking people and to convey a message of 'no questions asked' to the locals.

They said they would organise a large search party to leave Kathmandu on Thursday 16th. I was impatient but it would take them that long to organise men and provisions. They had also been out for virtually two weeks straight and needed some time to rest. I suggested they fly up to Dhunche but they declined. It would not allow them to acclimatise to the altitude properly. They would hire a minibus and drive to Dhunche on Thursday. After leaving Dhunche, they would need to stop in Shin Gompa to adapt to the altitude, but they could be in Gosainkund by Sunday, I guess it was the conversation I'd had with the psychic the previous evening that was making me anxious to get someone to Gosainkund as quickly as possible.

Carl and Ingo both had bills that needed paying, so I set about organising that while Tim and Andrew went into town to reorganise flights home. Andrew and I were due to fly out on the 27th, but Andrew felt he would need to leave before then.

I went back up to Blue Mountain to send off another fax.

During lunch the phone rang again. This time it was Lottie Weisse with another suggestion. She was good friends with the Chinia Lama and had been telling him about my brother.

'I'm sorry,' I cut in. 'Who is the Chinia Lama?'

He was a political and religious leader from the Helambu area, a man of great influence there. Now based at Boudha, he had already perceived we might be having problems getting information from the locals and was keen to help. Mrs Weisse explained that the people in Helambu were obliged by their beliefs to tell this man and his representatives the truth. I arranged to see him in the evening, after our meeting with Colonel Pun.

The colonel is a very nice man. The most experienced helicopter pilot in Nepal, he has flown a number of illustrious figures around his country, including Jimmy Carter. He confirmed he could redirect his training flights over the Gosainkund/Helambu area. He would land at

110

villages and talk to people for us and would distribute more reward posters and photographs. This could also be a good way to enhance our communications with the search parties. I suggested that the search teams carry brightly coloured banners to display if they had found anything important when the helicopter flew overhead. If Colonel Pun saw a banner he would land as close as possible. We decided pink and orange would stand out well against snow or jungle. After a few drinks we thanked the colonel and left.

'So, what now?' asked Tom. I explained that I was to meet with the Chinia Lama. I was happy to go by myself but Tom said he would come.

Mrs Weisse's house was up a lane. A servant let us through the gate. We knocked at the front door and a woman appeared at the top of the stairs.

'Come up, come up.' I recognised Mrs Weisse's voice.

Upstairs, we were in a dimly lit living-room. I was surprised by the number of people there. They had obviously been in the midst of a discussion, but all attention now turned to Tom and me. The Chinia Lama was a short, round man with a moon-shaped face. He wore a black topi and a scarf around his neck and spoke limited English. Tom told the story of James in Nepali. When Tom had finished, the lama said he was eager to help. His 'family' were nodding in agreement.

'What you must do,' he told me, 'is to arrange for a helicopter to take me up to the people. Then I will talk to them. If none of them know anything, I will ask others to go out and talk to everyone else. You must give me some money to pay these people.'

I agreed readily. We arranged to meet the Chinia Lama the next morning and organise a helicopter. The Chinia Lama also wanted me to go and see his Rinpoche. I was to return to Mrs Weisse's tomorrow and Kai would take me out to the lama's home at Boudha.

JOANNE: *14 January 1992*

'Jesus Christ! Who'd come to a place where you can't eat the food or drink the water?'

Andrew was feeling sorry for himself. I had teased him that he was suffering the effects of too much of the colonel's whiskey, but it was obviously more than that. We had both woken up feeling nauseous and with diarrhoea. Andrew was vomiting as well. It was surprising we had both been well for as long as we had. Only yesterday Maria had been telling me that you haven't 'arrived' in Kathmandu until you caught diarrhoea and everyone invariably 'arrives' within five days. Andrew would spend the day in bed. Apart from the need to rest, it was probably wise not to stray too far from a toilet. I left to meet the Chinia Lama again with Maria who came along for moral support.

The Chinia Lama lived in a two-storey house which was dark and cold inside. We took off our shoes as was the custom. I kept meaning to wear slip-on shoes but, invariably, would only remember as I struggled with shoe laces. We were shown into a sitting-room, seated ourselves and the Chinia Lama asked for tea to be brought.

Nepali tea is brewed with milk and sugar already added. It is very sweet. We sipped it from dainty cups and the lama explained his plans. Kai, Lottie's son, was able to translate. The lama suggested we charter a chopper from the private company at the airport. Their choppers were bigger than the army Alouettes and quite plushly fitted out. The lama said he knew the manager and could get a discount. We agreed to see if Graeme would go up with him to show that the lama was working with the embassy. I also felt Graeme knew the whole story and would ensure the correct facts were being passed on. Kai agreed to go as translator. Before we organised the helicopter, we went to visit the lama's Rinpoche.

We walked into a small courtyard, where the Rinpoche was waiting. The Chinia Lama took me aside and thrust a white scarf into my hand. 'You put some money into the Kata and put it on the table before the Rinpoche,' he told me. I did as he directed, approaching the Rinpoche nervously. Laying the flimsy scarf on the table, I sat before him. He picked up the scarf, removed the rupees and made a blessing before placing the scarf around my neck. Like the other Rinpoche, he picked up his prayer beads and ran them through his fingers, muttering under his breath. He spoke to the Chinia Lama in Tibetan. The Chinia Lama looked at me and said, 'The Rinpoche says your brother is alive. He is going to ask everyone in his gompa to pray for him.' I thanked the Rinpoche and he rose and left. The rest of the morning was spent organizing the helicopter and introducing the lama to Graeme at the embassy. When Kai and the lama had left, Graeme said he had a telephone number for Mateus/Mathial whose name was actually Mathias. The German Embassy had traced a Mathias Wasgelt with the passport number we had given them. Word had also come in from Australia that Mark Fulton was booked to fly out from Bangkok at 8.30 a.m. on Thursday 16th with Qantas.

'Thank goodness!' I said. 'The timing could not be better. Tim is flying out to Bangkok tomorrow, the 15th, and not leaving until

Thursday evening. He should be able to intercept Mark Fulton. We should ask an official from the Australian Embassy in Thailand to accompany him. I'll prepare a list of questions for Tim to ask. We should also send a list to the Australian Embassy in Thailand.' I would call Bangkok myself. Going through Graeme would mean having to go through Canberra first.

The two men who had been dropped at Dhunche by helicopter had also reported in, their mission thwarted by the weather. They had distributed many posters and had spoken to everyone they met but no one had any more information. Conditions were so bad, they had not been able to make it to Gosainkund. That meant the huts at Gosainkund had still not been searched.

Carl had suggested that the lama and Graeme try to get to Talu and Tharepati, where the lodge keepers from Phedi and Gopte were, and said it was imperative the lama land at his home town, where he would command the greatest respect.

When we returned to the hotel there were two messages to call Dad. They had extra information about Mark Fulton. Mark had travelled to Nepal with a friend. Where was this second person now? They had also been told that Mark had been due to fly out on 25 December to Bangkok but this ticket had been cancelled. Gaye had sought information from a psychic in Australia over the telephone. This psychic had told Gaye that James was still alive and that he was repeatedly saying 'leave me alone' and 'I'm deep down below' and that 'the pass was blocked'. This woman had also said that James was currently very distressed and confused and that Gaye and the family would never know what had happened.

I felt very disquieted by the time I had finished speaking to Dad. I seemed repeatedly to be running into brick walls. Perhaps there was one brick wall that I could do something about immediately. I tried Mathias's number. The phone was answered in German.

'Hello,' I said. 'Do you speak English?'

'Yes.'

'Can I speak to Mathias please?'

'Yes, speaking.'

'Mathias, my name is Joanne and I am calling from Kathmandu. You were recently trekking in Helambu?'

'Yes, that's right.'

'You remember there was a search for an Australian trekker and you left a note in Sundarijal to notify people that you were trekking alone?'

'Yes.'

'I am the sister of that trekker. He has still not been found. A group of trekkers thought they saw him, but we think it may have been you they saw. Can you tell me please, do you remember passing any other trekkers?'

'Yes,' Mathias answered. 'I passed a large group of trekkers between Tarke Ghyang and Shermathang on 30 December in the early afternoon.' A stab of disappointment hit me. That was where the French Canadians had reported seeing James.

'Do you recall anything about the trekkers?' I asked.

'Yes, they were speaking French.' There could be little doubt that Mathias had passed the same group. He continued, 'I only spoke to one of them. She was the last person.'

I recalled my conversation with the Canadian woman. She had been walking last in line. Mathias continued: 'She had very big eyes. I noticed them straight away.'

With a sinking heart I recalled the anomaly in the woman's eyes that instantly drew one's attention to them. What he said next meant there could be no further doubt. 'She asked me where I was from and I told her Germany.'

Mathias had repeated the exact words that the woman had told me. It was only then I realised how much I had been hoping against the odds that it had been James the Canadians had seen. I thanked Mathias for his help and thoughtfulness in leaving a note and hung up, despondent.

I think the fact that Tim was leaving the next day was adding to my depression. Tim was the last person we knew who had seen James alive. Tim and James had shared what was quite possibly the last weeks of James's life together. I could not help feel that saying goodbye to him was going to be like saying goodbye to a part of James.

JOANNE: *15 January 1992*

We arrived at the Downtown Guest House early in the morning. Tim was packed and ready to go. James's luggage was in two bags. I gave Tim the list of questions to ask Mark and a letter for him to take back to Calum. I had written it last night when I felt depressed. Tim said he would be sure to contact Gaye and my parents. It was also going to be difficult for Gaye and my parents to see Tim back in Australia alone: he and James should have returned together.

We said our goodbyes and Andrew and I took James's luggage back to our room. We then went up to Blue Mountain to pick up a fax we were expecting from Dad. We had barely walked in the door, when Tom called out, 'Quickly! Go to the embassy. They have found Mark Fulton. He will be phoning there any minute.'

Andrew and I ran back to the embassy and stormed through reception up to Auli's office. Tim was on the phone to Fulton. Auli had rung the Downtown Guest House just after we left and Tim had come straight over. Tim handed me the receiver.

'Mark,' I said, 'this is Joanne, James's sister.' We spoke for about forty minutes. Mark seemed very surprised to hear James had not shown up. Had he realised it was going to be this serious, he would never have left for Bangkok.

Mark told me that he had met James and Tim at Chipling on 20 December. He had no plans to cross the pass until James had said he and Tim were going to. Mark decided to join them and they would all attempt the Gosainkund trail. Tim was forced to turn back about an hour later with his sore leg. James and Mark continued on, staying at Mangengoth on the night of the 20th. Also staying at Mangengoth was an older German trekker with Nepali porters. In the morning, the two had left Mangengoth and arrived at Gopte at about 11 a.m. They'd had a cup of tea there and the lodge keeper told them they could continue on to Phedi that day.

'Gopte is on top of a ridge. You can just see Phedi from there,' Mark told me. 'We climbed down, then up and along the trail in the side of the ridge to reach Phedi.' They had spent the night at Phedi.

'Mark,' I said, trying to keep the anger out of my voice, 'why did you tell Tim that you stayed at Gopte?'

Mark denied he had. 'I said Phedi. We stayed at the foot of the pass. That's what Phedi means.'

I glanced at Tim who frowned and shrugged. I asked Mark to describe Phedi. He told me it had two huts: one where the lodge keeper and sherpas stay and the other for trekkers. The lodge keeper, his wife and their two children had been at Phedi. The lodge keeper had been very friendly.

'We've spoken to the lodge keeper from Phedi,' I told Mark. 'He says he doesn't remember you.'

'I find that hard to believe,' Mark replied. 'We bought his last chook from him. He was leaving to get below the snow the next morning, so we asked him if we could buy the chook and if he would cook it for us. He sold it to us for 200 rupees. We all ate it with dhal that night.'

On the morning of the 22nd, they had left Phedi at about eight o'clock, at the same time as the lodge keeper. There was some light

115

snow as they headed off. 'Perhaps two to three inches,' Mark said. As they had walked, the snow fell harder until there was only fifty to a hundred metres visibility. They had been following a path adjacent to a creek but had come to a place with a few stones (Mark thought they might have been a ruin of some kind) and lost the path. They thought they saw the path cross the creek so they had crossed and followed another branch of the creek. At this stage Mark said they were 'walking blind looking for the trail'. After following this second creek for perhaps a kilometre, they had come to what appeared to be a cliff wall. They could not pass this, so they retraced their footsteps. After about 500 metres, James said to Mark that he knew he could be back in Kathmandu in time for Christmas if he turned back then. Apparently James was very anxious to be back in Kathmandu for Christmas so he could phone his fiancée. And so they had separated.

James had continued back along the creek and Mark had climbed in a zig-zag fashion for the next two hours to the top of the pass. Once he got there, he realised they had been well to the west of where they should have been. Mark sounded amazingly unconcerned that he had been wandering around the slopes of a 5000-metre mountain in snow, trying to find his way. It was incredible that he had made it. I asked Mark if he didn't think it was very foolish of them to get themselves into such a position and then to separate. I did not want to deter Mark from giving us all the information he could but I could not help an angry and accusatory tone from creeping into my voice. Mark did not think they had done anything foolish. He said that all James had to do to return to Phedi was to follow the creek back. He never thought that James would have any trouble. He felt James had been overly concerned about the snowfall and altitude sickness, although he had not been showing any symptoms. As for himself, Mark said he had wanted to push on and try to clear the pass. If he had not found it by 1 p.m., he would have turned back.

After he had crossed the pass, the weather had deteriorated even further. He came to a lodge, probably at Gosainkund, and met up with an Israeli who was heading in the same direction and two Australians who were intending to cross the pass. The Israeli called himself 'Shai'. Mark stopped briefly to eat something and then had paired up with Shai. They had walked on to Shin Gompa where they stayed the night. The next morning, four hours' walk had seen them to Dhunche and then they had caught a truck carrying wool bales to Trisuli Bazaar. They had stayed at Trisuli overnight and travelled on to Kathmandu the next day.

Mark did not have an inkling of how lucky he had been in finding his way out. He verified that James had no matches or food, except for a couple of chocolate bars. He assured me they had parted amicably. I asked him about the information my parents had: he denied he had travelled to Kathmandu with a friend and that he had changed his flight between Kathmandu and Bangkok. He said my parents should feel free to contact him: he would arrive in Cairns at 11.55 p.m. the following evening. He gave me phone numbers for him and his parents and a description of how he looked and what he would be wearing. He also told me where he was staying in Bangkok.

I hung up shaking my head. James had been missing twenty-four days. I dreaded to think how much money had been put into the search so far, certainly well over $10,000. And we had not yet covered the area where James had last been seen. So far, no one had been above Phedi. James could be lying dead a mere fifty metres from where he and Mark had separated and we wouldn't know it.

Tim shook his head in disbelief. Not only had it been snowing when they separated, but they were completely lost as well. He said, 'Mark gave me no indication that things were so bad. He seemed to feel that James would have no trouble getting back. I can't remember him ever mentioning Phedi.'

I was very angry and frustrated. I had no doubt that Mark was telling the truth and that he had done nothing to harm James. What seemed amazing was how casual and unconcerned he appeared about it all. Therein lay the problem: Mark gave the impression he had no idea how much danger they had been in.

Andrew and I headed back to Blue Mountain to fax home this information. Things were looking worse and worse. We now knew that James had been heading back to Phedi, not Gopte, but the Phedi lodge keeper claimed to know nothing. I phoned Carl Harrison. When I described where Mark and James had separated, Carl said he thought he knew the spot and that he and Ingo would change their plans to cover the area between Phedi and the pass first. Maria offered us lunch but I felt too anxious to eat. Andrew had something and we went back to the embassy to wait for Graeme and the lama to return. I had a sickening certainty that they would have news for me.

We had not been waiting long. Auli had joined us for a cup of tea when we heard a phone ring and GK, the embassy's chief-clerk, appeared. 'Excuse me,' he said. 'That call was from some friends of mine in the village of Banepa. There has been a sighting of someone in the forest near there. A tall, red-haired man wearing a white T-shirt was asleep in the woods near a water well. When some children woke him, he jumped up and ran into the forest.'

I leapt out of my chair, my heart pounding. 'GK, where is Banepa?'

The map showed Banepa was a small village to the east and slightly south of Kathmandu. It was no more than one to two hours' drive away, on a road between Kathmandu and Helambu, where James might have reached.

I was staggered. 'But, shit! To be sleeping in a forest and running away from people. What sort of state is he in? Someone has to go there now,' I said. Auli organised for GK to go out with Andrew. I felt torn: I wanted to go out to Banepa but felt I had to wait for the helicopter. I was also a little scared: if this was James, I was not sure I could stand seeing him in such a distressed state.

After they had gone, I sank into a chair, numb. As always, there was nothing I could do except wait. I was shaking and my heart was beating hard. I made an effort to calm down.

'Auli,' I said. 'No matter what, my parents are not to be told of this sighting. I can't put them through another false sighting.'

Graeme returned just before 4 p.m. He had no further news. Using the Chinia Lama had been an excellent idea. The respect shown to the man was enormous. Everyone in the villages had come to greet him and they had been eating and drinking all day.

'I just know I'll have the runs tomorrow,' Graeme said. As promised, the lama had deputised fifteen people to go out and ask everyone in the local villages if they knew anything. Graeme seemed fairly confident that, if there was anything new to learn, this was the way to get it. Unfortunately, they had been unable to land at Talu due to the weather so the lama had not spoken to the lodge keeper himself, but his representatives should do so. Graeme said the Chinia Lama had organised a runner to report to him in Boudha with any news. The deputised villagers would be out a full five days. Graeme also said Colonel Pun had been to most of the villages already. The posters with the new rewards were everywhere, as were photos of James.

The two-way radio crackled into life. It was GK. The voices were very distorted and hard to understand. It seemed someone had been seen so they were going on a little further. Andrew came on the line.

'Yeah, look, I really don't think it's James. Everyone here is talking at once.' Nevertheless, he agreed they should go on to the next village. Despite this, I still felt hopeful that it might have been James.

'Do you want a cup of tea?' Auli aksed.

'I need something stronger,' I said, only half joking. She organised a rum for me. I was probably onto my third rum by the time GK and Andrew contacted us again. It was after five and they were heading back.

I was feeling much more relaxed. I had not eaten anything all day and the rum was mellowing me out nicely. It had been a hard day. We had received the devastating news that we'd spent the last twenty-four days searching in the wrong spot; I had expected Graeme to tell me they were bringing James's body back; and then I heard James may be sitting in a forest. I was sick of the stress, tired and I decided the only appropriate action was to have a few drinks and try to forget about things for a while. I asked Graeme if he could ring Himalayan Adventures and organise some men to go out tomorrow to Banepa. He said he would. Auli and Graeme suggested we wait somewhere else but I was quite happy. As their working day was over, they joined me in another drink.

Andrew and GK arrived back at 7. Andrew was convinced it hadn't been James. They had not been able to find out who had made the sighting and what had actually happened. Everyone had congregated around the vehicle and, eager to help, had spoken all at once. Everyone had their own story and no one was exactly sure about anything. We would send more search parties out tomorrow.

Auli asked us to stay for dinner. Tom and Maria, who had heard of the day's dramas, also joined us. Wine was served before and during dinner. By that time, I was extremely tipsy. I can't remember much of the meal, but Andrew informed me that I served myself huge helpings which I pushed around my plate without eating. Everyone waited politely for me to finish. I had not slowed down my drinking and, suddenly, I realised I was going to have to leave quickly. I grabbed Andrew's arm and said, in what I hoped was a whisper, 'I've got to leave. Can you come with me, please? I don't know if I can make it to the door.'

What a good friend! Andrew helped me outside into the cold night air. I stood beside Tom's jeep for a minute, unsure of what to do next. Tom came to our rescue. I had left my coat and my ever-present knapsack on the floor inside. He brought them out and drove us back to the hotel. With his and Andrew's assistance, I made it to room 427 and took myself straight to the bathroom where I was violently sick. I came out, feeling a little better. Tom and Andrew stood watching me with concern as I crawled into bed.

JAMES: *15 January 1992*

There was a glorious full moon. The stars paled in comparison. It was truly a sight to behold: a crystal clear night, icy cold, but the attraction was enough for me to poke my head out. Judging by the moon, I knew that it was almost four weeks since I had become trapped. I had stopped counting the days on 6 January.

That had been a hard day for me to cope with emotionally. Until then, I'd kept myself removed as much as possible from the grief and anxiety that would be suffered back in Australia. January 6th, however, was the day that Gaye was due to return to work. Things had not gone well for her in the latter part of the year and it was largely my fault. I'd had glandular fever in March and the virus hit Gaye more seriously in October. The doctor had recommended a couple of weeks off work but when she tried to resume her duties she found the nausea and tiredness too difficult to cope with so her employer suggested she take more leave and ensure complete recovery. That was at the beginning of November.

It was good, in a sense, as it gave us more time to spend with each other before I left for Nepal. In those three weeks, we'd been together every spare moment and grown closer than ever. I remembered how upset Gaye had been at the airport. But I had come to Nepal anyway and now was in a disastrous position with little chance of ever getting out. What a great fiancé I'd turned out to be! She would have been so much better off if she'd never met me.

During the day of 6 January I prayed especially hard that Gaye would be at work. My own prospects had taken a turn for the worse on that day when, around midday, the clouds that had been hovering over the southern end of the valley, blustered upwards, engulfing my mountainside in snow. I'm not usually superstitious but I couldn't help think that this change in weather coinciding with the day Gaye was to resume work was a bad omen. After a bit more thought, I'd come to the more logical conclusion that I had been lucky to have five days of good weather. Given the frosty temperatures within the valley, it was little wonder it was snowing again.

As I watched the heavy flakes of snow forming a powder layer, I thought how quickly all the good work of the sun was being undone. I tried to remain positive, thinking those five days of sunshine had not been a complete waste. After all, I had dried all my clothes and was much more comfortable. I had also been out to the knoll and seen the vastness of the valley, reassuring myself that it hadn't been through pure laziness that I was trapped here: it was physically impossible to get out. The sun had also lifted my spirits and fed the urge to keep going.

But one of the most significant findings I had made during that sunny period was how to get water without having to melt the snow or ice in my mouth. In the mornings, when collecting the snow in my sleeping bag cover, I would pack it in solidly, in order to fit as much in as I could. At times, I'd taken large chunks of icy snow and crushed them to as small a volume as possible, forming hard, compact balls of ice. Occasionally I made too many and would leave them sitting in the snow until my afternoon collection. On one of the clear days, some of these snowballs had been exposed to the sun. When I came back in the afternoon I noticed they had not shrunk at all. As I picked one up, water dribbled out the bottom. I immediately held the ball up to let the soothing water trickle onto my dry tongue. I bit into the snowball and was surprised by how wet it tasted. I put in to my lips and sucked out a satisfying quantity of water. I sucked it from every angle, drinking every drop. Here was a ready source of water without having to hold solid snow in my mouth until it melted. The taste of pure water was so good compared to snow. By sheer luck, I had discovered how to get pure water, free of the grit and dirt that mixed with the drips that fell from the rock.

My morning routine changed from that day onwards. I now made a series of rock-hard snowballs, some of which I put into the bag. I also made another pile which I set out to catch the sun reasonably early in the day. Using the snowballs in my sleeping bag cover, I could melt the snow in my mouth until the middle of the day. Then the snowballs would be ready to suck. When I had taken all the available water I put them in the bag for later.

It was the end of the day that I really looked forward to. These enormous snowballs waiting for me were perhaps twenty centimetres wide and a kilogram in weight, dripping with water. This afternoon habit became something of an addiction. The soothing trickle down my dry throat was one of the few highlights of the day and my mind would focus upon the pleasure for hours beforehand.

When the cloud and snow returned, the moment was often a letdown. In the freezing temperatures, after hours of anticipation, I often found the hard balls of ice had not thawed at all.

The change in weather began in a very dramatic fashion. On the night of 6 January, darkness seemed deeper than ever due to the thickness of snow and cloud. Then the winds picked up and I saw flashes of lightning in the distance. The soft rumble of thunder was barely audible at first. Gradually, the flashes became more brilliant and the sound of thunder increased. Within a couple of hours, the wind was howling, blowing the snow in all directions. The sharp crash of thunder would follow only seconds after the lightning. I kept my head out of the sleeping bag and watched in amazement and fear – fear for my own safety as the snow was now being swept under my shelter, covering the dry ledge where I lay. In the darkness, I groped around, collecting all the books, letters, shoes and clothing that were rapidly being covered by a thin layer of snow. I was huddled up against the back wall of my shelter, watching as an occasional flake would fall upon my sleeping bag. But, for the most part, about fifteen centimetres of dry territory remained between me and the snow.

In the early hours of the morning, the wind dropped. When I awoke later it was daylight. Snow was still falling heavily. My rocky ledge was mostly white but snow was no longer being blown under the overhang. I got up and, using my hairbrush, swept as much of the snow away from my bed as I possibly could. The dry space was smaller but adequate. It would be another week before my ledge was completely free of snow again.

The heavy snowfall continued for a couple of days and a pattern appeared to have set in. Each morning, I would wake to find the sky crystal clear and the sun shining brightly onto the wall across the valley. Southwards down the valley, I could see the cloud and mist waiting to creep up towards me. I would always hope they would leave me to enjoy my afternoon sun, but very rarely did this happen. As the tops of the nearby trees were catching their first rays of sunlight, the clouds would have insidiously edged their way upwards, ever so slowly. It would always be a race to see which would win. It would vary as to which came first but the clouds would come inevitably and, if I was blessed with any direct sun it was short lived. Several dumpings of snow ensured my continued imprisonment.

With the clothing I had for these conditions now dry, I could tolerate the cold much better. As well as sleeping during the day, I would usually catch a couple of hours at night which helped pass those long, dark hours quickly. Sleep was genuinely the highlight of my day, even surpassing the pleasure of snowballs laden with water. My dreams were so real that, when I woke, it was hard for me to believe I was back in this frozen landscape. The dreams of family and friends and food and home filled me with such delight that I looked forward to going to sleep.

The bear had left me four or five days after it appeared. I decided that it too was cold or hungry or both and headed for a more hospitable environment. In a morbid way, I missed it. Although its screams were terrifying, they certainly broke the monotony of night.

It was replaced by two other visitors. One day as I lay in my sleeping bag reading *Great Expectations* for the fourth time, I heard the fluttering of wings above me and spotted two large, black birds on a branch of the fir trees in front of my shelter. They had none of the daintiness or beauty of the smaller birds that kept me company. They were black and ugly and appeared as hungry as I was. Their beady eyes stared back. 'No bird's going to peck at my carcass,' I thought and squirmed out of my sleeping bag to chase them away. As soon as I bent down to pick up a rock, they flew off, cawing mockingly. They returned every day or so, obviously checking on my deterioration.

One day I decided to act dead and see what would happen. As I heard the cawing of their approach, I lay out flat with my eyes shut and arms spread out, even trying to hide my breathing. The minutes ticked by. I was on the verge of giving up when one hopped down, onto my ledge. I waited patiently with eyes shut, trying to sense where it was. Was it within striking range yet? Could I grab it now? Time passed by even slower and I had heard the occasional scuffle and hop, accompanied by a flap of wings. I wondered if I should wait for it to peck me before I grabbed it. I continued to bide my time until the rustle of wings seemed so close that the creature must have been within arm's reach.

I was completely relaxed, focusing my mind on how I was going to catch this bird. It was just like fighting someone. I had to look first, judge distance and attack the most vulnerable target. From a state of complete relaxation, I swiftly turned my head, fixed on the bird and lunged at its throat with my left hand. But the bird was too fast. Even before my arm was fully outstretched, it was in the air. I had missed another chance at food, but took some satisfaction in the trick I'd played and the fright I must have given the bird.

It was a couple of days before they returned but, after that, they visited frequently. They were more wary and never stayed long, just long enough to decide that I was not yet a carcass.

My hunger had largely abated by now. There were no longer painful cramps. Nor was there the same, desperate preoccupation with food. It had occurred to me how peculiar the sequence of my cravings had been. At first, it was the Christmas dinner that had monopolised my mind. Kentucky Fried Chicken had taken over when I was due to fly out to Bangkok. Shortly after, these thoughts were replaced by the hospital canteen lunches. The desire for these meals was replaced by cravings for fresh fruit and vegetables. Perhaps this was a direct result of the vitamin deficiency my body was experiencing, but the idea of a jug of fresh fruit juice would make my mouth water.

The yearning for fresh fruit had lasted longer. I remembered when Andrew and I had worked in a fruit shop. In the heat of a Brisbane summer we would sneak into the cold room and shovel handfuls of grapes into our mouths, savouring their sweet taste. Eventually, the longing for fruit faded and all I wished for was a glass of water. The roaring stream somewhere far below increased my thirst. Sometimes I felt tempted to battle my way down to the creek again, just so I could drink the fresh, flowing water. But I knew this would be an insane and suicidal act.

Gathering my snowballs one day, I was amazed to find a caterpillar sitting on one of them. I had seen no other insects or spiders. It was possibly three to four centimetres long with smooth, green skin. Disappointingly scrawny, unlike the fat, juicy grubs I had seen flourishing back home. Nonetheless, I ate it without a second thought, savouring the morsel of protein that it would provide. It had no distinct taste, just a soft squidginess as I chewed. I sucked on a snowball and washed it down.

It had been in the initial fifteen days when I had noticed the fastest loss of weight. I could now easily count my ribs and my abdominal muscles bulged without a layer of fat to cover them. The musculature of my arms, legs, back and chest had dwindled considerably at first, making me look and feel scrawny. The drawstring of my trousers had to be tightened every few days and my ski jacket, which had once fitted snugly, now seemed to hang off my shrinking shoulders.

Like the waning of my muscles, growth of my beard and nails had slowed. My body was conserving energy. Its metabolic rate must have slowed drastically since I had become lost. Although I was still losing weight, at least the muscle no longer seemed to be wasting away at the same alarming speed.

I had not washed for close to a month. There was little I could do about it, except to keep my hands clean and there was no point worrying. My nose and mouth had bled at various stages and I knew that there was blood caked in the grimy hair covering my face. This, combined with the mucus that regularly dribbled from my nose, made me relieved not to have a mirror.

I'd had difficulties with a cold and sore throat which presented two problems. Blowing my nose had failed to clear it and so I had begun to pick away at the inside using my toilet paper, making it bleed. More importantly, the blocked nose meant that I had to breathe the cold air through my mouth at night, causing it to dry and crack. The unpleasant, salty tang of blood as it oozed from the mucosal ulcerations would nauseate me and I would grope around in the dark for my sleeping bag cover with its snow balls. I would try to melt the ice in my mouth which only made it worse, burning the roof of my mouth and gums.

I had some local anaesthetic for relief of mouth ulcers. At first, I had just dabbed the liquid onto the spots that were most painful. I was surprised, not only by the relief it brought me but also by how good it tasted. It was tangy, a huge contrast to the snow and ice. I'm sure that, had I been well fed, the taste would have made no impression but the way it stimulated my taste buds now made me hungry for more. I began using it more frequently. Even though my mouth would be numb, I applied the substance for the taste alone. As the days passed, more ulcers and cracks appeared. Before long, the small bottle was empty. I filled it with snow and kept it in the sleeping bag with me to melt. The diluted mix still helped a little but I developed more ulcers which took longer to heal.

I looked through my medication in case there was something else that might help. I had various antibiotics, anti-diarrhoeals and anti-emetics. I tried one of each. The only palatable one was imodium, an anti-diarrhoeal. It had a chewy, gluggy consistency. It was probably unwise to eat too many. Not yet halfway through my seventy days, I rationed it to one capsule a day and looked forward to it like a child anticipating a treat.

My bowels hadn't moved since the second morning and the immodium would probably ensure no change. Through the thinning wall of my abdomen I could feel the accumulated faeces. I was pleased that I had no urge to go to the toilet as I wasn't sure I had the strength to squat.

My feet presented another problem. Snugly protected in multiple pairs of dry socks, they began to thaw. I wrapped my ski jacket around the bottom of my sleeping bag to add to the heat. As they warmed, the blue disappeared, replaced by a searing pain which stopped me sleeping day or night. I thought it would only last a couple of days but the pain only seemed to increase. In the end I removed the ski jacket and the socks and let my feet regain their numbness. I spent the days juggling with the socks, trying to balance the pain against damage from the cold. I went back to wearing only one pair of thicker socks

125

which provided just enough warmth to prevent the complete loss of sensation.

Life had become difficult in some ways, though the suffering from cold and hunger had eased considerably. I recalled others who had suffered far worse fates. I thought about soldiers captured during the wars. In addition to cold and hunger, they had suffered brutality and humiliation. I kept reminding myself that things could be a lot worse and counted the few blessings I had. The single goal of staying alive for seventy days was at the heart of my will to survive – even if I had to crawl out on my hands and knees. I had so much to live for, so many people that I loved so dearly. I was determined to fight every bit of the way.

JOANNE: *16 January 1992*

The morning of Thursday 16th found me feeling considerably better than I probably deserved to.

We met Carl and Ingo in the hotel lobby after breakfast. Both agreed that the most important area to search now was between Phedi and the pass, where James and Mark had actually separated. They were surprised Mark had assumed James would have no trouble finding his way back. According to Ingo, there were many creeks and it was extremely easy to get lost. Ingo was also most interested to hear that Mark and James had spent the night at Phedi. 'Ah! See, I told you I was not happy about what the Phedi lodge keeper was saying.' I told them what Mark had said about buying the man's last chicken.

In light of the new information, they decided that it would not be wise to go up via Dhunche. With further snowfall, the pass could well be impossible to cross. If they approached it from the Phedi side, they could at least be sure of reaching where Mark and James had separated. They decided to drive to Melamchi Pul Bazaar, the starting point of the eastern arm of the Helambu trek. This was as far as the road went. They would then trek to Tarke Ghyang and on to Gopte and Phedi. Ingo reached across the coffee table.

'Whilst we are following this route,' he said, indicating a path on the map, 'I know there is a trail here that has not been searched by anyone.' The spot he was pointing to was a trail between Mangengoth and Mahankal. It looked like a short cut between the western and eastern arms of the Helambu trek.

'You see,' he continued, 'looking at the map, you would think that there is a road to Mahankal.' He was right. According to the map, the road that they would be following that very day to get to Melamchi Pul Bazaar continued on to Mahankal. 'We know that it is not passable to vehicles, but perhaps your brother came down to Mangengoth and thought he would take a short cut and get a ride from Mahankal.' This was possible if James had made it back through Gopte. Part of the search team would follow this trail to be sure. I handed Carl some lengths of orange and pink fabric to signal Colonel Pun's helicopters.

We arrived at the embassy just after 9.30. Graeme had already sent five men from Himalayan Adventures to Banepa to cover the village and surrounding area. 'I think we should get more people out there,' I said and Carl had given me the name of a company where he employed guides.

Colonel Pun phoned to say he had landed and distributed posters at many villages but had no news. It had been too windy to land at Gosainkund but he would try again today.

A fax arrived from my mother to say Mark Fulton had failed to board his flight to Australia. The Australian Embassy in Bangkok were trying to find out what Fulton was up to. I was stunned. I had told Mark that Noel Ryan might be at Cairns airport to meet him. Perhaps that had scared him off? But he had seemed so co-operative on the phone . . . What on earth was he playing at?

Eight people from Tashi Taki Trekking arrived. We gave them bundles of black and white photos and posters, told them what we knew and showed them where to go. With their help, we would cover a wide circle around the area of the sighting. I asked them to get to Banepa this afternoon, stay overnight and search all day tomorrow. As always, I explained to them how important it was that James be found. 'You must speak with everyone you meet,' I told them.

We were having a quick cup of tea with Graeme when a message came through on the two-way radio. It was from the helicopter division at the airport. Colonel Pun was on his way down from Gopte and wanted someone from the embassy to get to the airport as soon as possible. He had said it was very urgent. A wave of fear swept over me.

'Why?' I asked.

Graeme was already pulling on his jacket. 'I don't know.'

'They've found his body, haven't they?' I was shivering uncontrollably.

'I don't know,' said Graeme.

'What else could it be? You tell me! What else could it be?' I was nearly shouting. It was the only time I saw Graeme react to me with

127

anything like anger. He turned to me and raising his voice slightly, 'Joanne, I am telling you. I don't know.'

Graeme told Andrew he should stay with me. I returned to my chair and tried to compose myself. My reaction rather scared me. I thought discussing daily the likelihood that James was dead would somehow prepare me but this was not the case: one radio message – which we could not be sure even spelt bad news – and here I was a shaking wreck.

'Graeme?' He stopped and turned towards me. 'If they've found James's body . . . please don't tell me over the radio. Ring up. I don't want to hear it over the radio.' Graeme nodded. We heard the four-wheel drive start up and watched it head down the drive.

'Nothing to do but wait, I guess,' I said. My shivering would not stop. Andrew gave me his jacket as well. It didn't help. We didn't talk much. Auli arrived back a short time later.

'What's happened?'

'They may have found a body,' I responded. No tears now, just the damn shivering. Auli organised more hot tea. I stood up. 'I can't stand it,' I said to her. 'Radio Graeme and find out what's happened. I'll wait outside.'

I heard Auli transmit to Graeme and put my hands over my ears so that I would not hear the answer. Visions of a filthy, frozen corpse being roughly thrown into the helicopter tormented me. I kicked at some pebbles. So unfair. So un-bloody-fair. Cautiously, I lowered my hands. It sounded as if they had finished. I went back inside.

'It's okay,' Andrew told me. 'It's nothing.' I felt giddy with relief.

Although Andrew thought it was nothing, Captain Koirala of the helicopter division would probably disagree. Graeme told us the story when he returned. The message had obviously upset him too. He had raced all the way to Colonel Pun's office. When he barged in, the colonel had looked up from his desk.

'Look at my co-pilot,' he said. Graeme turned to see Captain Koirala covered in mud with a large rip in his trouser leg.

'What happened to you?' Graeme asked. Captain Koirala opened his mouth to explain, but Colonel Pun took over. He had landed the helicopter at Gopte and the captain had carefully picked his way through the snow to the door of the first hut. He had barely stepped inside when he shot out the door like a bullet out of a gun, yelling, 'Take off, take off!' In his haste to return to the chopper, he had fallen in mud and ripped his pants leg.

'What was it?' asked Graeme.

'A wolf,' Colonel Pun replied.

'An enormous wolf,' Captain Koirala broke in. 'I have never seen such a big wolf. He wanted to eat me. There were two of them. I have never been so frightened.'

Another officer walked into Colonel Pun's office, took one look at the co-pilot and burst out laughing. Colonel Pun, also, could no longer contain himself and started laughing too. Captain Koirala seemed a little hurt at the lack of sympathy.

Colonel Pun had not known that the huts at Gopte had already been checked and seeing the wolves had made him wonder if James's body might be inside, hence his urgency.

'I told him that the huts had been checked and we knew there was no way James's body was in there,' said Graeme.

Relieved, my mind turned to the other search parties. The men heading for Talu up the Tadi Khola had been out for several days. I had been assured they would contact me but I decided it would do no harm to ring Amadablam and see. To my consternation, I found the search teams had arrived back yesterday. The secretary put me onto Mr Ravi who was most apologetic. He told me Balaram had to return home because his father was ill. He immediately sent a car to collect us.

Mr Ravi's office was roomy and light. He stood to greet us and offered tea. 'Some of the men who searched are waiting. I'll get them.'

He called out the window in Nepali. A short time later three or four men appeared. Mr Ravi made them stand and report what had happened. It made me feel like a strict school teacher listening to naughty children. One little man, who gave a particularly detailed report, stood with his hands clasped behind his back and his eyes flickering nervously around the room the whole time. To cut a long story short, they had found nothing.

One group had followed the Tadi Khola, starting well to the west of Kathmandu, from a town called Ranipauwa. This village was on the road between Kathmandu and Dhunche. They had gone along the river until just south of Talu. There they had been told that the area above had already been checked to no avail by other searchers (Carl and Ingo's group, no doubt). They had taken it upon themselves to head west from below Talu, on a path roughly parallel to the Gosainkund trail, but further south until they met up with the road between Dhunche and Kathmandu just south of Dhunche. I had mixed feelings about their efforts. I was glad they had decided to check this other area, but still no one had checked the path between Talu and Phedi. Harrison had approached Talu from Tharepati, not Phedi.

To my annoyance, the second group had merely followed the route up to Tharepati that James and Mark had travelled. This route had already been searched at least once by Harrison's party.

'No, no,' I said. 'They were not supposed to go up that way. They were supposed to follow this other branch of the Tadi Khola to get to Talu.' This meant that the area due west of the Helambu's western arm remained unsearched. Even though James would have been seen on his way there, passing through Talu or another of the higher villages that had been searched, I was annoyed there was yet another area that still had not been checked. At times like this I would seriously doubt the effectiveness of the search parties. I had no way of knowing whether or not they did a good job and I did not like having to put so much trust and responsibility in the hands of others. Unfortunately, I had little choice.

I thanked them all for their help and told Mr Ravi that his bill should be sent to the embassy for payment as they had control of all the funds. He told me not to worry about money at the moment and offered to provide guides, free of charge, if we wanted to go anywhere.

We opted for a quiet night with dinner in the room. James's luggage was sitting in the corner. I would have to go through it. Perhaps there was something in it that could help. As I unpacked the bags, I could not help smiling. James was never renowned for his tidiness and, in typical style, his clothes had been stuffed into the bags. There seemed to be dirty clothes amongst clean ones and a vile-smelling sleeping bag cover with a damp towel. There were also the gifts that James had written about in his letters. A beautiful suede jacket for Gaye and carpets for my parents and the Ryans. He had not written much in his diary before he left for Helambu. A stethoscope lay right at the bottom of the second bag. I repacked the bags, putting all the gifts into one and kept the dirty clothes for the laundry.

Just before bedtime, Lottie Weisse rang. 'Joanne, I have been speaking to my Chinese friend again. She says you must get up to Gosainkund quickly. Your brother is there, waiting for you to collect him. He is in one of the huts. He has made a flag from some cloth and put it outside. All he wants is for you to come and get him.'

Again, I hung up feeling very shaken. I was aware that I had still to get a search team to the huts. I expressed my fears to Andrew.

'Bloody psychics. I don't know why you listen to them. What would James be doing in a hut at Gosainkund?'

'I don't know. Maybe he's injured or something.' Andrew was disgusted that I would even consider the woman might know something.

In bed, the idea still weighed heavily on my mind. For the sake of my own peace if nothing else: I was going to have to get someone up to Gosainkund.

JOANNE: *17 January 1992*

That morning, like so many others, we made our way up to Blue Mountain, sent a brief fax home and walked to the embassy. Graeme had spoken to the men from Himalayan Adventures who had gone to Banepa yesterday morning. They had nothing to report. They hadn't even spoken with the people who had supposedly made the original sighting. I said I wanted them to go out again and stay overnight, like the team from Tashi Taki. I told Graeme of my decision to send some men to Gosainkund. I fancy he and Andrew exchanged at least one glance under raised eyebrows as I went over the psychic's call.

'I want it checked as soon as possible,' I said. We then rang Colonel Pun to see if I could charter a helicopter to go up the next day. He told me that would be fine. I still had to find two men to go. The colonel explained that it might not be possible to lift two passengers to the high altitude of Gosainkund. He might have to land at Gopte, take one up, then return for the other. Because he could not carry a lot of fuel at that height, the men would have no more than forty minutes to cover the 300 metres from the helicopter to the huts and back. He would have to take off if weather conditions changed suddenly, perhaps leaving the men behind. They would have to be well-equipped, experienced mountaineers. I decided that Amadablam was probably my best bet and made the call. I also wanted searchers to cover the area that the last group had missed.

From the embassy, we walked for a while and caught an autorickshaw to the hotel for more posters for the Amadablam groups. The screaming engine made conversation impossible, leaving us with our thoughts and the bone-rattling road.

While we were in our room Gaye called. She sounded very distressed. A relative of hers had been told some upsetting information by a psychic. James was supposedly still alive, but had only twenty-two hours to live. He was lying somewhere 'low down', and was 'bleeding'. He was somewhere 'between a rock and a creek' and 'someone was with him'. The psychic had said that there was 'lots of blood, especially from James's ear' and that he kept 'calling for help but there was no response'. She had said that he was 'somewhere the search parties had already been and that we could expect to hear some news tonight'. She predicted that the situation would be resolved by 25–28 January. As I listened, I found myself shivering again. It is hard to describe just how upsetting information like that can be. We were very vulnerable and clutched at any hope cast our way. But this information also made me furious. I tried to speak gently.

'Look, Gaye,' I said, 'what you are telling me is impossible to act on. All of Nepal is rocks and creeks. We have searched an area of over 1000 square kilometres. We can't cover that in twenty-two hours.' I could hear her crying.

'I know,' she said.

'Okay, Gaye, tell me what you want me to do about this. Because I don't know what to do. But, whatever you tell me, I'll do.' We both realised nothing could be done. The information was counter-productive. It gave us nothing we could act on, but was still extremely upsetting. I felt guilty, since it had been my visit to the Rinpoche that had initiated all this psychic business. However, I also maintain that seeking the opinion of an enlightened person in Nepal was very different to talking to a psychic from the Yellow Pages in Brisbane.

Gaye also said there was to be a press release in Australia the following morning, Saturday. I groaned inwardly. Auli and Graeme had both commented how good it was that the press had been kept out of it to date. Once the press got hold of the story, they could expect to be besieged by phone calls from the media and anxious relatives of other trekkers. As we had experienced first-hand, communications to and from Australia were time-consuming and frustrating.

But it had reached the stage where my parents felt that people had to know. Friends were regularly asking how James's trip to Nepal was going. It was just too painful to have to keep explaining. In addition, James and Gaye's engagement party was to have been held on the 24th. Many of the 150 friends he had invited were phoning to accept and my parents were having to tell them about James. They decided a newspaper article would be the best way and the Courier-Mail, a local Brisbane paper, would run a story the next morning.

I hung up and told Andrew. We tried to call Colonel Pun but were informed that he was unavailable. We went to Thai Air who reconfirmed Andrew's flight on the 22nd and that James and I still had valid seats for the 27th. They also gave us written clearance for the extra luggage it looked like we would have to take back.

We left the offices and headed back to Amadablam and our meeting with Mr Ravi. I stopped frequently to tape up posters. Every time I did this, a group of people would gather round. There would be much discussion as the posters were read.

We walked along the road opposite the royal palace. There were high walls on either side, ideal for displaying posters. The area also seemed to be full of beggars. One man we often saw had pencil-thin arms and legs. He was unable to stand and the limbs seemed to be twisted around themselves. I was surprised by how quickly we had become immune to the poverty and the begging. When young kids came up to me with large, brown eyes and outstretched hands, I now had no qualms telling them to go away.

We were due to see Mr Ravi at two o'clock but he was unavailable. While we waited, we phoned Auli to warn her about the press release and again tried to contact Colonel Pun. He was still unavailable.

It must have been about 5 p.m. when we finally saw Mr Ravi. As always, he was quite charming and apologetic. He explained he always had a late lunch as he often did not eat dinner until ten or eleven at night. I guess Andrew and I should have had a better understanding of Nepali time by then anyway and realised that 2 p.m. could mean any time before 7 p.m.!

He quickly got together the men who were going to cover the area that had been missed before. We decided they would go by taxi to Budhanikantha and then walk up to Talu. Mr Ravi suggested they should also carefully search the Chisopani forest. In his experience, that was the most dangerous area for lone trekkers in Helambu. I was pleased to see that the small man who had been so conscientious in his report last time was going to join this team.

Then we met the two mountaineers who would go to Gosainkund. Mr Ravi suggested they take a camera to prove they had reached the huts. Although this was an excellent idea, I did not have a camera. Looking somewhat pained, Mr Ravi offered his.

I used his phone to ring Colonel Pun and at last got hold of him. Unfortunately, the colonel sounded quite annoyed. He said I had left it far too late to arrange a flight for tomorrow. This, in turn, made me angry. I retorted that I had been trying to call him all day but had been repeatedly told he was unavailable. He asked to be put on to Mr Ravi. After some discussion, Colonel Pun agreed to go up on Sunday with the two men.

I was in bad form as we climbed into a taxi. I could not understand Colonel Pun's anger and was disappointed that the chopper was not going up until Sunday – even though I was still not convinced that it was the right thing to do anyway.

'I can't believe you are sending the helicopter up,' Andrew said as we turned out the driveway. 'It's going to cost you a fortune. Those climbers can get to Gosainkund by foot just a day later. You can't tell me a day is going to make any difference. I can't believe you're going to waste all that money.' His comments struck a nerve.

'That's great, Andrew. Just great. You sit in the office and don't say anything and now it's all arranged you tell me I've done the wrong thing. Fantastic!'

'Well, it's obvious you're not being logical.'

'All right. Fine. I'll cancel the goddamn helicopter and get them to catch a bus tomorrow. That's going to make me look like I'm really thinking straight, isn't it? That will impress Colonel Pun no end!' Nonetheless, I knew Andrew was right.

Our taxi coughed and spluttered and came to a halt in the middle of the road. Now I could vent my anger on the driver as well as Andrew. 'Great. Now what?'

Without a word, the driver got out and started rummaging around in the boot. I crossed my arms, settled back into the seat to observe the traffic manoeuvring around us and heaved a sigh of disgust.

'Oh, shit. Where's he going?' said Andrew.

I turned around to see our driver cheerily heading down the road, swinging an empty jerry can. He was obviously making for a petrol pump a short distance back. He didn't seem to care that his vehicle was totally obstructing one side of the road! I opened my door.

'What are you doing?' Andrew asked.

'I'm going to walk.'

'Don't be stupid. It's miles,' Andrew replied. We then had an argument about how far away the hotel was.

'Look, Andrew,' I said. 'You just told me I'm an idiot and that I should cancel the flight and send them by bus, so that's what I'm going to do. But I'll have to do it soon or it will be too late for them to leave tomorrow.' It was then we saw our driver returning.

'Just wait. It should only be a second now,' said Andrew. Hah! The driver fussed around for a while looking concerned, before lifting a sheet of paper from the floor. He rolled it to make a funnel and poured, losing almost half the petrol on the ground. All this time I was getting more and more annoyed. Eventually, we were ready to go again. We drove a short distance up the hill, around the corner and there was the hotel.

'I told you it was close,' was my final retort to Andrew as I left him to pay the bill.

I marched into the reception area and asked to use the house phone. I got straight on to Mr Ravi and told him I had changed my mind and wanted the two mountaineers to be on the bus to Dhunche first thing in the morning. He said that would be okay. I then bit the bullet and rang Colonel Pun. He sounded more affable. I explained to him I was very sorry for all the inconvenience I was causing but had decided to send the men by bus instead. To my relief, it didn't seem to bother him at all. He added that he still might fly up for interest's sake on Sunday anyway.

JOANNE: *18 January 1992*

It was still dark when the phone wrenched me out of a dream. I'd not had a restful night, continually plagued by dreams of mountaineers not reaching Gosainkund. I sat up and switched on the light. It was just before 6 a.m. It had to be Australia calling. I picked it up.

'Mr Andrew,' said the operator, 'it's a call from Australia.'

I was surprised to find the caller was a reporter from one of the Australian television stations. Then I recalled the press release. It would be after 11 a.m. in Australia now.

'Hello, is that Joanne Robertson?' The reporter identified herself and asked if we'd heard any more news.

'Listen,' I said, 'do you know what time it is here?' There was a short silence from the other end of the phone. 'It's 6 a.m. and you've woken me up.'

The caller apologised, mumbling something about having been given the wrong information by Telecom about the time difference, then asked again if there was any news, had we found James? I contained myself, merely saying there was no further news, no we had not found James and they could be certain that as soon as I had any news, I would tell my parents who could then pass word on to them if they chose to do so. As I hung up, I wondered if I had handled them properly. I really wasn't sure what I was supposed to say. I wondered if the embassy was receiving similar calls.

I could not get back to sleep. Tom and Maria had asked us up for brunch at ten. So I wrote another fax home.

We taxied up to Blue Mountain and had a delicious meal. Auli and Larry were there with their son, Angus. After we had eaten, I phoned home. I chose a bad time. Mum was in the middle of being interviewed for television. The cameras were actually filming as she was speaking to me. She sounded quite distraught. I kept the call reasonably brief, telling her I would phone again later. The clichéd image of the news report my calling could generate ('Anguished parents receive word from Kathmandu as our cameras roll'), didn't impress me.

I then rang Tashi Taki and Himalayan Adventures. No news. Their search parties were not back. Tom suggested we should go for a drive in the afternoon. There was nothing we could hope to achieve by remaining in the city. There was no word from Banepa, Colonel Pun wasn't flying and Harrison's group would only just be reaching Phedi. I thought a change of scene would be nice and I asked if we could go towards Banepa.

This was my first trip out of the city. As we began to climb the rim of the Kathmandu valley, I caught my first glimpse of the Himalayas. Snow-capped peaks majestic against the sky, looking almost like cardboard cut-outs through the hazy Kathmandu light.

We climbed through picturesque farmlands, with quaint thatched houses squatting on terraced hillsides, their bright, ornate window and door frames standing out against the greenery of young rice. Children chased hoops along the roadside.

Banepa is an ugly, noisy village. We went straight on and ascended to the village of Dhulikhel and stopped for some ginger tea. Further up, Tom turned off the main track and climbed to a high point. I got out and took in the view, mile after mile of undulating hills, thick with vegetation. Small houses and farms were scattered here and there and innumerable tracks wound their way around the slopes. In the distance stood the Himalayas. I had spent hours looking at maps of the area, but only now was I getting an inkling of what it was actually like. I suddenly realised the size of the task I had undertaken. Trying to find a solo trekker was like looking for a needle in a haystack. It had to become even more difficult as the altitude increased.

Three old men wearing topis, tattered jackets and scarfs came by. When Tom told them about James they said they had seen the announcement on the television. I wondered where on earth these old men with their missing teeth and shabby clothes would get to watch television! One told Tom that he wished he could find James. He would never have to worry again: he would have enough money in this life to be comfortable and, having performed such a good deed, he could be sure that this next life would be looked after as well!

We returned to Kathmandu after dark. There was a message from Dad waiting for us. Although it was after 11 p.m. in Australia, I rang. All was still not right with Mark. Auli had discovered he had rebooked for a later flight. He had apparently arrived on the flight he was supposed to be on, but had walked straight past Noel Ryan who had a placard with his name on it. This was making everyone suspicious. It certainly was most unusual behaviour. Dad also said that Kimberley in Canada had spoken to her psychic and that I should call her myself. Reports of James had been on news bulletins right across Australia. Mum and Dad had been giving interviews most of the day and were dismayed at the way the reports exploited any emotion. Mum had spent half an hour being interviewed by Channel Nine. She had calmly told the whole story except for one brief moment when she broke down and wept. This was the only part that was broadcast.

I called Kimberley before I went to bed and we had a long talk. Her psychic was sure James was still alive. He had said that James was 'somewhere near Kathmandu' and was able to contact us but that he wouldn't. He was involved with a group of 'very bad' people and there would be an 'act of violence' committed. He predicted two possible outcomes. One was that James would break away and come forth; the other was that James would be encouraged to commit suicide. I asked if we could get a geographical situation so we might know where to search. She said she'd see what she could do and let me know. I hung up and told Andrew what the psychic had said. He was furious.

'That's bullshit,' he stated. 'That's an absolute insult to James. I don't know how you can even contemplate his being mixed up with other people. And to say he won't come forth is ridiculous. If James were alive and able, nothing would stop him getting back to Kathmandu. It's an absolute insult.'

'Furthermore,' he went on, 'you were just on the phone for twenty minutes. Do you know how much that call cost?' Without waiting for my reply, he continued, '$170.'

I was too stunned to speak for a moment and did a quick mental calculation. He was right. I didn't need Andrew to tell me what else that money might have been spent on. I went to bed feeling chastised.

JOANNE: *19 January 1992*

Sunday found us back at Tom and Maria's by mid-morning. Before long, Andrew would return to Brisbane. I was staying on for at least a further five days. Tom and Maria had invited me to stay with them after Andrew left and I had accepted.

We were sitting down for lunch when Dad rang. It seemed the Mark Fulton mystery was growing by the hour. Noel Ryan had rung Foreign Affairs who had contacted Mark's parents. Only with this prompting had Mark rung Noel. Noel wanted to meet with him but Mark refused. Noel had offered to pay Mark's taxi fare to his place and again Mark had refused. The reason Mark gave was that he had to have lunch and then go swimming!

At Noel's suggestion, they were trying to get the Federal police to speak to Mark but the police needed a request from Nepali authorities saying that a statement from Mark was necessary for the continuation of the search. Dad asked me to see what I could do. I rang Graeme to discuss it.

He agreed that Mark's behaviour could have been better, but maintained it was not enough to warrant Federal police intervention. The more I brooded on it, the more ridiculous it seemed that we could not get a statement from Mark. I decided to change tack.

I rang Graeme back and asked him if it would be a good idea to get, not an interrogation, but a police statement from both Tim and Mark. James was still missing – twenty-eight days today. Surely it would be sensible to have a written account of what they both felt had happened? Graeme felt happier about helping with that and said he would cable Canberra.

It also occurred to me that it might be possible to get confirmation of Mark's story from other sources. He had told me about the Israeli fellow he had met up with at Gosainkund. I decided I would try my luck at immigration again the next day. Perhaps Shai could confirm Fulton's story.

JOANNE: *20 January 1992*

I knew the next few days were going to be particularly difficult. Andrew was leaving the day after tomorrow. He would arrive back in Australia on Friday 24 January, the day that was to have been James and Gaye's engagement party. Tomorrow, 21 January, was James's birthday.

Maria drove us to immigration. I went in the back entrance this time and straight to the office of the man who had been so helpful last time. He remembered me. I explained that I needed to find another trekking permit.

After a few hours, I was able to give Graeme Shai's details. He said he would contact the Israeli Consulate to help track him down. Despite the full co-operation of the Israeli Consulate, we were never able to make contact with Shai. The other search parties returned from Banepa with no news. Not a great deal had been achieved today.

Andrew wanted to buy some presents to take back, so we went into Thamel where there are many souvenirs on sale. I occasionally had a fleeting urge to buy something, but then I wondered whether I would ever want to be reminded of my time in Nepal. Andrew got the things he wanted and then we had dinner at the Old Vienna Inn. We decided to make a night of it and went on to Tom and Jerry's.

I would sometimes start with surprise when I found myself having a good time in Kathmandu. Was it right that I should have a night out? Andrew was sure that James would have wanted us to have some time off and to still be able to laugh. It was also good for me to talk to other people about things apart from my missing brother. Sometimes it seemed I spent every waking moment trying to find an answer to what had happened to James. I wondered how I would readjust to life if nothing was ever found.

I am not accustomed to failing. Yet, realistically, there was now virtually no hope of finding James alive. Even I was starting to accept that James had never made it down to Gopte or to Talu. That left two possibilities: he had either died somewhere near Phedi or had crossed the pass. Andrew was certain James was dead. He kept saying that, knowing James's willpower, somehow, some way, he would have made it back to Kathmandu by now if he was alive. I knew that until a body was produced, we would always be wondering if he could still be alive. It was also obvious that in Australia they were refusing to accept that James was dead. I could hear the hope rise in their voices at even the slightest positive news. My father was taking it especially badly. Any time I tried to broach the fact that James could have died, he would pass the phone to my mother. It was going to be horrendous to find a body, but far worse to be always wondering.

JOANNE: *21 January 1992*

I rang Mum and Dad at 8 a.m. No one mentioned James's birthday. They both sounded tired and depressed. Mum later told me that that was the day she really began to lose hope. They had succeeded in finally talking to Mark Fulton and had, at last, come to the conclusion that he had been telling the truth. He was guilty only of a shockingly casual attitude.

Dad had also talked to Linda Griffith who mentioned how dangerous the countryside was. She said that, being near the Tibet border, there could be drug running going on. Kimberley's psychic's 'bad people' might be drug runners. Kimberley's husband, Mark, was flying to Toronto with a map in case the psychic could pin-point a more exact location.

They told me that they'd had a request from Foreign Affairs for more money to be sent over. Mum's relatives and friends in the UK and South Africa were sending some money direct to Kathmandu and they were also receiving gifts of money from people in Australia for the search fund. I was relieved to hear that money was still not a problem.

Graeme had told us the ambassador had returned several days earlier. I was surprised we hadn't heard from him: I had, after all, sent him a letter. No doubt he was very busy but it would have helped if he had taken a minute to call and see how we were going.

It was becoming increasingly apparent how much friends and family were doing to provide help and support. The number of letters my parents were receiving was overwhelming. Money was coming in from all sorts of people: from relatives, from James's karate dojo, medical students and people who worked with James and my parents. We needed about $50,000 for the search costs and most of this was supplied by money donated. It was also through friends that we managed to get the police statement from Mark without having to cope with the Foreign Affairs bureaucracy. Countless people were praying for us every day all over the world. The support of so many people gave us a lot of the strength we needed to keep searching and hoping.

We went back to the hotel room and Andrew started packing. He was relieved that I had decided to go and stay with Tom and Maria once he had left. Every time I thought of his leaving, I wanted to cry. I was going to miss him dreadfully. He was my voice of reason, the one who told me when I was being ridiculous. I didn't know how I would cope without him. Perhaps my greatest fear was that he was the only other person in Kathmandu who knew James. If James's body was found, I did not know how I would find the strength to look at it.

'If they find a body, just get yourself on a plane, Joanne. Don't you identify it, don't you worry about anything except getting yourself home,' said Andrew. 'Everything else will be taken care of.'

Andrew was going to take James's luggage back. I sat on the hotel room floor and gazed at James's bag. The dirty clothes had been returned freshly laundered. I pulled out James's stethoscope. One way I could repay some of the kindness shown to me was by looking at any animal problems. A stethoscope might be useful. I also pulled out a complete set of spare clothes for James. Andrew looked at me curiously.

'I just want to keep one set of clothes, Andrew. Just in case . . .'

'Jesus Christ, Joanne,' Andrew said, 'if you find him alive, you can buy a whole new wardrobe.'

Stubbornly, I refused to put them back. Sending all of James's clothes home would feel too much like giving up.

JOANNE: *22 January 1992*

The day of Andrew's departure started eventfully with an early morning call from my father. He sounded quite excited. They had a new lead.

He had received a message written on the back of a pre-paid airmail envelope. The postmark showed it had been posted in Brisbane on 20 January. It had been addressed to 'Professor Scott, Faculty of Medicine, University of Queensland'. Handwritten on the back was:

'The best bet to find your son is Amnesty International; this may sound off the wall but intellectuals or students are highly suspect. You're prominent in status (Chinese standards). There is a political prison SW of Tibet by 10kms. Find informants there.'

We had thought of many possibilities but not that James might be being held as a political prisoner. My parents had no idea who had written the letter. I admit I thought it was one of the longest shots that we had been given. Interestingly, my father had been one of the first Western scientists to be allowed to visit Communist China. He had travelled to many remote parts of the country and he currently had two Chinese researchers working with him. One of these had been vocal during the recent uprising in China. So there was a tenuous connection. But what was the likelihood that someone had followed James and captured him? And what purpose would it achieve? If that were the case, I later joked to Tom, I should watch my back very carefully.

We were about to leave when Lottie Weisse rang. Her psychic friend claimed to have been in telepathic communication with James. She said that none of the searchers we had out now would reach him at Gosainkund. Even though I knew we had two very experienced mountaineers heading there now, I found her call very upsetting.

Andrew and I arrived at Blue Mountain to find that Dad had faxed the letter through and Tom had already found contacts for Amnesty International in Kathmandu and London. We agreed that we had nothing to lose by taking the message seriously. We drafted a letter, listing James's details and summarised briefly what had happened to date. I also told Tom about Lottie Weisse's call. Tom wanted to ring Colonel Pun about the anonymous tip-off anyway and suggested we see if he would fly up to Gosainkund. I was sure Colonel Pun would be beginning to wonder about my state of mind. It seemed every few days I asked him to fly people up to Gosainkund then backed out of it! Nonetheless, I knew the only key to my own peace of mind was to get the damn huts checked once and for all. If that meant Colonel Pun thought I was the most erratic, fickle person he had ever encountered, so be it!

Colonel Pun said that he did not believe there were any prison camps so close to the Tibetan border. Virtually the whole of Nepal's northern border is formed by Tibet, so reference to a prison camp '10 kms SW of Tibet' is far from helpful. Colonel Pun was prepared to fly up near Gosainkund tomorrow, but we would need to find another two experienced mountaineers if we wanted the huts there searched. I rang Amadablam and left a message for Mr Ravi.

Andrew was running late for check-in by the time we arrived at the airport. I had been trying to write a letter to send back to Calum with Andrew. I hastily scrawled a few lines leaning on Andrew's luggage and handed him the letter. I had resolved to be brave and decided to keep it as brief as possible. I thanked him for all he had done and we hugged each other goodbye.

'James could never have had a better friend,' I said and quickly walked away so that Andrew would not see the tears rolling down my cheeks.

I cried all the way back from the airport. Tom kept passing me tissues and every time I nearly got my emotions under control, James's face, as captured on the hundreds of posters now distributed throughout Nepal, would flash into my mind and start me off again. I was feeling dejected, depressed and despondent, very pessimistic and very tired.

On the way back to Blue Mountain, we dropped in at Amadablam. Mr Ravi was still not in, but the receptionist said they would try to organise two men. Tom dropped me at the embassy and I found Graeme in his office. Andrew had already filled him in on the latest hunch. For once, even Graeme could not disguise his scepticism. Shaking his head he said to me, 'Joanne, if James is found in a political prison I'll give you a Porsche!' I told him I would hold him to that. He also said he had still not managed to get in touch with the Chinia Lama. He added that the ambassador was upstairs and had said I should see him if I called in.

I spent some time with the ambassador. He expressed his concern that James had not been found and thought the situation was very grim. He gave the impression I should be coming to terms with the inevitable and thinking about leaving Nepal. He acknowledged my letter which he had passed on to Canberra for a response. He said I could now use the fax and phone facilities at the embassy. They would monitor the length of any calls and bill me. By that time I already had an alternative system sorted out. However, I hope other Australian citizens that find themselves in a similar position will be allowed to use the embassy's facilities from the outset.

While I was back at Blue Mountain, Amadablam Trekking called to say they had no mountaineers available for the next day. I rang several others but no one could help. Lastly, I tried Tashi Taki. Initially, it looked like the same story there before Tom took the phone. Speaking in Nepali, he had two mountaineers organised for early the next morning in a matter of seconds. I was grateful for his help, but found it frustrating that he could accomplish something in seconds that I had been unable to do in hours. Obviously, speaking the language gave him a head start as did, I suspect, being male.

JAMES: *22 January 1992*

I lay in my bag, a bundle of misery. Very little had gone my way. Every day was harder to deal with. The suffering seemed relentless.

It was no surprise that I had developed an infection in my upper respiratory tract. The weather conditions and the lack of nutrition to support my immune system left me very vulnerable to disease. One day, however, whilst applying chapstick to my cracked lips, it struck me that perhaps I could soothe the painful ulcerations within my nostrils by using the same medication. I rubbed the chapstick upon a finger and applied it to the inside walls of my nose. It brought immediate relief and cleared my nasal passages in an hour or so. From this time on, I used it regularly, especially at dusk, so that my nose would remain clear throughout the night. It may seem like a minor discovery, but at the time it meant one less hardship.

I experimented with a stick of Old Spice deodorant, in case it might do once the chapstick ran out. It burned painfully and had no effect on my blocked nose but the smell brought a flood of memories of home. I took to sniffing it when my spirits were low.

Despite these small improvements, I was finding the conditions extremely difficult to bear. My earlier coping mechanisms were no longer working so well. I reflected mockingly at the way that I had torn at my hair and pinched my skin to try to relieve the hunger and pain of those early stages. The inadequacy of those defence mechanisms showed how naive I had been. Since then, I had developed a variety of mental tricks to pass the time and ease the stress. The major force had been the hours spent recalling positive memories each day, moments of my life which, to me at least, had been exciting.

One night I tried to relive the year I'd had with Andrew in Europe. I tried to recount every day of that adventure. Although there had been ups and downs, all I remembered were the good times.

My trip to Asia was another holiday which provided me with much food for thought. I found the culture fascinating. How I wished I could go back again, especially since Gaye speaks Japanese.

I went over the week spent with the Queensland karate team in New Caledonia, one of the best times of my life. I recalled the extraordinary hospitality and the camaraderie I'd felt with the rest of the team.

Even the days that had seemed so monotonous at university, slogging away through text books and seeing patients, were full of fond memories. Events which I had taken for granted now, in isolation, gave me much pleasure.

Possibly my most effective coping mechanism, however, had been established through rigorous karate training over the previous six years. The philosophy behind karate of never giving up until the battle was over had helped me go beyond the boundaries of pain from hunger and cold, to persevere. When the pain became insurmountable, I would reflect upon my karate training, focusing on the physical techniques themselves. An important aspect of my training had been through kata, a sequence of techniques flowing together that would represent a battle against a number of opponents. Many years ago, kata had been used like a library. It would be practised by students of karate to enable them to learn and remember a repertoire of movements which they could draw upon if ever necessary. It is still a major part of modern training. In my mind, I would practise kata. I could do this for hours on end if necessary, for many of the kata are very complex, with extremely difficult and detailed movements. As I lay there in the dark, cold nights with nothing else to provide sensory stimulation, I would picture either myself or my sensei, performing the kata. In my own mind, the more I practised, the more correct the techniques would become. The stances would be stronger, the movements faster and each punch or kick would be delivered with devastating power and accuracy. Despite my own body weakening, the kata I performed in my mind had grown stronger daily. The concentration required in recalling every minute detail was so great that all my surroundings would be blocked out. It was like a dream over which one had full control, leaving myself oblivious of all that was going on around me.

Even this was now beginning to fail. Negative thoughts kept surfacing. The goal of seventy days was no longer shining like a beacon, but a distant, fading glow.

'I have to make that seventy days,' I kept trying to tell myself. But, as I watched the snow fall more heavily than ever for the second day in a row, I started to wonder if it would even be melted by day seventy.

The odds of one in a million that I had given myself of getting out of this desperate situation alive had grown even longer. I had begun to hope for other events to occur that might bring about my rescue. As I looked at the ranges of mountains surrounding me, I pondered the possibility that one of these peaks might erupt as a volcano, spilling lava down into the valley, attracting people to the area. Occasionally, I had thought that I had heard the sounds of aircraft engines. I knew that joy flights were carried out regularly around the Himalayas. I thought, 'If one of those planes was to come through the valley, maybe someone on board would see me.'

In my own egocentric way of thinking, I even contemplated the possibility of a commercial airliner crashing in the area, initiating a search that might result in my rescue.

The chance of any of these occurring was ridiculously remote but I had nothing else to hope for. The straws I was clutching at were so feeble, I wondered whether it was worth persisting in the struggle to live. I'd been able to overcome cold, but without proper nutrition I knew it was starvation that would eventually kill me.

These negative thoughts were strong on this day due to the increasing feelings of isolation. My pen had lain in the dirt untouched for at least a fortnight. I had a desperate desire to reach those back home. Of course, there was no guarantee that they would get the letters, but I knew I had at least to write something. I blew the dirt off the pen and scribbled on the paper. It still refused to work. It was so filthy now, covered in dirt, yet the ball on the nib was rolling smoothly. There was still ink in the barrel, but it would not flow onto the ball. I looked at the end of the barrel to find it blocked with grime. The ink could not move down. It would have been like holding your thumb over the top of a straw filled with water. I cut midway up the plastic shaft and snipped off the blocked section with my scissors. A few quick flicks to

145

push the ink downwards, a scrawl on the paper and the ink was flowing freely once again.

This give me a small sense of achievement. At least something was going right. I drew out my writing paper and continued my letters, first to my family and then to Gaye.

> Dear All, I have lost track of the days, date and time. You will all be surprised to hear that I believe if I haven't yet passed my twenty-third birthday, I must be close. My pen was broken for all this time, but today I have managed to get it to function again. I have been lost for about one month. It has been a time of very mixed emotions. I have been depressed far less than one might expect. Frustration is probably a better word for how I have felt at times. As time is not of the essence any more, let me write to you the exact circumstances leading up to this ridiculous and wasteful affair.

I then went into detail, writing several, long pages that recounted how I had ended up under my rock. I explained the hardships that I had undergone on those first two and a half days before finding my shelter. I even mentioned I was prepared to signal a helicopter if one should come.

I talked of the first few cold nights and then the sun drying my clothes and my attempt to walk out to the knoll. I went on to describe how I'd tried eating all the plants, but nothing was edible. I wanted them to know that I had done all that I could to try and survive.

> I thought if I could extract 1500 calories per day, just to get through January and February, I was sure that, as spring came around, there would be more opportunity for food. But as I look around now, I can't imagine where I can get these calories. Water isn't a problem as there is snow everywhere. Just as the snow melts down, a new batch comes across. Today has seen some of the heaviest snowfall since those first couple of days.
>
> Of course, I've lost a lot of weight. I couldn't estimate how much, though I'd be surprised if I am greater than sixty kilograms. Cravings for food were far worse in the first days. I still think about meals etc, but not with the same morbid preoccupation as I did.

It was most peculiar, one day recently when I'd become particularly bored and couldn't stomach reading Charles Dickens for the fifth time, I had flicked through my guide book to Nepal. I came across the restaurant section in Kathmandu. It described in detail the specialities at various restaurants and the delights of each meal. If I had read that section in the first ten days, I think it would have driven me insane but I could read it now, thinking casually to myself how nice it would have

146

been to have tried that dish. There was no longer the same anguish over my lack of food.

It is frustrating to think that I had so much ahead of me and that it has all been thrown away. I can't describe how much I miss you all and how much I'd like to come home to each of you.

John, congratulations on getting your black belt. That certainly is an achievement to be proud of. I love you very much, my dear brother, keep working hard.

I will keep writing as long as I and my pen last. I don't have a lot of faith in either. I do have a lot of Christian faith, however, and I know that this is but the beginning for me. I have a debt, my dear parents, that I can never repay. I owe you both so much. You are both such wonderful people and I love you both greatly. Anyway, I'll sign off for today. All my love and heartfelt regret,

Your everloving son and brother,

James.

I read over the letter, feeling happier that I'd had the opportunity to express my feelings towards my family again. I continued writing, to Gaye this time. I started where I'd left off, on the same piece of paper.

I have no idea what date it is. I know that at least three weeks have passed since I last wrote. My pen broke and obstinately refused to work until today. I've written a long letter to my family who I miss very much, but I wish to devote far more ink to you, my darling.

Very little has changed. The weather has cycled between sun and snow. The last couple of days have been snow, with last night's fall creating a pure white atmosphere. It is still cold, though more of my clothes have dried and I am comfortable. There is nothing to eat which is unfortunate. If I could find food then I am sure I could last through the winter and make it to a town once the snow has cleared. I grow thinner each day though, blessedly, the pangs of hunger subsided a time ago.

I have read and reread a Charles Dickens' novel, *Great Expectations* which I have thoroughly enjoyed. Because it was written so long ago, his style of writing gives me much to think about. There is a certain, peaceful harmony in the way he writes. The book has a melancholic theme which rests easily with me at the moment.

I think and dream a lot about you. I think of the engagement party we were supposed to have, our wedding and our honeymoon, the car we were going to buy and the children we were to raise. I find it frustrating to think about all that I have given up and lost. I cannot help but think I may be saved yet and all these things might become . . .

I had intended to write 'a reality', but the ink faded to just a depression on the paper. The pen was empty. I pressed hard and continued. It was no longer ink, just an impression of the words, saying, 'My pen is out of ink. I love you! I love you forever!' I tossed the pen back into the dirt. Those were the last words it would produce.

My spirits had lifted while I had been able to write, but now my isolation was even more depressing than before. I had so much more to tell Gaye. My feelings towards her were stronger than ever. It was now more than two months since we'd been together and I was missing her terribly. I remembered the wonderful weekend we had spent together on the north coast, shortly before my departure from Brisbane. On the Saturday night, we had remained at the unit, feasted on spaghetti bolognaise, before settling back to watch *The Sound of Music* on television. Gaye hadn't seen it before and I hadn't watched it since I was a young child. Snuggled together, it was so peaceful. As thoughts of that night flooded back, I found myself singing the chorus of *Edelweiss*. It had such a lovely melody that, even through my own, cracked, off-tune voice, it brought me immense pleasure. I lay there for a long time, repeating the chorus, enjoying the sound of my own voice and not feeling so lonely any more.

I read over my letter to Gaye and was happy with most of it, except for the space devoted to *Great Expectations*. But the novel had been another mainstay for my sanity. The fact that I had read it four times in a short period and had enjoyed it more each time was quite incredible. Never had I reread a novel in such a way before. There was one part of the book that I always enjoyed. Towards the end of the novel, the central character, Pip, finds himself in a situation which, in many ways, was similar to how I now found myself. He receives a note telling him to go to a secret meeting place where he is confronted by an enemy from his past, someone he had long ago forgotten. This man, however, has not forgotten Pip or the injustice he feels Pip has caused him and plans to kill him.

Pip is bound and taunted and teased, as the man explains his plans. He tries to come to terms with the fact that he is going to die shortly and his heart becomes heavy with regret. He reflects on how he has betrayed the people from his humble youth to reach his higher status. Pip's captor tells him how, once he is dead, his body will be thrown into the lime kiln and never be discovered. I thanked God I had no regrets about how I had treated people in my life.

Just as Pip is about to meet his fate, his best friend, Herbert, barges in and saves him. I used to think to myself, as I read this passage, 'Wouldn't it be wonderful if someone like Herbert would come in and rescue me just as my time was running out?' The thought would bring a grin to my face. A 'Herbert' was extremely unlikely but the thought was so comforting it became another straw to clutch.

Now, as the blizzard continued around me, the seventy-day goal, the Herbert rescuer, the commercial airline crash or the volcanic eruption seemed more remote than ever. I lay there and contemplated the weeks that had passed. I was probably twenty-three. I was dirtier, thinner and smellier than ever. Grit and grime coated me from head to toe. My ribs stuck rudely through the walls of my chest. My hips were devoid of fat or muscle and it was uncomfortable even to lie on my bed of dirt. The fact that I'd ended up in such a filthy, degraded, starving state appalled me. From being an average university student, I had sunk lower than most miserable, mangy animals in Kathmandu. How wrong things had gone!

At times, I had considered taking photos of the surrounding environment but I had no inclination whatsoever to record my shocking appearance. From my letters, my family and Gaye would have an unrealistic impression that things weren't too bad. A photograph would reveal the reality of the suffering.

As my self-esteem fell to an all-time low, the grey clouds around me seemed to sink across my own mind. I felt my situation was absolutely hopeless and seriously questioned whether it was worthwhile persisting.

JOANNE: *23 January 1992*

It was pitch dark and quite cold when we arrived at Colonel Pun's office with the two mountaineers. He ordered tea, which soon arrived in china cups with floral designs. They seemed incongruous in the otherwise Spartan surrounds. A number of maps clung to the drab walls. The floor was cement and the seating rather shabby. He put a kerosene heater in front of me and we brought him up to date on all the searchers still out. I told Colonel Pun about the psychic who kept telling me that James was at Gosainkund. Given that two men had already gone up on foot, he could see little point in flying up with two extra men. If the men on foot could not get there, there was no way he could land anyway. If he took civilians up, I would have to pay for the helicopter; if he went up on a training flight, he could check out what was happening at Phedi and it would cost me nothing. It was logical.

Tom and I went to the upper floor of the building towards the radio room, a cold and depressing place. What looked, at least to my uneducated eye, to be a very primitive communications device sat on a table in a dark, claustrophobic room. There were two wooden chairs and an urn in a corner of the room. Underneath the urn was a plastic container full of grey water with a banana skin floating in it. This was used not only to catch drips from the urn, but also as a washing up container for the tea cups. I grimaced as I thought of the cup of tea I had just finished. A soldier brought me the kerosene heater from Colonel Pun's office.

About twenty minutes after take-off, Colonel Pun radioed that he had found the search party snowed in at Phedi. Voices over the radio are distorted and gravelly and take on a spooky, almost sci-fi quality. In between transmissions, there is the eerie wail of static.

Colonel Pun had been surprised by the amount of snow. He estimated there was at least two metres of snow at Phedi. There were no signal banners on display. Several men had raced out of the huts at Phedi and run a short distance up the hillside where the helicopter could land. They had started to shovel snow out of the way, some of them using their bare hands, but it was useless.

Nothing had been found and Colonel Pun had instructed them, using a combination of sign language and shouting, to keep searching. He then made for Talu, where he was able to land. There was snow even there. In the little village, he met up with Ingo. Obviously, the search team had split up. Ingo had found nothing either. His intentions were to search between Talu and Phedi, but there was nothing he could do until the weather cleared and some of the snow thawed. The search would take at least two or three days.

Whilst Colonel Pun was up in the mountains, a thick mist had covered the city. This meant that he had to land at Tokha, an army base high above the valley.

I was annoyed that the weather was so bad up there. It really seemed everything was against us! I had no idea of how much of the area above Phedi had been searched. I was worried that the search party would run out of food, so I decided to organise some food supplies and get Colonel Pun to drop them off. That way, they would not have to return to Kathmandu to re-stock.

JAMES: 23 *January 1992*

My head was still wrapped in the sleeping bag when something broke the silence of dawn. It was too cold to begin my daily routine. I lay there sullenly, aware that it was a clear day outside. I could tell by the light that filtered through the layers of my sleeping bag. Without even having to remove my head from its covers, I would know the morning's prevailing weather conditions. After a quick glance to the south of the valley I could predict whether or not it would snow that day.

The noise, now clearly audible, was unlike anything I had heard in my weeks on the mountain. It had a howling quality about it. As it grew louder, it took on a more rhythmic, mechanised tone. No force of the environment could produce such a regular racket.

'It must be a helicopter!' I thought. I unzipped my sleeping bag and got to my feet. As I was struggling to get my sandshoes on, the chopper soared high above me, heading northwards towards Phedi.

I made my way to the right-hand edge of my rock, tying up my shoelaces and grabbing my sleeping bag along the way. The helicopter had taken no time at all to ascend to Phedi. It was now far away, circling above the village. Although so distant, I felt with the blue sleeping bag and my maroon, thermal underwear, they might still be able to see me. I stepped out into the snow, surprised at its depth. It was now well above mid-thigh and it needed a huge effort to wade out to the clear area. I could only get about a quarter of the distance out, just clear of the trees. Undoing the drawstring of my trousers, I pulled them down, all the while furiously treading the snow beneath my feet in the hope of compacting it. It was important that I was as elevated as possible and exposed as much of my coloured thermals as I could.

I had been out in the snow for five minutes and the helicopter was still circling. Every time it flew towards me, I waved my sleeping bag desperately. Whenever it turned its back to me, I took a brief rest until the next opportunity to wave. This continued for about fifteen to twenty minutes and my arm grew weak, though I was able to stand the entire time.

All the time, I knew the chance of being spotted from so far away was very slim. Yet, I could not let any opportunity slip by. It was certainly more likely that the pilot would spot me than a volcano would erupt, I reminded myself. I sent an urgent, silent prayer that it would come back via the valley and not continue up over the pass. Every time it circled and swung above Phedi, I couldn't help but fear that it would continue upwards and over the mountain range.

After twenty minutes, the helicopter abruptly turned and raced down my valley. It was a couple of kilometres away and well below me, seemingly clinging to the opposite wall. I screamed with all my might, 'Don't leave me here!'

As it disappeared into the distance, I strained my ears, hoping it would come back. I had imagined, if I was ever to be spotted by a helicopter, it would have to do circles within the valley, sweeping close to the wall where I sheltered. I had often pictured a helicopter doing just

151

this. It didn't seem fair that the helicopter, having actually come, had disappeared so quickly without giving me a chance.

I stumbled back to my rock. What a coincidence! I had only written the day before about my parents sending up a helicopter and one had been sent up. I knew, of course, that the helicopter had not been sent up for me. I had been lost so long by now, that any search my family undertook would have been given up long ago.

On the way back, one of my sandshoes came off. I felt through the snow with my hands but couldn't find it. I cursed and went on. I would need both of them on day seventy when I crawled down the mountain to the village.

The helicopter had brought me hope. Yesterday I had struggled to justify my continued existence. Now, I reasoned, if one helicopter had been sent into the valley, then maybe another would follow.

The way it had hovered around Phedi was curious. Accompanying the lift of my spirits was a depressing suspicion about the helicopter's mission. With the last two days of heavy snowfall, other trekkers must have attempted the pass and met a fate similar to mine. If they had made it successfully to Phedi, the helicopter would have winched them out of there. But the way the helicopter had returned made me fairly certain that the search had been unsuccessful. What also occurred to me was how quickly the search had been instigated. For helicopters to be used in the search, someone of authority must be missing. This was good for me since more searches might follow.

As I looked down to the south of the valley, I knew the rest of the day would be fine. This was another good omen. I would bask in the sun that afternoon, I thought, and I set to preparing my snowballs to enjoy later that day. That one helicopter flight had brought me back from the brink of despair. It was proof that the world outside was continuing and it give me renewed hope.

JOANNE: *23 January 1992*

Once back at Blue Mountain, Tom got some breakfast together while I read a fax from Dad. They had made contact with Amnesty International in Australia. Kimberley's psychic was now saying that James was 'with a group of people, to some degree Westerners'. The psychic said they were drug dealers, operating in a roughly triangular area just above Dhunche. He had said the best way to gain information was to work through the local lama. He also stated that James was 'emotionally troubled' and would 'show up in two months'. I virtually disregarded the last statement, but some of the other comments were interesting, as they tied in with Linda Griffith's opinions about drug trafficking.

I phoned Amadablam to see if they'd heard how their two teams were going. I was told that the mountaineers who had gone to Gosainkund were back. Again, I was very annoyed that I had not been contacted.

'I told you I wanted to know as soon as they were in. Why didn't you call me?' I demanded. The receptionist, obviously deciding not to trouble herself with my complaining, immediately put me on to Mr Ravi. He apologised for not letting me know. The men had got as far as the Laurebinayak Pass and had found nothing.

'Did they search every hut at Gosainkund?' I asked. Mr Ravi said they had. I felt a stab of disappointment. Despite Andrew's scorn, a part of me had been hoping desperately that James would be there.

'What does it take to get them to do as I ask? I said. 'If I didn't keep chasing them up, I'd never hear anything. Don't they realise how anxious I am to hear from them?'

Graeme called to say he had talked with the Chinia Lama who had still heard nothing. We were well past the five days of searching by the people he had deputised. I was concerned by their lack of results. Using a helicopter had not made it a cheap exercise. I wanted to know what had happened, even if they'd found nothing. I wanted to know if they'd spoken to the Phedi and Gopte lodge keepers and hear what they had to say.

I rang Amnesty International in London. They had read the fax but were not prepared to issue what they termed a 'full alert' on the basis of our anonymous letter. They'd need to analyse it more closely. I was to call in twenty-four hours.

JOANNE: *24 January 1992*

After one night at Tom and Maria's I wondered why I hadn't stayed sooner. Maria did her utmost to ensure my every comfort. I had more blankets than I knew what to do with and had been sent to bed with a hot-water bottle. Beside my bed was a tray with a thermos of water, tea, coffee and milk. I had my own little bathroom, with sink, shower and toilet. The water from the shower was often a bit difficult about going down the drain hole and the toilet wouldn't always flush, but I could easily live with those small inconveniences in return for the welcoming, caring atmosphere.

Cuddled up with my hot-water bottle, I'd had a reasonably restful night. The telephone sounded at 8 a.m. In Nepal, offices don't open until 10 a.m. One can't do much until mid-morning. Of course, 8 a.m. in Nepal was 1 p.m. in Australia. And Dad decided that was the best time to call.

Dad wanted to let me know that at the suggestion of Linda Griffith, he was going to meet with Mr Gautam, Nepal's Chief Secretary. He was on a trip to Australia and currently in Queensland. I thought it was an excellent idea.

As I got off the phone, I wondered what Dad's meeting would achieve. If it proved to be fruitful, I would be annoyed in some respects as Mr Gautam had been in Nepal when I first arrived. I knew the Australian Embassy had seen him off to Australia from the Kathmandu airport. If meeting with government officials from the Nepali Government would help, I would have thought it the Australian Embassy's place to try to arrange something like that for me. Still, having said that, Gautam was not on his home turf and would be eager to promote positive politics by doing things like meeting with my parents. Also, my father held a considerably more important position than I did. We'd have to wait and see.

I questioned Dorrilyn about the procedure when a body is found. Being a nurse, I wondered if she knew what was involved in shipping a body. Suddenly, I found myself in tears. She was very understanding and explained that the body would be brought back in a body bag and taken to a morgue, most probably at the American Embassy. It would take five days to get clearance to fly the corpse out of the country. During that time, they would probably have to embalm it. She told me gently that it would all be taken care of and reminded me that if James still had a passport or another form of identification on him, there would be no need for me to identify the body. She said the best thing I could do would be to get home as quickly as possible. One thing I knew for sure was that I would not want to be on the same plane as James's body. Knowing that a coffin bearing my brother's corpse was lying in the hold below me would be more than I could bear.

At midday we collected the photos taken at Gosainkund by Mr Ravi's team. The shots showed the men wading through waist-deep snow. The huts looked deserted. One photograph showed where they had pinned up a wanted poster for James in the window of a hut. The lakes were completely frozen over and I could see no sign of a trail anywhere. There could be no doubt that the men had not only reached Gosainkund, but had gone to considerable trouble to do so.

In the afternoon Tom drove me into Thamel to Tashi Taki. They'd done a good job with the food parcels. There were three wrapped up in hessian. It should last the party for at least another week. However, Colonel Pun was unable to take it up until Monday 27th. I hoped that none of the food would begin to rot. The last thing I wanted was to send the men at Phedi a supply of gastroenteritis!

I tried to ring the Chinia Lama, and was told he was at Boudha. They gave me an alternative number which I rang, only to be told he was at home! It was beginning to dawn on me, uncharitable though it might be, that the Chinia Lama might have used me for a publicity stunt. Doubtless it had impressed his villagers no end to have their leader descend on them from the skies, flanked by an embassy official.

I rang Lottie Weisse and told her the mountaineers had checked every hut at Gosainkund and James was not there.

'Oh. My friend was very certain you would find him there.'

'Well,' I said, 'she was wrong. Tell her thanks anyway.' After all, the lady had only been trying to help me. I asked Lottie if she'd been in touch with the Chinia Lama. She hadn't, but said a very prominent lama had died and everyone was very busy with his funeral arrangements. Perhaps the Chinia Lama was involved.

At 8 p.m. I phoned London again. This conversation with Amnesty International proved more fruitful. They advised me to notify the Nepali Government and to contact the Chinese Embassy and see what they came up with.

JOANNE: *25 January 1992*

Saturday morning found me looking for something to do. I decided to go for a walk, feeling some sunshine and exercise would do me good. Despite the poverty and the number of people wandering along the roadsides, Kathmandu seems a fairly safe city. Quite a lot of people watched me, more in curiosity than anything else. I was, by now, almost immune to the stench of garbage in the streets, the guttural sounds of men and women spitting, the skulking, bedraggled dogs and the weaving vehicles. I found myself instead noticing the shy smiles and murmurs of 'Namaste' as I passed, the vivid colours of a fruit and vegetable stall and the beautiful saris worn by the women. I watched children laughing as they played along the roadside. I was developing a fondness for this strange, exotic, filthy, but animated city. I was beginning to understand why James had come here and why he had enjoyed it so much.

Tom and Maria were just about to have lunch when I got back. Following my conversation with London Amnesty International last night, Tom had, as always, a contact he thought might be able to help us. This lady, Indra Ban, had many friends in political office and she was currently in Sydney. Tom suggested my father call her.

As we were discussing this, Dad telephoned. The Federal police in Australia were going to help with some of the more irregular leads. A Federal police officer was with him and offered to get a colleague of his in Pakistan to call me.

Indra proved to be a great help. After Dad called her, she made several calls to India and Nepal and suggested we contact the Minister for Forestries, a good friend of hers. When Tom tried, he was not available but agreed to see us early tomorrow morning. As a courtesy, we rang the Australian Embassy to advise them and ask if someone wanted to accompany us. We were told no one would be available.

There was not much more I could do that day. Dad called after his meeting with Gautam. The Chief Secretary was most concerned to hear about James and said that it was not common for a person to disappear as James had. He dismissed the idea of James being held in a political prison, saying that, if that was the case, Nepal would know about it by now. He told Dad that I should go and see him once he returned to Nepal on 1 February.

JOANNE: *26 January 1992*

January 26 is Australia Day, a public holiday. In Kathmandu, the Australian Embassy was hosting a cocktail party to celebrate the occasion. Auli had organised an invitation for me. January 26 was also Graeme's last day in Nepal before a month's leave.

I had been dismayed to hear that Graeme was going away on holiday. I had come to know him quite well and knew he was genuinely concerned about James. He'd been very co-operative and anxious to help. The ambassador had made no further attempts to see me since the first meeting. Whereas both Graeme and Auli had offered me hospitality, the ambassador and his wife did not once ask how I was coping, if I had somewhere to stay or if I was being looked after. I was going to miss Graeme when he left. First Tim, then Andrew and now Graeme . . . I felt I was being deserted.

Tom and I were on the road by 7.30 a.m. We drove across town to the home of the Minister for Forestries. Leaving our shoes at the doorway, we joined a crowd who were waiting patiently. I was wondering how long it would all take when a stocky man wearing a topi appeared in the doorway of the room and came directly across to us.

We stood and greeted him in the Nepali fashion, saying 'Namaste'. He sat down beside us. Tom and he conferred in Nepali for a while. I kept track of what was being said as best I could. The minister frowned, shook his head and looked at me sympathetically. He listened to our entire story, asking questions and nodding his understanding. When Tom had finished, he said the best person to help us would be the Minister for Tourism who lived close by. He told us how to find his house. I could not help but think the buck-passing had begun.

Tom and I arrived there to find a similar set-up, but the only other person in the waiting area was an old man dressed predominantly in white. He asked Tom why we were waiting. Tom replied, telling him briefly about James. Tom had not said much before the old man interjected. He had already heard about James, the Australian missing in the Helambu/Gosainkund area. When Tom asked how he knew, he replied that word of James's disappearance and the reward had travelled as far away as North-Western India where he had recently been.

It was only a few minutes before someone came and indicated we should follow him upstairs. As we left the room, I whispered to Tom, 'But that other man was here first.'

Tom replied, 'Yes, but he's not a Westerner.'

The Minister for Tourism was a lean man with grey hair. He looked a little dishevelled, with untidy strands of hair sticking up and a large shawl swathed around his upper body. I wondered if we had got him out of bed. We seemed to be in a lounge room of sorts. He sat across from us on a wooden chair and we were seated on a couch with a crocheted rug thrown across it. Tom went through the whole story again. The minister listened and then said he would see what he could do, but the most important step for us to take was to write letters formally requesting help. These letters should be directed to him, the Home Ministry and the Minister for Foreign Affairs, who happened to be the Prime Minister. My heart sank. I imagined writing letters, putting them in the post and, if they ever made it past the desks of the myriad assistants (something which was far from certain), having them placed at the bottom of a non-urgent pile for the minister's eventual reading pleasure. We thanked him, said we'd get onto it straight away and left. I expressed my concerns to Tom. He had different ideas.

We went back to Blue Mountain and quickly composed a letter. Tom told me that we would then try to hand-deliver them. The embassy's social event was going to stand us in good stead, as was the fact that the last thing the Nepali Government wanted was for any waves to be created between China and Nepal.

We began the letters to each of the officials by saying we were waiting on the advice of the Australian Federal police, Mr Gautam and Amnesty International. We then outlined the story, mentioning that Dad was a scientist of 'world renown' and presented the anonymous message. The final paragraph read, 'My family and I are beside ourselves with grief and anxiety. We feel that under the circumstances, all leads must be taken seriously and investigated fully. We can also not accept that someone can just disappear without trace. I have written to Amnesty International. They have also advised me to contact the Chinese Embassy in Nepal, but I felt that I should seek your advice prior to doing so.'

This was yet another time when I realised how unbelievably fortunate it was that I had met Tom. He understood so well how things worked in Nepal. By making my family and I sound as important as possible and by mentioning involvement of the Australian police, we were much more likely to create a strong impression. Also, the thinly veiled threat to go directly to the Chinese Embassy would prove a most useful catalyst. The last thing the Nepalis wanted was for me to go marching up to the Chinese Embassy and accuse them of holding James in a political prison camp.

Tom's talents came to the fore in delivering the letters too, especially at the Prime Minister's office. Tom tried to talk an official into letting us see him. The official said it was impossible. Tom then said he had a very important letter for the Prime Minister from the Australian Embassy. This caught the official's attention. He said we could still not see the Prime Minister, but if it was an important letter, we should see the Prime Minister's secretary. We were directed to another office.

Tom spoke to the secretaries in Nepali, showing them the letter and obviously impressing upon them the importance of its contents. As he spoke, the men seemed to become more serious, nodding and listening intently. Tom handed the letter to one of them and asked for a receipt as proof the letter had been delivered. As we left the room, I said to Tom, 'I hope that letter gets to the Prime Minister.'

'Don't worry about it,' said Tom. 'I guarantee it will.' He told me he had told the secretary that the letter contained information of vital importance to the Australian Embassy. At the cocktail party the embassy was hosting tonight, the Australian Ambassador would most certainly wish to discuss the contents with the Prime Minister. It would be most embarrassing for the Prime Minister if he had not read the letter before attending!

We had still heard nothing of the party from Amadablam that had gone to search the area between Kathmandu and Talu. They'd been out for over a week now. Surely they were back? I was willing to wager that, as usual, Amadablam hadn't let me know of their return. The receptionist knew me by now and, no doubt having categorised me as difficult, passed me straight on to Mr Ravi.

'I am calling to find out if the last search party is in,' I informed him.

'Yes,' he replied. 'I assumed you knew already. They got back on Thursday. Didn't you hear? A body has been found.'

Maria looked up in surprise as I abruptly sat in the chair beside the phone. My voice trembled as I tried to quell a surge of nausea.

'What? I know nothing. Tell me.'

Mr Ravi said that the search party I had sent out had been returning through Chisopani. The lodge keeper there had told them that the body of a European had been found in the north of Helambu near Tarke Ghyang. Word had it that the Nepali who had found the body was now in police custody in Kathmandu and other locals from all over Helambu were racing to Tarke Ghyang in the hope of claiming a reward.

'Of course, it could just be a rumour,' Mr Ravi finished.

'Great. Just great,' I thought. I asked Mr Ravi if he had any more information. He didn't. I broke the connection and tearfully told Maria. I had no way of knowing how much truth there was in the story. I was trying to pull myself together when the phone rang.

'It's your father,' Maria told me. 'Can you talk to him?' I nodded and took the phone from her. I can't remember much of the conversation, except that it seemed ridiculous to be talking about government officials and letters when it could be that the mystery was solved and James's body had at last been found.

Once I hung up, I rang Graeme. I started to explain but my voice broke. Taking a few moments to regain control, I tried again and managed to tell him what I'd heard. He said he would see what he could find out. Within half an hour, he'd called back. He had not been able to find anyone who had any information. I decided to call Anoop Rana, recalling his connections with the police. Anoop said he would do what he could and was back in touch within ten minutes. He had spoken to the local police who knew nothing of any of this and would speak to all of the local districts tomorrow. I was breathing more easily at this stage. If no one here knew anything, I felt there was a good chance it was all just rumour.

I also managed to reach the Chinia Lama. He confirmed he had still heard nothing and said that he might have to send a messenger up if no word came through in the next day or so. I was becoming increasingly exasperated and questioned the need for a messenger. I thought he had instructed a runner to come to him. He said he had and was surprised that one hadn't arrived. We left it that we would see what the next twenty-four hours brought.

I had not thought to pack anything to wear at cocktail parties when I hurriedly stuffed my suitcases back in Brisbane what now seemed an eternity ago. I had offers of clothes, but decided I could probably find something that would do. Maria lent me some jewellery and make-up and, in between power cuts, I managed to assemble enough to attend. The ambassador's house was brightly lit and the noise of chatter and clinking glasses filled the air. We were greeted at the door by the ambassador, his wife and Auli. The lounge room was full and people were spilling out onto the patio and into the garden. Waiters were carrying trays of drinks and hors d'oeuvres. I took a glass of white wine from a passing waiter and surveyed the room. Knowing virtually no one present and not feeling in a very sociable mood, I wondered if it was going to be a long night. It was then that a handsome, bearded Nepali man in a suit introduced himself.

'Dr Robertson? My name is Niranjan Koirala. I am the adviser to the Minister for Tourism and the nephew of the Prime Minister. You must come with me. There are many people here who are most anxious to meet with you.' Amazed, I obeyed. We were near the entrance foyer when the Minister for Tourism came over. I was telling Niranjan we had already met when a tall man dressed in white and wearing a sash across his chest apparently broke off his conversation with the ambassador to come across. As he extended his hand, I realised that this was none other than G. P. Koirala, the Prime Minister of Nepal.

He took my hand and said, 'I am very sorry to hear about your brother. We should have been notified a long time ago.' The ambassador had followed the Prime Minister over and, as the Prime Minster said this, I glanced at the ambassador.

'Is that so?' I commented. The Prime Minister went on to say that he would do all he could. He told me I should stay in touch with Niranjan and take details of all areas searched to him tomorrow. He did not think it likely that James was in a political prison but he surely had to be somewhere.

As the Prime Minister left me to mingle with other guests, I felt triumphant. I had, with little help from the embassy, managed to create an impression and meet the Prime Minister. Who knew what new avenues this might open to us in terms of resources?

I sipped wine for the remainder of the evening. Anoop Rana was there. He told me he felt that the talk of a body being found at Tarke Ghyang was purely rumour. I remember he took me away from the noise to sit on a garden wall. I gathered he had decided to try to talk some sense into me. He told me I should leave Nepal. He said either James was dead or didn't want to be found and that I was causing myself a lot of unnecessary grief. I retorted that I fully accepted that James was probably dead, but that I had to know that I had done everything possible before I left Nepal and that we would never rest until we had found out what happened.

After the cocktail party, we went to Auli's house. I told her what Anoop had said. She said she was sure James was still alive. She couldn't explain it: it was just a feeling.

It was after 1 a.m. when we left. I had said a very tearful goodbye to Graeme. I had forgotten that we were due at the airport with the food parcel at 6 that morning.

JOANNE: *27 January 1992*

By 7, Colonel Pun had taken off with the food parcels and I was sitting in the radio room. There was no kerosene heater, which made it very cold. I tried to sit beside the radio, but was still shivering. Instead, I began to pace the verandah outside.

Eventually the radio crackled into life. Colonel Pun had managed to fly to Phedi although the weather was bad. The tiny village was now deserted. He had also landed briefly at Talu. Ingo was no longer there. Colonel Pun was flying back to Kathmandu.

'Damn!' I said. What did this mean? Were the searchers on their way back to Kathmandu because they had run out of food? Had the weather cleared enough for them to continue on up and over the pass?

On his return, Colonel Pun could tell us no more than he had over the radio. I watched grimly as the food parcels were unloaded. We had no idea where the search team was and we had a heap of food supplies with a limited life span. It had not been a productive exercise.

I kept myself occupied for the rest of the day. The Australian Federal police officer in Islamabad called. I explained to him what had happened so far and asked him to think if there was anything at all he could do to help. I faxed him copies of all the letters I had sent and a map. Maria and I also went into the Ministry of Tourism to see Niranjan Koirala who assured me that all police and army forces in the area were mobilised. I sent a fax home, tried to call the Chinia Lama who, to my frustration, wasn't there and rang Debbie Harrison to let her know that the parties were no longer at Phedi.

It's difficult, in retrospect, to look back and attempt to describe how I was feeling by this stage. I was certainly very weary. James had been missing for exactly five weeks and one day.

The repeated advice that he could never have survived so long had penetrated. I knew, logically, we were looking for a body and that the hard fact of the matter was that we would be lucky to find it. The repeated reports of the severe weather conditions would mean that there was going to be a limit to how much more searching could be done. It was too dangerous for men to subject themselves to two metres of snow, especially when they believed they were only searching for a body. I could understand that. The last thing I wanted was for anyone else to die. I felt that Anoop's comments last night advising me to leave Nepal probably reflected the thoughts of most local people. I suspected that I was considered quite mad by a number of people. I felt even the efforts of the government officials were an exercise in placation rather than expectation. What people thought didn't really bother me. What did matter was that when I left Kathmandu I should know that I could have done no more. I also realised that perhaps the hardest thing I would ever have to do in my life would be to get on that plane back to Australia having failed. I knew interest was waning. Once I left, it would go altogether. James would become another statistic, another trekker lost forever. That was why it was crucial that I never appeared to have given up hope. No matter how outlandish the suggestion, if there was a shred of possibility to it, I had to portray utter positivity that we were finally on the right track.

A part of me did not accept that James had died. I had spoken to Gaye on the phone at one stage and she had told me she didn't feel that James was dead. I knew what she meant. Some part of me was convinced that I would know if James had died. I couldn't stay in Nepal forever, but I wasn't ready to leave yet.

Andrew phoned early in the evening. I had spoken to him once or twice since his return to Australia. He had seen my parents on several occasions. He had told me how much they were suffering. Dad was refusing to accept that James could be dead. I had asked Andrew to describe the terrain to them and prepare them for the worst.

Given this, it was strange that I reacted so badly to Andrew's news.

They were going to organise a memorial service for James – not a funeral, a celebration of James's life. He told me something had to be done to draw this nightmare to a close so we could get on with our lives. They would wait until after I got back from Nepal and Andrew suggested I consider leaving as soon as possible.

I bit back tears. They could call it whatever they liked, but to my way of thinking it was a funeral. They were convinced James was dead. It was giving up. I felt I would never have the strength to attend such a service. I was not ready to say goodbye to James yet. And what if we went through all of that, just to have James's body recovered in spring? That would mean another service and a burial. I couldn't face it.

A while later Dad called back. He refused to discuss the memorial service but said, 'Joanne, only once you leave Nepal will we know there is no hope for James.'

JAMES: *27 January 1992*

While trying to psych myself into leaving the warmth of my sleeping bag, I'd watched the light of another clear day creep down the valley wall opposite. It had been an interesting few days since seeing the helicopter. It was three, perhaps four days. Time meant very little to me now. The weather had been kind and I had watched the snow slowly melt away. The two black birds had returned. I took little notice of them now. Nonetheless, I was determined that there would be no way they would be allowed to pick away at my body. I was weakening but when the time came, I would make sure my sleeping bag well and truly covered my body so that my corpse might not be disturbed.

I'd had a fright a couple of days earlier. Whilst reading, I'd heard faint barking in the distance. The thought of a pack of wolves descending on me was horrifying. I knew I would be unable to defend myself, easy prey for the wolves to tear me to shreds. If they looked like attacking, suicide with my scissors would be far preferable. But the barking of the dogs faded away.

I had contemplated suicide from time to time, especially over the few days before I'd seen the helicopter, when the snow was so heavy and my spirits had sunk. How easy it would be to just plunge the scissors into my chest! After a brief moment of pain I would know nothing more about it. I thought of how I could use my shoelaces. I could tie them to a stick and wrap them around my neck. If I twisted the stick behind my head, I would soon be unable to breathe. It would

163

be a quick end. The most painless method would be to make my arm numb by placing ice over my brachial artery. A quick, precise incision would do the trick. Any of these would bring a quick end, a comparatively easy escape from pain and loneliness.

As hope had faded, the idea of suicide became more enticing but the helicopter had changed all that. It had rekindled my spirit to fight on and I had sat patiently waiting for another to come.

Today my patience was rewarded. I heard the howling of the rotor blades again. The noise quickly grew louder and I leapt up with my sleeping bag. Putting my remaining shoe on my right foot and a sleeping bag cover on the left I raced into the centre of the clearing. I was going to give it all I had. Before the helicopter passed, I was in position, waving my sleeping bag.

The helicopter zipped past, almost level with me, heading straight for Phedi. I waved my sleeping bag crazily. Its rustling was even louder than the din of the helicopter. My trousers were down around my ankles, to show my maroon thermal underwear but the helicopter, a good kilometre away, sped up the valley, oblivious of me.

In seconds they were hovering above Phedi but I continued to wave. Although far away, the helicopter stood out very clearly, so incongruous in the snowy mountains. It did not stay long and I watched with glee as it came back down the valley, this time heading straight towards me. It was moving slowly and much closer to me.

I waved even more frantically now, mustering all my strength, trying to jump up and down to attract their attention. I watched it slowly soar past, not more than 300–400 metres away. I could see the two pilots in the cockpit, both of them looking directly towards Kathmandu. Their heads never turned left nor right.

My heart sank as I watched the helicopter fade into the distance and disappear around a bend. I stood there, hoping desperately that it might fly up the valley once more. I knew the chance was very slim but, having made the effort to reach this position, I was not willing to return to my rock too quickly. I stood quite still, a speck on the vast mountainside. I would not see that helicopter again today. I clenched my teeth, trying to rise above this depressing set of circumstances. They had been so close this time and yet so far . . . Was that to be the last opportunity I would have? I stumbled back to my rock. I was nearly there when I found the heel of my missing sandshoe peeking through the snow. At least that's something, I thought.

Back at my rock, I tried to remain optimistic. I thought if two helicopters have come up, there's no reason why a third shouldn't. I wondered how long it would take for a third helicopter to arrive. I had been there thirty days before the first one came along, perhaps these were army manoeuvres and not search parties? Perhaps it would take another thirty days. Time was no longer on my side. And I prayed, as I towelled myself down, that God would give me just one last chance.

JOANNE: *28 January 1992*

Repeated barking by Bluey during the night, the sound of scampering feet and half a banana missing in the morning led us to the conclusion that a rodent of some sort was sharing the kitchen with the rest of us. I tried to convince myself that it was probably a little field mouse, but the impressive quantity of fruit missing suggested that we were deal-ing with something larger.

We were sitting down to breakfast on Tuesday morning when Carl Harrison rang. The search teams were back. I organised to meet them at the embassy around 11.30 a.m.

I arrived early to chat to Auli. I asked her if she would mind trying to speak with the Chinia Lama. I was thoroughly exasperated with him by now and hoped that the weight of an embassy official might help.

Carl, Ingo and Ang Phury turned up and we met in the usual conference room. Needless to say, they had again found nothing. Carl had taken a group of men to Phedi and felt confident they had covered the area above the village thoroughly. Ingo had taken three porters and the dog and gone directly to Talu.

'The lodge keeper from Phedi now remembers your brother,' Ingo said. 'As soon as I mentioned the chicken to him, he remembered.' I was very relieved to hear this. Ingo told me that the lodge keeper had left Phedi at about 10 a.m. on the morning of the 22nd. On the way down there had been very heavy snow.

Between the two groups, they had also covered the path between Phedi and Talu. It had not been easy. Carl described thigh-deep snow which hid huge holes and chasms. He had usually led the way, testing the depth in front with a shovel. At one point, the shovel disappeared into a very deep gap. They'd also had to lower men by ropes in some places. Ingo said there was so much snow that both groups had nearly become lost themselves. It was only the dogs' tracking abilities that helped his group find a path after they lost it. Carl's group also had lost their way briefly. Ingo had been out searching above Talu when he saw Carl's group in the distance, walking in the wrong direction. His shouts alerted them to their near error. There was one remaining area between Phedi and Talu that had not been searched.

'It's a huge valley,' Carl told me, 'with boulders the size of this room. It is very dangerous, full of ice, forest and deep water pools.' Ingo likened the conditions to a refrigerator. It was freezing and full of snow. They told me it would be impossible to search the area on foot until summer. It would take at least fifteen days without snowfall before they could even contemplate sending a search party. Carl and Ingo both thought it was highly likely that we would find James's body in this valley. They explained that the route the trail followed between Phedi and Talu did not really make sense. One would expect the path to follow the Tadi Khola. Instead, it takes a very winding route. If one were unable to locate the trail and instead followed the river, as James was likely to have done, one would end up in this valley.

Ingo had left plenty of rubber gloves with the local people who would not handle a body without them. They had agreed to go out and look after Lhosa (the Tibetan New Year in April). He had also met people the Chinia Lama had deputised. They had found out nothing. Again, I was convinced that Carl and Ingo had been extremely thorough. Carl told me that they had actually found another body, a Nepali who had died about two years ago.

It looked as if James had wandered into this valley. Without food, shelter or a way of making a fire, he would have died within days. I would have to resign myself to the fact that this valley could not be searched until the summer.

The only other alternative would be to send up a helicopter. After all, I had the word of the Prime Minister that they would do all they could to help. Why not try for free use of a helicopter? Neither Carl nor Ingo had ever been into this valley before. Perhaps from the air they would be able to map a route in preparation for a summer search. There was a chance they could see something as well, perhaps a ruck-sack not fully buried by snow? This was highly unlikely but I knew I would feel happier if we'd at least tried. Although I knew he was not overly fond of flying in choppers, Carl said he would make the flight.

Carl and Ingo both presented me with bills. Carl's account was in American dollars. Only the embassy had access to the trust fund. They told Carl a bank cheque would be ready on Thursday and he pointed out that he had men to pay not later than Friday.

The ambassador and Auli said they would talk to someone in the army about using a helicopter.

I returned to Blue Mountain and sent another fax home. Tom

suggested that someone in the helicopter should take a video camera to give me an idea of the terrain and something to show my family. This last search answered many questions. I still kept in the back of my mind the area Kimberley's psychic had selected: the triangle above Dhunche. But it was not with any real hope of finding James alive that I considered this. 'I think I have to accept that James is gone,' I said softly to Tom.

'You know, Joanne,' he replied, 'if James has died, he couldn't have chosen a more beautiful spot in the entire world. Up there in the mountains is like nowhere else on earth. But . . . you know, I have this feeling. I think he's alive somewhere. I really do.'

I passed the afternoon on the phone. I phoned Niranjan who had spoken to the ambassador and said he would keep me informed. Auli called a short time later to say the ambassador would be meeting with the Commander-in-Chief of the Nepali army tomorrow and did I want to go.

'Of course I do!' I replied. I was the only person I trusted to brief the general fully. I was to be at the embassy by 10.45. The meeting with General Rana was at midday, but the ambassador had another meeting first. I would wait in the car. I quickly called Carl to see if he wanted to come along. He felt anything he could offer I already knew, which was fair enough. He wanted to take Ang Phury on the flight, someone he could trust to be on the lookout as well.

I also got a call from the accountant at Amadablam. He more or less demanded that I pay their bill immediately. I was dumbfounded. Every time I had mentioned finances to Mr Ravi, he had told me not to worry about it for now. I got a little abusive back, saying that it had been made clear from the start that the embassy was handling all the accounts, that I didn't even have access to the money and that, considering I'd had to chase up every damn search party that had been out and returned, it was probably a good thing I wasn't the one paying as I might well not do so.

I decided to give the Chinia Lama another try. Even though I knew his men had found nothing, I considered it a matter of principle to chase him up. Amazingly, I managed to get through to him. He had heard nothing and was very concerned and said I should give him some money to pay for a runner to go up and find out what had happened. I'm afraid I did not react very positively.

'Listen,' I said, 'I have already given you money to pay people who have not done as they were supposed. I also paid a lot of money for you to go up in a helicopter and you promised me some answers. I am not going to pay anyone any more and I still expect to hear what happened.' The lama said he would see what he could do and hung up. I knew he wasn't very impressed, but then neither was I.

JOANNE: *29 January 1992*

The usual eight o'clock call from Dad got me out of bed, although I had been awake for ages. During the night, the rat had visited the kitchen again. My room had a gap between the bottom of the door and the floorboards. I lay in bed hoping the rat would not come in.

Dad had some new information from psychics that had been passed on by a family friend. Ever since the huts at Gosainkund had been found empty, my tolerance for psychics had been diminishing. They kept saying James was in a brick building above the pass. I appreciated they wanted to help but I figured if a psychic here in Kathmandu who was 'visited by a female god' couldn't get it right, I wasn't going to hold my breath on the predictions of someone from Brisbane. Nonetheless, I listened patiently. I told Dad I'd see what I could do.

It was probably about 9 when Ingo turned up at Blue Mountain. Something was bothering him. Yesterday, at his request, I had given him a copy of Mark Fulton's statement. Ingo mentioned the morning they had set out by bus for Melamchi Pul Bazaar on the way up to Phedi. He had spoken then about a trail in Helambu that had yet to be searched, one that ran from below Mangengoth on the western arm of the Helambu circuit, joining the eastern arm at Kiul. He had brought it to my attention because it was a route James may have considered using as a shortcut if he had made it back into Helambu.

'Remember, I told you it was a very dangerous trail. It's sometimes called the "broken ankle trail".' I nodded.

'I remember, Ingo, but you said you would search this trail on the way up to Tharepati.'

'I said that, but it was not searched,' he replied.

'Why not?'

It seemed that there had been a difference of opinion. Ingo had wanted to check the trail but Carl was against the idea. Obviously, Ingo's wishes had been overridden. I was not surprised to hear that Carl and Ingo were having some conflict. They were both used to being in charge and were very different. Ingo was, in many ways, quite spiritual. He believed that to find a lost person, you had to understand the way they were thinking and the decisions they might make. He was the type of person who would play by hunches and intuition. Carl was more objective. He looked at the facts, determined the most probable outcome and investigated that.

'Your brother,' Ingo said, 'I believe he is very strong-minded. He will not sway from a decision once it is made.' I agreed: James could be stubborn.

Ingo raised his voice. 'Then he did not cross over the pass. Once he turned back he would have kept going.' Ingo explained that, although he accepted the valley above Talu was a strong possibility, he was concerned about this still unsearched trail. I began to protest, saying that James had not been seen and, with the number of small villages, it would have been difficult to get to Mangengoth without a sighting.

'No. That is not so,' Ingo told me. It seemed the lodge keeper from Gopte had left the same day as the keeper from Phedi, the 22nd. James would not have been seen at Gopte. Tharepati was a busy village. Many people pass through. 'They may well have not seen your brother.'

Mangengoth, the next town down, comprised a lodge and a small army base. Ingo told me that the army quarters were separated from the lodge. It was conceivable someone could walk past them and not be seen. He also said that the lodge keeper from Mangengoth often went away for the day. Ingo claimed he had been at Mangengoth for over thirty minutes before someone noticed him. 'And I was whistling!' he said. 'And look at this.' Ingo pointed to Mark's statement. Mark had said, 'I think that James would have taken the track the way we came but he may have taken the way to Mahankal to try to catch transport.' Ingo's broken ankle trail would be the shortest way to reach the road.

'I think I must search this trail,' said Ingo. He was also still bothered by the Chisopani lodge keeper who was adamant that James had passed back through his village. I told Ingo we were sure he was thinking of Tim on his return journey.

'The lodge keeper said this person wouldn't eat dhal bhat. He bought a chocolate bar and that was all he ate.' Tim was probably sick of dhal bhat, I thought to myself.

'Ingo, you must go and search this trail. I'll call Mark and see if he and James actually discussed the possibility of a road to Mahankal. I will also phone Tim to see if he ate chocolate at Chisopani.' Ingo would leave on Saturday, in two days' time, and would not be back until the middle of the following week.

'I am supposed to fly home on Monday,' I told Ingo, 'but perhaps I should stay until you return.'

169

'I think you must stay a little longer,' Ingo replied.

One of his large dog crates was still at the embassy, and one of the dogs was unwell. I offered to deliver his crate tomorrow and have a look at his sick dog.

When Ingo left I realised it was nearly 10.45 and I was due at the embassy. Grabbing my rucksack with the usual assortment of photos and maps, I made my way quickly along the road. I was probably only 100 metres away when I saw the white Mercedes pull out of the embassy gates and turn towards town. To my relief, the vehicle stopped. The Australian ambassador must be the only person in the whole of Nepal to be on time for anything, I thought to myself. I apologised for being late as I hopped in. The ambassador seemed a bit annoyed. I couldn't blame him.

He told me they had received an official statement from the Nepali Government confirming that there were no political prison camps in Nepal. He criticised the use of Blue Mountain letterhead to write letters to government officials and Amnesty International. He said it didn't look very good. My gut reaction was to reply that I didn't really care, but I managed to bite my tongue.

Promptly at twelve, General Rana stood as we entered his office. He and the ambassador shook hands as a photographer took advantage of what was apparently a great photo opportunity. Quite a large man, General Rana was impeccable in his uniform. I was introduced, we were seated and tea was ordered.

The ambassador left most of the explaining to me. When I produced a map there was a momentary flutter as an aide found the general's glasses. Suitably bespectacled, he listened to all I had to say. He then assured me that all army posts in the vicinity had been notified and that extra patrols had been sent out. In addition, he would organise another patrol to go up on foot from Talu. I gladly accepted his offer, although I thought they would be unlikely to cover any ground the search parties had not already checked. Carl had been a little sceptical of army patrols, suggesting they were likely to turn back at the first sign of anything like snowfall.

I asked about the possibility of using a helicopter free of charge to fly over the deep valley still unsearched. The general was very dubious. If we were sending up civilians, I would really have to charter the helicopter. I was disappointed but understood.

Back at Blue Mountain, I put together a list of facts for the general. To my surprise, we had already used more than seventy men in the search. I calculated a total of over 640 man-days had been spent looking. I took over one of the many maps I had of the Helambu/ Gosainkund region. I could probably draw a map of the area in my sleep! Using highlighter pens, I began to shade the areas covered by the search parties so far. When I'd done that, I took out a blue highlighter and circled three areas: the unsearched valley above Talu, Ingo's 'broken ankle trail' and the triangle above Dhunche. I collected it all and went down to the embassy.

Auli and I sat outside in the small courtyard between the offices and her house. I showed her the three unsearched areas on the map and asked if it was still worthwhile sending a chopper to check the valley. The chances of seeing something were remote. Was it worthwhile sending a search party to scour the area above Dhunche, and check any gompas or religious structures?

'They're the only areas left,' I told her. Auli looked directly at me. 'You have to check them, Joanne. You know you have to do it.' She was right. I went to see Mr Ravi and arranged to meet Balaram. I wanted his help.

Back at Blue Mountain, I rang Mark Fulton. He could not recall discussing transport from Mahankal with James but he still thought it was possible that James had headed there. Then I rang Tim who confirmed that he had eaten only chocolate at Chisopani. I was more convinced than ever that the lodge keeper was getting Tim and James confused.

That night I lay in bed clutching my hot-water bottle. I turned my mind to what I had to do tomorrow. After delivering Ingo's crate, I would organise Colonel Pun and Carl to go up in the helicopter and search the valley. That would only take a day. Ingo would leave Saturday and be back next Wednesday. If Balaram could also leave by Saturday, he should be back next Thursday or Friday. I would cancel my flight out on 3 February and re-book for the 10th.

I wondered how Calum was coping. It had now been over three weeks and I hadn't even telephoned! 'Just one more week,' I promised myself.

JOANNE: *30 January 1992*

Thanks to Auli, I was able to use an embassy vehicle to take Ingo's dog crate back out to Sundarijal.

Sundarijal is the start of the Helambu trek. Ingo runs a trekking information centre and a first-aid post which offers trekkers advice, basic first-aid or a night in his lodge. Many locals also go to Ingo for first-aid. If they are too sick for him to treat and have no money of

171

their own, he will find the finances to send them to hospital in Kathmandu. Beyond Sundarijal, the hills rise steeply. I took one look and reckoned I would last about ten minutes as a trekker!

We got a warm welcome from Ingo and a crowd of Nepali children. A couple of his dog handlers were smiling shyly in the background as Ingo proudly showed me his dogs. They were fine-looking specimens except for one, a bitch that had whelped not long ago. Her abdomen was distended by fluid, but she appeared bright enough. I had warned Ingo that, without the proper equipment and facilities, there would be little I could do. I had brought James's stethoscope and my basic examination suggested a liver problem. Without further tests, I couldn't be more accurate. It struck me Ingo might have thought it ridiculous to contemplate diagnostic tests on an animal when they were probably not available for humans.

I followed Ingo around the back of the building for tea in a little wooden pagoda-type structure. We were joined by a wizened, little man with a drooping moustache. Brown eyes twinkled from his leathery face. This was Lopsom. He had been to see his Rinpoche and still believed James was alive.

The tea arrived. I had become very used to drinking an assortment of tea now: black or white, with sugar or without. I told Ingo I had spoken to Mark and Tim. Ingo said he would leave on Saturday and walk up via Melamchi Pul Bazaar, crossing the trail east to west. If he found nothing, he would return by Chisopani, perhaps having a quick look through the Chisopani forest. I would be grateful if he did anything he thought was necessary and would expect to hear from him late next week.

On the way back to the embassy, we spotted Carl waiting for a taxi. He was going to collect his cheque. He had to pay his men tomorrow and would be free on either Saturday or Sunday to make the flight. I told him I would let him know.

At the embassy, the ambassador's wife was filling in for Graeme. I wandered down to his office to find her eating her lunch at the desk. I know I must have been staring at her plate of fresh prawns, no doubt imported from Bangkok. 'Excuse me,' I said, 'Carl Harrison is here to pick up his cheque.' It was not ready as promised. 'He needs it to pay his employees and has made a special trip to collect it.'

It seemed there was nothing humanly possible that could be done. Either Auli or the ambassador had to sign it. Auli was in town and the ambassador was at his residence. I apologized to Carl and offered to deliver the cheque myself later in the day.

Having seen Carl on his way, I joined Tom and Maria for lunch on their sun-deck. I called Colonel Pun who said it suited him to fly over the valley on Sunday. When Tom mentioned taking a video on Sunday, the colonel said we should get a trained cameraman from the army. The chopper would be stationed at Tokha on Saturday night, so it could take off on Sunday morning regardless of any fog in Kathmandu.

I returned to the embassy where I approached the ambassador about asking General Rana for the services of the army cameraman. In the middle of my question, the ambassador walked away and headed for the stairs to his office.

'What? Do you want me to wait here or am I supposed to be following you?' I asked. He said I should come up. The cheque was still not ready. The ambassador was annoyed. He didn't want to be held up as he had a meeting to attend.

Auli and I went out to the courtyard to have a cup of tea and another Australian turned up, bag of golf clubs over his shoulder, wondering if the ambassador was ready for his round! The cheque was eventually produced.

'Excuse me, madam.' I looked around to see one of the embassy drivers standing behind me. He handed me two photographs of James that had been in one of the cars. They were photos I had not seen before. I guessed Tim must have taken them. In one, James was wearing his straw hat and knapsack. The shot was taken against a magnificent backdrop of snow-covered mountains. The other showed James sitting on the ground with several children. He was wearing his maroon tracksuit pants and a brightly coloured jumper. I recognised the jumper. It had gone back to Australia with Andrew but not the pants. James must have them with him, I thought. He looked healthy, relaxed and happy. His bright red hair shone in the sun. It was how I would like to remember him.

I was putting the photos away when Balaram turned up. He was as obliging as ever. I reached for my map and told him that many psychics were saying that James was above Dhunche. I asked him to go and check in every gompa and shrine. I wanted him to speak with every lama and sadhu he met. Balaram seemed quite prepared to do it and would leave by bus in the morning with two men. He would return about the same time as Ingo.

When I delivered Carl's cheque, we chatted over tea and I told him the helicopter was arranged for Sunday morning. We would pick him up at six. I said I would be in Kathmandu for one more week. If

173

nothing was found, I would have to rely on him to resume searching in the summer.

JAMES: *31 January 1992*

The night had been particularly harsh. The sky was crystal clear, the moon was barely a sliver and the stars shone brightly. But there was still a vast blackness around me. Unlike other nights when I lay for hours taking in the beauty of the sky, tonight I was full of disturbing thoughts. I was growing more aware of the dramatic changes in my body. The cold seemed to penetrate more deeply than ever. I could no longer pinch the fat off any part of my body and I realised that this loss of insulation was making me more susceptible to the cold.

I had always been solidly built, especially around my calves, thighs and buttocks. Running my hand over my body now, I could feel how my thighs had dwindled away to thin straps. My buttocks were just bones jutting against the skin. I could no longer keep my hand warm by nestling it between my thighs. In fact, whereas my knees were once forced apart by having my hands flat in this position, I could now easily push a clenched fist between my legs and keep my knees together, without touching either thigh.

It was not just the cold that made me uncomfortable. With so little padding, I felt every rock and pebble that lay beneath me. Other physical symptoms had appeared. Nausea had come on a couple of weeks ago. It had been slight at first, just an uneasiness in the pit of my stomach I could ignore. As the days passed, the queasiness increased and, over the past few nights, it had reached a point where I would find myself uncontrollably retching. In the darkness, I had to lift my head from the protection of my sleeping bag, gasping in the cold night air, trying to relieve the urge to vomit. Only once had I actually thrown up, after swallowing a lot of water.

The night the retching started, I thought my life was at an end. It was so difficult to gulp in air between the retches. The pattern had continued night after night. Along with the nausea, the discomfort in my feet had returned. It had started as an uncontrollable itchiness which had progressed to sheer pain. I couldn't understand the reasons for these symptoms. All I knew was that death was closing in and, despite my mental struggle to fight on, my body was conceding defeat.

The new moon told me I had been trapped here for nearly six weeks, just over half of the seventy days I had hoped to last. It was only now I really accepted the fact I was not going to be alive when the snow

174

thawed. If I was going to survive, I would have to walk out now rather than wait for the snow to disappear. As the days dragged by, more slowly than ever, there had been no further sign of the helicopter. If it had been on a search and rescue mission, it must have been abandoned. I could not envisage the helicopter returning in the time I thought I had left. I faced reality: if I had a chance of surviving, I would have to act.

I spent the rest of the night psyching myself up for the journey ahead of me in the morning. I believed Gopte would only be ten kilometres away and, if I headed north-east from my rock, across the steep slope, then I might make it. The more I thought about it, the more I persuaded myself it would not be too hard. There had been only one day of snowfall since the last helicopter and yesterday had actually been a full day of warm sunshine. Hadn't I seen all that water rush over the edge of my rock as the tonnes of snow on the hillside above had melted? Hadn't I seen those tree-stumps emerge through the white blanket of snow? Maybe the snow was only knee-deep now! Maybe I could cover three kilometres a day! I'd find shelter at the end of each day and try to rest before setting off again. Why, I'd be in Gopte within four days! Back with other people, enjoying food and a warm fire. I couldn't understand why I hadn't made a successful escape earlier. Hadn't karate taught me that I must always put in my maximum effort? That I must work to my fullest potential if I wanted to win?

The rest of the night, my mind was at ease. I felt happy that I had, at last, made the decision to get out of this situation once and for all. I believed that nothing could stop me and, suddenly, everything looked hopeful.

As the light from the rising sun edged slowly down the opposite side of the valley, I continued to build up my self-esteem. My belief in my ability to get out of this had reached a peak as I emerged from the sleeping bag and considered what I would need for the journey. Without standing, I put on my sandshoes and, over these, I tied the two sleeping bag covers. I then emptied my backpack and replaced only the bare essentials: a couple of pairs of socks, one jumper, my scissors and elastoplast and a spare pair of trousers, I decided to take *Great Expectations* as a memento.

With great effort, I staggered to my feet. The world appeared different. I saw double of everything, one image lying just above the other. I had no idea why but there was nothing I could do about it. In comparison with the task in front of me, my visual problem was insignificant.

I reached down and picked up my backpack and was surprised by the weight. Although it could have weighed no more than four kilograms, it felt like a heavy dumbbell. I threw the pack over my shoulders and fastened the buckle of the strap that now hung loosely about my waist, even in its tightest position, some ten centimetres from where it had been. This meant the weight of the pack, instead of being distributed evenly between my shoulders and my waist, was now concentrated on my shoulders. The small weight pulled me backwards. I had to bend forward to prevent myself toppling over.

I felt relieved looking over the vast valley and the towering mountains for the last time. So little had changed, yet I had never become bored by what I saw. The great expanse of mountains, the rugged cliffs and the sunlight reflecting off the snow had always enchanted me and today was no different. Perhaps one day I would return warm, comfortable and well-fed – with the security of knowing I could leave when I wanted.

I took my first step, tensing for the icy cold I knew was waiting. The wind blew across my face, the only part of me that was now exposed, and stung my nose. My hopes for escape soared even higher as I walked out from under my rock and the snow did not even come over the tops of the covers on my feet. 'This won't be so difficult,' I thought, despite feeling my thighs quiver.

It seemed, however, that positive thought and a strong desire to escape were not to be enough. Within five steps things had taken a turn for the worse. As I moved into territory that I had not interfered with, my feet plunged through the soft slush until the snow reached mid-thigh. I had hoped it would be shallower, but I supposed I wasn't really surprised it was this deep. I dragged my legs upwards, trying to lift my foot clear, so that I could move it forward without resistance. The effort needed was so great that nothing I had done in my entire life would begin to compare.

I felt a sudden desire to eat the snow. I began shovelling large amounts into my mouth, swallowing it frozen, regardless of the harm I knew it would do. This was the first time that I completely failed to discipline myself. I had a craving for calories and illogically felt that snow could supply the energy to continue. I trudged on, feeling my trousers becoming sodden. Water trickled down my legs into my shoes. The pain in my feet heightened. It was different this time – a sharp burning concentrated in my toes and the soles of my feet; the same pain as when I had allowed my feet to thaw several weeks earlier.

I stumbled continually and fell over. In between, it took all my concentration to remain upright.

I struggled this way for what seemed like hours. Halfway across the clearing, a gust of wind sent my straw hat hurtling. It landed about four metres directly below me. I ignored it. It would be a waste of energy to attempt to climb down the steep bank after it.

The further I got, the more shrubs and trees there were. Eventually, I was confronted by thick scrub and bush. The snow here was shallower, for the ground had been protected by all the trees but the vegetation made the going difficult. A wave of nausea swept over me. I bent forward, leaning against the stump of a long dead tree, and started retching uncontrollably. Clear fluid gushed from my mouth, melting the snow where it fell. Simultaneously, I started shaking and shivering, going into rigorous spasms, as the cold overcame me.

My vomitus was tinged with bile, and left a bitter taste. As one wave of nausea was replaced by another, the retching continued though there was nothing more to bring up. After what felt like an eternity, I was able to control the urge and take some deep breaths. I spat dis- tastefully into the snow. To my horror, the spittle was bright red with blood. I choked back the impulse to vomit and shoved some snow in my mouth which I allowed to melt slowly. This diluted the coppery taste in my mouth. I spat out the mix of water, blood and bile and repeated the exercise several times. Each time the redness was less pronounced.

I looked back at my rock to gauge the distance I had covered. I was exhausted. It felt as if I had been walking for hours. My heart sank as I saw that, despite effort and suffering, I had made little headway – barely one hundred metres. The rock no longer seemed the friendly haven that had protected me all those days and nights. It jutted from the side of the mountain like a scar on a beautiful landscape. I could only think of it as my captor, a captor from which there was no escape.

The decision whether or not to continue was made for me. Huge, dark clouds had gathered and were creeping up the valley towards me. The wind was increasing, and I would make little headway before the storm. Reluctantly I turned back.

It was slightly easier on the way back. My footprints were there to retrace and it didn't need the same effort to heave my feet in and out of the snow. I kept my eye on the clouds that seemed to be racing me back to the rock.

I came to the point where I had lost my hat and stared down at it angrily. It reminded me of when I had dropped my water bottle into the creek on the first day I got lost. That day seemed a long time ago, but I could clearly recall the feelings. Losing the water bottle had echoed losing control over my circumstances. Seeing my hat well beyond reach rekindled those feelings. I knew now that things were hopeless, far more so than before.

I began to envy my hat. Soon it would be covered with snow. How easy it would be just to lie there and let the snow cover me as well. It would be painless, a quick end to suffering. Just sit down and wait! There would be nothing more required of me and I wouldn't have to continue living in this nightmare.

And then I thought, why not go back to the rock and die in a peaceful, protected manner? In a way that would be painless, and in a place where my body would be protected until it was found?

I turned and trudged back to my rock. I felt no pain now. No unhappiness. Just a general contentment that everything would soon come to an end.

As I reached the ledge again, I was concerned about the mess I had made. Clothing, pieces of notepaper, books and medication were strewn everywhere. I set to work tidying it up. Before long, I had everything neatly packed away in my rucksack. I laid out my sleeping bag again. I took the covers from my feet and removed my sandshoes. I pulled off any wet clothing and fastidiously dried myself with my towel. I dressed myself in all the warm, dry clothes I had and put the wet ones out to dry. I climbed into my sleeping bag and, resting my head against the rucksack, lay back exhausted and content.

Today I had tried as hard as I could to reach civilisation and I had discovered it was impossible. Failure was not due to any laziness or lack of effort.

I now knew that the situation was completely hopeless. I was obviously not going to last until the snow thawed. I thought back over all I had endured. And for what purpose? Despite all my efforts, I was going to die. I wished now that I had died on the first night. Why should I go on? Nothing was going to change. For the first time, I was overwhelmed with despair. My will to survive ebbed. I decided to accelerate the inevitable.

At that moment, I broke the disciplined routine that had helped keep me alive for so long. I made a conscious decision not to drink any more snow or water. I would dehydrate myself. It was a perfect way to bring on the end. My body would be found and there would be no signs of any suicide. It would be assumed that I had died naturally, either from the cold or starvation.

I remembered the last words in my letters. I had written of my will to survive. Should my body be found and the letters passed on, no one would ever know I had given up.

I even convinced myself that dehydration was a natural way to die and would not be looked upon as suicide. Even if suicide was a sin I reasoned that God would forgive me for dying this way. Surely He would realise the hell I had been through? Surely He would not punish me for trying to escape it? I lay there content with this logic and prayed for my family, my friends and Gaye. Then I prayed this would be my last day in this world.

JAMES: *1 February 1992*

I rolled over, faced outwards and spat. It was impossible to dispel the salty taste of blood coming from my cracked lips and gums. The spittle was almost pure blood and stuck to my tongue. I wiped my mouth on my shoulder, leaving a red stain. With no fluid intake, the suffering had increased immensely. If death had not been so near, I could not have tolerated the pain.

I decided to urinate before the sun set completely. I struggled to my feet, finding it very hard to keep my balance. In thirty-six hours of dehydration the deterioration had been incredible. Before, I'd managed to wade a hundred metres through thigh-deep snow. Now, it was an enormous struggle to take the few paces to my latrine. I supported myself with my hand against the roof and urinated into the gully. All the signs indicated death was near. Just minutes earlier, with grim satisfaction, I had been able to pinch the skin on my abdomen and lifted it up a good six centimetres. When I let go, the fold fell over flatly. There was no natural elasticity to snap the tissues back into position, a sure sign of serious dehydration. My mouth was parched dry, I no longer produced saliva, and now I was struggling to urinate. A small amount trickled into the gully. Its grotesque brown-black colour reinforced just how dehydrated I was.

I staggered back to my sleeping bag and fell painfully on my back-side. There was no padding left to protect my hip bones. But the pain didn't matter any more. It would soon be over.

I watched darkness come for what I hoped would be the last time. I was tired, extremely tired. I was careful to put my head under the sleeping bag and to tighten the cord around the top, tucking the top fold under my head so that it could not be opened easily. I didn't notice coldness any more, I didn't feel any hunger, just thirst and pure

179

exhaustion. My dehydration plan had gone well. I hadn't been sure of the will power needed to stop drinking. Surprisingly, it had not been all that difficult. I had a new goal now, to die as quickly as possible.

Night fell and I repeated the string of prayers that I'd said over all those previous weeks. I finished with the Lord's Prayer and prepared myself for leaving this planet. I lay there content and drifted off to sleep.

As I slept, one hand tucked under my bony head and the other seeking warmth between my thighs, my mind drifted back home, thousands of kilometres away. I was reunited with everyone in Brisbane. I dreamt that I was standing on the verandah of my parents' house at our engagement party. The dream was so vivid it was as if I really was there. On the verandah, to my right, stood my family. To my left stood Gaye, exceptionally beautiful. Friends from school, university, karate, work and friends and relatives of the family were on the lawn – all the people I had been praying for over the past weeks. I could see each face in detail. They were talking amongst themselves and sipping drinks. Everybody looked so very happy.

They turned to listen to me speak. I had no prepared speech, no notes to follow but I spoke from my heart. I thanked them for celebrating such a wonderful occasion with us. I told everyone what a wonderful family I had and how dearly I loved them. I expressed special thanks to my parents who had done so much for me over my twenty-three years.

And then I spoke of Gaye and how lucky I was. I went on to tell the crowd how fortunate I'd been, what a good life I'd had and how much I looked forward to the many years ahead. It was all so vivid, so tangible.

It was, therefore, a terrible shock to me when I awoke to find myself in this cold, painful place. I involuntarily gagged with nausea, an action which wrenched me into a state of complete alertness. It was then I realised just what I had done. I had taken smug satisfaction at the acceleration of my own death. I had given up on the one in a million chance I might get out alive. I felt nothing but depression and despair. In giving up, I'd let everybody down. Why had I given up? I couldn't believe what I had done to myself. How stupid I had been. There was nothing I could do right then to fix the damage already caused. To get out of my sleeping bag now would be fatal. I would have to wait until daylight to collect snow and try to rehydrate myself.

I lay there all night, a miserable wretch, the mental anguish that tormented me now far outweighing the physical discomforts. You've got to fight on, I kept telling myself. There is always hope. And, even though the chances of my survival were now so slim, when dawn arrived I would do everything I could to amend things.

JOANNE: *2 February 1992 a.m.*

I woke well before the alarm went off at 5.15 a.m. and lay thinking about the day. I was still toying with the idea of going up in the helicopter. I wondered how Ingo and Balaram were going. It was early days yet for either of them. I felt Balaram was our only real chance of finding James alive, but the idea of James holed up in a temple was a little far-fetched. The most we could hope for from the flight was that Carl would see an easy way in for his summer searching and that I would have a video tape of the area to take home.

Tom and I left at about 5.45 and drove to Carl's house. The streets, that an hour or so later would be swarming with people, animals and vehicles, were relatively deserted.

We arrived at Carl's at the first light. We waited outside but could see him fastening his boots on the verandah. I introduced him and Tom.

'I've heard a lot about you, Carl,' said Tom.

'I've heard a lot about you,' replied Carl.

'Well, let's hope now that we've joined forces, together we will find something.'

I smiled at Tom's optimism. It was a nice sentiment, but their chances were not good. A few minutes later we collected Ang Phury and headed out to meet the colonel at Tokha base where the weather would be more suitable for take-off.

As usual, before take-off, over-sweet Nepali tea was served in clear, plastic cups. Tom organised someone to take a photo of us all in front of the chopper. I stood next to Carl and joked that it would probably upset Dad to see me even this close to a helicopter!

I stepped back and the blades started spinning. The familiar red light flashed on the chopper and the engine rose to a deafening wail. The wash from the rotor buffeted the grass and my hair. The bird rose straight into the air, hovered for a moment just off the ground, then took off over the mountain, its steady beat fading quickly into the distance. I watched until it was no longer visible and headed back to the car.

The journey back to the airport wasn't too bad. I was fortunate not to meet anyone coming the other way until I was well and truly off the mountainside. I followed the basic principles anyone who drives in Kathmandu must: don't trust anyone, don't follow any rules and honk your horn frequently. It seemed to work. At least the drive had kept my mind occupied. Nonetheless, as I walked towards the helicopter headquarters, I felt the familiar fluttering of butterflies in my stomach and rise in pulse rate. I ignored the sign saying only authorised people could pass this point, and climbed the stairs to the radio room.

'Any contact with Colonel Pun?' I asked.

'No. Nothing,' the operator replied.

I sat down briefly beside the radio, then got up and went onto the verandah outside. Two monkeys played in the tree opposite. A few soldiers were walking in the compound. The usual sound of people expectorating regularly broke the distant hum of planes on the tarmac. The early morning Royal Nepal flight took off and several people wandered into the radio room.

'Army base, this is army two-nine. Come in.'

I raced inside, my heart hammering against my ribs. Despite my many mornings at the base, I still felt trepidation every time a message came through. The radio operator answered calmly, 'Army two-nine, this is base. Come in.' Colonel Pun answered in Nepali. The radio operator handed me the microphone.

'Colonel Pun, this is Joanne. Go ahead.' My mind was in turmoil, as it always was at the first transmission.

'Joanne. This is Colonel Pun. We have spotted a person above Talu. Alive. I repeat, we have spotted a person above Talu. He is alive. We think it could be James. Over.'

I was speechless. Had my mind just played a trick on me? Had I been wanting to hear something like this for so long that I had imagined what the colonel said? No! That was what he had said – alive. How could he be alive? It was forty-two days today. No food . . . I felt tears forming in my eyes and rolling down my cheeks.

'This is marvellous. How could it be? Where is he? What are we going to do? Can you get him out now?' I realised I was babbling non-sensically into the microphone. Through my tears, I could see the radio operator watching me curiously. 'They think they've found my brother,' I explained to him. He still didn't understand.

'Joanne, this is Colonel Pun.' The steady monotone of his voice against the whistle of background static caught my attention. 'I repeat, we have spotted someone above Talu. We think it could be your brother. We are on our way back to Kathmandu now to work out a strategy. We will land in ten minutes. Over and out.'

I ran out of the radio room, along the verandah and down the stairs onto the tarmac to wait. My thoughts were racing. If this was James, it was a miracle. But maybe I was getting ahead of myself. We didn't know it was James. It could well be someone else. I worked on calming myself down. I felt sick with anxiety mixed with a sense of elation.

Carl and Colonel Pun were the only occupants in the helicopter. Carl jumped out as the blades slowed. 'What's happened?' I demanded.

Carl explained in his usual precise manner. 'We have spotted someone above Talu,' he said shaking his head with disbelief. 'He is in the most incredible place, halfway up the side of a cliff, in a cave. He cannot go up and he cannot go down. He came out from his cave and waved a blue sleeping bag at the helicopter. He started out by standing up, but collapsed by the end.'

On the first flight, Carl said it had just been him, the colonel and Captain Koirala. They had left the video people behind so the chopper would be lighter and allow more time for searching. They had spotted a man and circled several times trying to get a clear view. They had returned to Talu to pick up Tom hoping the magnification of a video camera might show more. Even after the second flight they were still not sure it was James but this person obviously needed help. They dropped a packet of noodles out of the helicopter before leaving.

'I think,' said Carl, 'that I will have to rappel out of the helicopter to get him. Then we can winch him into the chopper.'

I looked at them both. 'Have either of you tried anything like this before?'

'It will not be a problem,' replied Colonel Pun, evading the question.

'Carl, have you rappelled out of a helicopter before?' I insisted.

'It's just like doing it off a cliff. It will be fine.'

'How long would it take people on foot to reach Ja . . . this person?'

'About six to eight hours,' Carl reckoned.

'It doesn't matter,' I said, 'whether this person is James or not. We must get to him today. I will never forgive myself if it is James and he does not make it through another night. We must get there today.'

Carl nodded and we set off to collect the necessary equipment. I was still in a daze.

'This can't be James, can it?' I said to Carl.

He shrugged. 'I think it could be him,' he said.

'It would be a miracle. It's six weeks today! How could he have survived? What makes you think it's James?'

'Well,' Carl explained, 'he's European . . .'

'How do you know that?' I interrupted.

'I just know he's a European. He has a blue sleeping bag and a red hat.'

My heart sank. I couldn't for the life of me remember what colour sleeping bag James had . . . Blue was pretty common. And a red hat . . .

'James didn't have a red hat,' I said.

'Well, it was something red left in the cave. We could just see it.'

'A rucksack?' I eagerly suggested.

'Yes, it could be.'

'What about his hair? What colour was his hair?'

'His hair was dark. About your colour.'

Again my hopes fell. 'James has bright red hair,' I commented.

'It could be dirty,' Carl observed reasonably.

I felt sure in my heart it was James but common sense kept telling me not to get my hopes up.

It seemed to take hours to get to Carl's house and put the abseiling equipment and a medical kit together. Then we had to detour past Ang Phury's house to get his trekking gear. He had not thought it would be necessary to leave the chopper and had gone up in casual day clothes.

We arrived back at the helicopter unit around midday. Colonel Pun was in his office, ready to go. As they were about to take off, I found myself close to tears again. I wanted to go back up with them. I even wanted to abseil out of the chopper with them but I knew I would only be a hindrance.

I took Carl aside and said, 'Please get to him today. Be careful, but do all you can. If it is James, please tell him two things. Tell him that Gaye says she loves him very much and tell him to hang on for us.' Carl hugged me goodbye.

JAMES: *2 February 1992 a.m.*

Dawn found me very weary. I felt incredibly weak and extremely ill. I thought of some of the terminal cancer patients I'd seen in the wards. Like them, I had a terminal disease, starvation. How often I'd seen those patients clinging desperately to the last threads of life. That was what I was to do that morning.

I unzipped the sleeping bag and crawled shakily to the right-hand side of the ledge. It was too much effort to get up and walk now. I sat by the edge of the snow, collected a handful and put it in my mouth. The taste of that first mouthful, the only snow I had eaten in almost two days, was like heaven. It melted quickly in my mouth, alleviating the pain of the cracks and ulcers. I continued letting each mouthful melt slowly while I filled my sleeping bag cover with snowballs.

It was barely dawn. Only the caps of the opposite mountains had caught the sun's rays and I could not help but admire their beauty once again. How often I'd seen that sight. Such a beautiful range of mountains. I knew that I had little time left to admire them.

I crawled back to bed. I had to rehydrate myself, but was careful not to consume snow too quickly. It was still hard for me to justify this attempt to revive myself. I knew I had done considerable damage to my body over the past couple of days. Just looking at the colour of my urine yesterday evening made me question my kidney function. I doubted I would last more than two days, even with fluid.

Yet, the dream the night before had been an important lesson to me. That one in a million chance, although remote, was still there. That dream had made me realise how important it was to cling to hope. The sheer pleasure of the water from each mouthful of melting snow trickling down my throat was incentive.

I wasn't in the mood for reading that morning. I wanted to spend whatever time I had left thinking of those back home and the happiest moments of my life. I lay there and relived those moments, cutting off my hostile surroundings.

My thoughts were disrupted some time later. The light had crept well down the opposite mountains. I heard, far in the distance, the howling, hurricane-like noise that I knew would be a helicopter. I can't believe it, I thought. Another chance. My initial response was pessimistic.

'It will probably shoot straight up the valley to Phedi, hover around and fly off again.' I doubted if I would even have the strength now to get out into the centre of the clear area. Driven by the memory of my dream, I knew I had to try.

I unzipped my sleeping bag and, mustering what strength I had, groped around for shoes. I tied the laces into simple knots: my fingers couldn't handle a bow. I pulled on my gloves. My hands seemed no bigger than a child's and swam in them. I pulled the velcro strap to its tightest position, hoping they would not slide off.

I staggered to my feet, swaying unsteadily and leant against the roof of my rock until my balance returned. The world in front of me went white. Ten to fifteen seconds later, my vision returned and everything slipped into focus – in double. Whatever I looked at I saw two. One above the other.

I closed my mind to everything but the roaring of that helicopter. I stumbled into the snow, dragging my sleeping bag behind me. The increasing noise urged me to move more quickly. I found myself continuously falling over.

It seemed to take only seconds to cover the twenty metres to the clearing. I tore at the knot in the drawstring of my trousers and they fell loosely to the snow at my knees. I hoped my maroon longjohns would stand out. As I watched the helicopter come up the other side of the valley, I started waving my sleeping bag frantically.

Why couldn't it be on my side of the valley? I thought. But I was determined not to give up. It continued slightly past before banking and turning directly towards me. It flew in a wide arc as it raced for me, changing direction again a couple of hundred metres before reaching me and then circling almost immediately back to the other side of the valley.

The helicopter now did giant circles within the valley, all at approximately my altitude. With each circle, the chopper flew slightly nearer. The noise was deafening as it screamed past quickly, before arcing widely and heading back to the opposite wall. I felt my strength ebbing, my legs buckling under me. Suddenly, I lost my footing and fell down on my backside. I struggled to stand, but could not get up. My shoulders and arms ached as I swung the sleeping bag through the air. I knew, without my maroon longjohns and the blue sleeping bag, I would look just like a stump in the shadows.

The way the helicopter was circling was exactly as I had fantasised for all those weeks. Until it soared in a circular manner, systematically searching the walls of the valley there would be little chance of them spotting me. Now, after all this time, they were doing it right. As I had dreamt they would.

I was shivering, one bony arm propping my body up in a sitting position while the other continued waving. I conserved my energy, only waving when they were very close and resting when they flew away. I wondered how much longer they would continue to fly in this way, for the cold was making me impatient for some type of signal. I thought there was a good chance they might have seen me, but I could not be sure. I noticed from the red emblem on the tail of the chopper that it belonged to the army. Even if they had seen me, maybe they thought I was a villager and wouldn't bother to act on my sighting. Maybe they were just curious, wondering what in hell anyone would be doing standing in the snow on the side of the mountain.

And then, during one of those great arcs where they flew so incredibly close to where I stood that I felt I could almost shout out to them, they broke their circular routine and screamed off down the valley.

I sat there in the snow, alone once again, feeling exhausted and confused. I could not decide whether this latest helicopter was reason for rejoicing or resentment. Will they bother to do anything? I wondered. As the confusion subsided, I became aware of my vigorous shivering. I felt the cold, just as I had on that first night under the smaller ledge. I must have been sitting out in this wet, slushy snow for fifteen or twenty minutes. Whatever the result of that flight, it was now completely out of my hands. All I could do was fight to stay alive as long as possible. Pulling my trousers up, I began to crawl back on my hands and knees, dragging my sleeping bag behind me. I would have been a pathetic sight as I crossed that clear patch of snow, still dazed by the events that had taken place. Unlike the few seconds it had taken me to reach the clearing, the return journey was desperately slow and I felt myself quickly succumbing to the cold.

About halfway back, I heard them returning. A tinge of anger mixed with my confusion. I was still some distance from my rock, but fir trees would now partially obscure me. I considered trying to signal the helicopter from where I was. But, I knew that I would not be doing justice either to myself or those back home. I had fought this long in the hope of seeing them again. I wasn't going to give up now.

Bracing myself against the wet coldness, I crawled back out to where I had sat before, hauling my sleeping bag behind me. It felt as if I was dragging a large sack of potatoes. The helicopter flew close to where I sat and I feebly attempted to signal it with the sleeping bag. I no longer had the strength to do this. Dropping the sleeping bag, I concentrated on pulling my trousers down to my ankles. I still wasn't certain they had spotted me. I knew their return was a promising sign, but did not dare allow my hopes to be raised.

Having dragged my trousers down, I tried sitting up but was unable to do so. I no longer resisted the pull of gravity and lay flat in the snow. Fortunately, the hillside was so steep, it would almost appear as if I was standing anyway. The helicopter now hovered about 150 metres away. I tried to focus, bringing the two images together as one. I waved my right arm back and forth, looking desperately for some signal they understood my predicament. I was almost certain they had spotted me, but I wanted to know, I repeated to myself over and over, Please have spotted me, please have spotted me. After what seemed an eternity, someone waved.

Yes! They've spotted me! For the first time in almost six weeks, I had been given a true indication that there was still hope.

I beckoned them to come closer and lower their ropes or winches. I waved my arm downwards in front of me but the helicopter hovered as if the pilot could not decide what step to take next. I was getting colder by the second, the wind from the rotor blades rushing over and freezing the water in my clothes. I gritted my teeth, fighting hard against the harsh wind, trying to remain out in the snow to allow them to rescue me.

It came to a point where I knew I must turn back to my rock. Under these conditions I would be dead withing a matter of minutes. The helicopter pulled away and shot off down the valley. Clasping my sleeping bag, I crawled back to my rock, colder and wetter than I had been in days. The hour in the snow had been horrific. Now every motion of my arms and legs seemed to sap away at my last reserves. With each forward movement, I wondered if I could continue. Every couple of minutes, I stopped, gasping for air. I made it just to the edge of the rocky overhang and struggled to remove my outer clothing, drying myself down. Every movement was an effort. I looked longingly at my usual bed site, but could not be bothered struggling the extra, short distance. I felt completely drained, utterly defeated.

As a part of my karate training, I had watched people fight opponents who were far superior. Occasionally, I had seen people get slowly ground down, each blow draining them of their spirit, until their hands fell by their sides and they became completely defenceless. It would be with one mighty blow that they would be sent to the floor, their spirit crushed. That was how I felt as I zipped up my sleeping bag and feebly ate some snow. My spirit had been crushed and all the will to live had left me. Never had I felt so defeated.

The howling began once again. All I could do now was turn my head and look at the helicopter. It hovered and I was fully expecting a rope to come dangling out into the snow. Would I have the strength and courage to get back out one more time and harness myself up? I felt so weak now, so desperately exhausted, that I doubted I could.

I was never put to the test. The rope never came. Instead, a flash of white shot out of the helicopter and landed two or three hundred metres below where I lay. The notion of even attempting to collect it was completely ridiculous. As I continued to rehydrate myself, my mind in turmoil, I wondered what it could have been. I decided it had to be some type of radio transmitting device to mark my location. That was an excellent sign that something positive was being done. A step had been taken towards my rescue.

I could not understand why they hadn't sent down a rope or a winch. Maybe the Nepali army didn't have the equipment? I went through other options. A party might be sent up on foot and take three days to reach me. The other option was for a better-equipped helicopter to be flown in from another country. I doubted any of the surrounding countries would have helicopters much better equipped than those of Nepal. The search party coming by foot was the most likely option. I would need to stay alive for three to four more days. There was no guarantee I would be able to do this but, as I continued to take in fluid, my optimism grew. My initial goal had been seventy days and now all that was required was three. It was the first time in the last forty days that I had any real chance of survival and I was not about to let it slip away.

JOANNE: *2 February 1992 p.m.*

I looked out from the verandah near the radio room, glumly survey-ing the wooden huts and rough roads of the helicopter base and des-perately wished we were back in Australia. How different the situation would be there! We would have an emergency medical team on stand-by, ambulances, paramedics, good hospitals . . . Instead, I was going to have to make do with a four-wheel drive and a Third World hospital. Still, there was no point crossing bridges before we came to them, I told myself. Just wait and see if it is James for a start and take it from there. There was a familiar burst of static as the radio leapt to life.

'Army base, this is Army two-nine. Come in.' The weather had closed in at Talu for now. They had all the gear ready and would take off as soon as it cleared. Hopefully, the clouds would blow over, but it was also possible that the weather would not improve enough for the helicopter to go up again today.

By two o'clock, I was becoming more and more frantic. What if the weather didn't clear? According to Carl, it would take six hours to get there on foot.

'Joanne. This is Colonel Pun. The weather is still not good enough for us to attempt the rescue by air. Carl has just left with a ground party. They will be in the area late this afternoon. They have a walkie-talkie with them. You should go and come back around 5.30 p.m. I will not be transmitting again until then. Over.'

Shit, shit, shit! I thought to myself. 'I understand, Colonel. Over and out.'

Maria came out to get me. Although the embassy vehicle was still there, the ambassador had rung to tell the soldiers I was not to drive it.

189

I had resumed my restless pacing up and down her kitchen. There was no way that I could relax. Apart from being worried about James (if it was him), I was terrified that Dad would call. There was no way any-one in Australia should hear about this. I tried to read, but could not turn my thoughts to anything.

The temperature was dropping and daylight was already fading when we left at 4.15. We picked up Debbie Harrison and returned to the airport radio room to wait. The soldier who had been manning the radio all day was still dutifully huddled beside it.

We sat in the adjacent room. Debbie and Maria chatted whilst I sat in silence. The radio brought me to my feet. It was now nearly 6 p.m. and very dark outside.

'Please let them have reached him tonight,' I prayed.

'Joanne. This is Colonel Pun. The search party are in the vicinity but have not reached the person as yet. It is also too late for us to return to Kathmandu tonight, so we will have to remain here at Talu. I am going to shut the helicopter down until morning. I will begin transmitting at 6.45 a.m. Please advise the radio operator to be here at that time.'

'Roger, Colonel Pun,' I replied. It was bitterly disappointing news. I would now have to wait until at least the next day. A long night stretched ahead.

JAMES: *2 February 1992 p.m.*

I felt stiff and sore when I awoke. Had I only dreamt the helicopter? I pulled the sleeping bag from over my head and found I had rolled into the snow and could feel the dampness was soaking through. It was dif-ficult to know the time in the heavy cloud surrounding me.

I staggered back to my normal bed and spread the sleeping bag out. I knew it would not dry today so, as I climbed back in, I put a T-shirt between me and the wet patch. My sleeping bag cover was full of snowballs from which I began to suck water, still desperately thirsty. I noticed the elasticity of my skin had not returned. I picked up one of the three parts of the dilapidated Charles Dickens novel and began reading absent-mindedly. I knew the story so well that I could take it up from any page.

As I had always done when my routine was so disciplined, I moderated my snow intake, one mouthful of snow per two pages of Dickens. I could predict what would be said in the next paragraph as I read and it required little concentration for me to follow the story.

The comparative silence of the afternoon was interrupted by the howling. I did not even bother to sit up. The noise of the blades was distant. The cloud was so thick, the helicopter would be in danger of running into the side of the mountain if it came too close. But it was comforting to know that a rescue operation was under way or, at the very least, my presence on the mountain had attracted enough attention for them to come back and see what was happening. A hideous thought crossed my mind. What if that helicopter was like those two birds? Maybe it would just return each day to see if I were still alive. I quashed this stupid idea as quickly as I could. Thinking like that wouldn't get me anywhere. I had to stay alive three days, an easy task compared with the seventy I'd initially set myself.

I was rehydrating myself slowly. It was hard to estimate just how much damage I'd done. Would my intestines be able to absorb enough water to get my body fluids back to normal? I imagined all those little villi, with the cells lining row after row, working overtime, not letting a drop of water escape.

It was a hazy afternoon. My mind kept flitting from subject to subject, unable to concentrate on any one thing for long. I was calm and tired. I was going to do all I could to survive for as long as I could. Everything else was out of my hands. The day drifted on endlessly.

Using my abdominal muscles and my arms, I tried to pull myself up. I wanted to urinate. I got to an angle of about thirty degrees and fell back exhausted. I tried again, this time only managing to bend my neck and lift my head. I considered trying to roll over and drag myself on my stomach to the urinal but wondered what I would do once I got there.

I lay contemplating this problem for a while, quite anxious about it. It wasn't that I had a desperate need to urinate then and there but I didn't feel I could hold on for three days. The other problem was that my supply of ice was low. I had enough to see me through the night but somehow I'd need to find the strength to get up next day to gather more.

As for relieving myself, I had little option but to do it where I lay. I decided to use the only container I had – a shampoo bottle. I only produced a small quantity of urine, once again reinforcing how dehydrated I was, but I felt the fact that I could produce any at all was remarkable. I emptied the bottle as far away as I could, making sure it would not trickle back towards my bed. I pulled the sleeping bag over my head and said the usual prayers that accompanied nightfall.

As I said these prayers, a soft voice answered in the distance. At first it was a muffled shouting which I strained to hear. I was not sure if I was hearing voices, hallucinating or if they were real people. Concentrating, I waited until I was certain what I was hearing was real.

'Namaste,' the voice called out, still far away. Then a shrill whistle. I waited to hear it again before I responded. This was all too much. I had thought, in the past, that the only people who were likely to wander up here would be poachers hunting the rare snow leopard. Reluctant to get my hopes too high, I couldn't help but think that whoever was shouting must be part of a rescue party. I took my head out from the cover of my sleeping bag and screamed, 'Namaste! Namaste!'

My voice cracked. It felt so strange to be using it after such a long time and, now, I was not just talking but screaming at the top of my lungs.

The voices responded, I grabbed my Nepali guidebook and looked up the translation for the phrases, 'I am sick' and 'I can't walk'. I shouted these out in Nepali. The only response was 'Namaste!'

'Please come here,' I shouted out in Nepali, for I feared that whoever was up on the mountain with me had settled somewhere way below and was expecting me to walk down to them. I started to whistle, using my fingers. It was loud and echoed throughout the valley and was much less tiring.

All the time, the voices grew louder. I could now distinguish two separate voices slowly but surely making their way towards me.

It had become too cold for me to leave my head out. I continued to whistle, occasionally shouting out. I was bewildered that they had come up so quickly but I was desperate they reach me as soon as possible. Finally, I could actually hear their voices clearly. Amidst their shouts, they were chattering excitedly in Nepali. I could hear them breaking bushes and trudging through the snow. I peered out from my sleeping bag to see who my rescuers were. They were somewhere below me. I was no longer frantic, just excited, and I called out, 'I am up here! Under the rock.' Their voices came back, closer now.

In what seemed like no time at all, I saw two Nepali heads pop over the ledge. One of them was wearing the straw hat I had lost two days ago.

They were barely able to suppress their excitement and greeted me in the usual Nepali fashion, hands clasped in a prayer position in front of their chin and heads bowed. 'Namaste,' I returned their gesture weakly, somewhat bewildered by the events of the day. These were the first people I had seen in six weeks. I could not believe they were standing here in front of me.

With great agility, they leapt up onto the ledge and one of them asked, much to my amazement, if I was James Scott from Australia. It was inconceivable that anyone could have been searching so long. Maybe the helicopter had gone back to Kathmandu and had looked at people reported missing in the district and they had got my name that way.

'Yes, I am,' I responded, still baffled.

At that, tears came streaming out of their eyes. They raced up and started hugging and kissing me, paying no attention to my filthy condition. They just seemed so overjoyed, so overwhelmed to have found me. I choked back tears and fired questions. They replied in an unintelligible mixture of Nepali and English. There was something about my little sister in Kathmandu and another Australian on the mountain who had been searching for me. They sat marvelling at me, stroking my hair and face.

'James Scott, you are a god,' one of them finally said.

They managed to convey that no one had ever survived more than ten days in the mountains. They told me, in Nepali, the number of days that I had been there. I couldn't translate but said, 'No, God kept me alive for all that time.'

They squatted nearby staring at me and touching me frequently as if to check I was real. It was only then I became aware their clothing was old and flimsy. One of the men was actually in bare feet. The bravery of these two men was astounding. They had risked their lives to continue on in the darkness, through hostile country, simply because they knew someone was in desperate and urgent need of help. Inadequately protected from the cold and with no source of light in the dark, they had ploughed up the mountain in deep snow, putting their own lives at stake so that I might be spared another night alone.

After a very excited and emotional time for all three of us, one of the men volunteered to get the rest of the search party. I talked more quietly and calmly with the man who stayed. Even though our conversation was very basic, it was so wonderful to hear another person's voice again, I didn't care that I couldn't understand most of what was being said.

The rest of the search party strode up the hill through the night and joined us under my rock. A quietly spoken, confident man introduced himself as Carl Harrison. He asked again whether I was James Scott from Australia and said he'd been searching for me for a very long time. All I could think of was the suffering and grief that my family back home must have felt over the past six weeks and I was only able to control myself for long enough to say, 'I'm very glad to see you', before I wept like I hadn't done since I was a very young child. The emotional shutdown that I had experienced all that time on the mountain was completely swept away. The floods of tears that I wept in those first moments acted as a release for all the negative emotions I had kept suppressed for so long. I knew I was going to be rescued and I would see all those back home once again.

I struggled to regain control of my emotions. There was no longer reason to maintain the defensive barrier I had held up for such a long time. I now had company, a fire was being made and I was given a ski jacket which I was told came from my sister in Kathmandu.

Everyone was very silent until I stopped crying. One of the first things I asked for was water. Carl warned me to sip it very slowly. It was wonderful to be able to enjoy the taste of pure water from a container and not to have my lips scorched by burning ice. With the water came comfort and I immediately felt better. I was now warm, not so thirsty and enjoying the glow of the fire and human company.

Carl spoke in a quiet, reassuring voice and described the events of that day. He told me how everyone had thought I had died long ago. I was stunned by this and said, 'Surely others have survived this length of time?'

He replied, 'No, I think you've set some kind of record up here.'

'How could you have kept looking for so long?' I asked. He went on to relate, in fairly simple terms, all the work that Joanne and her friend, Andrew, had done.

'She's quite a detective, you know,' he commented as he described how they had managaed to pinpoint my location to this valley. I felt numb with disbelief at the persistence she had shown in searching for me. I asked who Andrew was. Carl did not know Andrew's last name but the only Andrew I could think of was Andrew Ross. It seemed unbelievable someone would give so much of themselves to help in the search for me. I asked about all those back home, especially my parents and Gaye.

'They're fine,' he said. 'They'll be overjoyed to hear the good news.' This did not help the guilt I felt for having put everyone through so much and the thought made me break down once more.

Through the sobs I said, 'How will I ever be able to repay my family?'

Carl was interested in just how I had managed to find myself in this spot. He'd set off at about two that afternoon and the first men had found me about five hours later. I felt acutely embarrassed that they had got to me so easily and I hadn't managed those extra few hours walking to reach safety. As I told my story, I felt humiliated. I told him of the cliff and deep snow, the nights under the rocks, but I couldn't bring myself to be entirely honest. I didn't think he would understand why I had stopped walking after just two and a half days. I was purposely vague about the time I had walked and exaggerated my disorientation. Those few moments were going to be the first of many in the months to come when I found myself in the frustrating position of feeling very vulnerable and humiliated. At the start of the trek, I had very little fear of anything. I had felt I could hold my own with others around me. That night, wasted away to a miserable bag of bones, I realised just how humbled I'd been by the experience. I was no longer a match for anyone, not even a child. Stricken with grief, illness and starvation, I was completely defenceless.

I wept as I recounted those early days. Carl's only comment was that, when trouble hits, you've got to stick together. He tried to console me by saying I had made the right decision to head back to Phedi instead of continuing on in the blizzard and that Mark had been extremely lucky to get across the pass. It was little help. Just another half a day's walk and I would have been at Talu. I had momentarily forgotten the deep, powdery snow that had trapped me. I'd also forgotten the weakness I felt after two and a half days without food and the thick vegetation that was too difficult to negotiate. Carl and the rest of the search party had seemed to make it up so effortlessly to where I was. At that point, all I felt was shame and guilt.

They had some biscuits, chocolate and bread which I was sparingly fed. I was well aware of the dangers of refeeding. Tasting the first real food in six weeks was incredible, even though they were just plain, dry biscuits. With each small bite I was sure that life was slowly but surely returning. I was also fed some chocolate. The energy would help keep me warm that night. It is hard to describe how much I appreciated all that I had been given within those few hours. I felt like a king.

The Nepali rescuers were still talking excitedly amongst themselves. Carl said they still had trouble believing I was alive. Every so often, one of them would come over to touch me and run excitedly back to the others. They would chatter and stare at me in amazement as they sat around the camp-fire. I could still scarcely believe it was true.

I said, 'We must get a photo of this.' I wanted something that would be a memento of one of the most amazing moments of my life. I told Carl my camera was in my rucksack and he and Ang Phury took several photos. I asked Carl if he knew any good restaurants in Kathmandu. Carl told me he actually owned a restaurant in

Thamel and explained its location. I hadn't eaten there though I remembered it. I said that I would have to try it when I came back to Nepal.

He seemed surprised that I was already talking about coming back, but my love for the country had, if anything, grown rather than waned in the six weeks. I assured him that I would return to do more trekking. Perhaps next time, I would use his trekking agency! I told him how grateful I was and hoped his business would derive a lot of good publicity for all his hard work. I was so genuinely thankful to this man who had done so much. I felt I owed him my life.

He explained the plans for the next day. A helicopter was to fly up if it was a cloudless day with little breeze. The helicopter would hover fifty metres off the ground so a rope could be lowered and fastened to the harness I would be wearing. Carl had taken the extra precaution of getting a harness that provided support for me between my legs as well as under my shoulders. Army harnesses rely on the individual being able to hold their elbows by their sides but he felt that I would need the extra support. I appreciated his foresight. Carl added that, if the weather conditions were unfavourable, they'd have to carry me down. 'It's very difficult for a helicopter to hover at this altitude,' he told me.

Not having seen a stretcher, I asked what they would carry me on. Carl simply replied, 'Their backs.'

'Will we make it?' I asked.

'It'll be difficult,' he conceded. I was left wondering which would be the lesser of the two evils: to dangle from a rope underneath a helicopter or to be carried down on the back of some poor, little Nepali man through snow that was more than knee-deep. Neither option was particularly appealing but I decided I'd just have to accept whatever fate brought. Carl was in charge now and I was confident he would get me out one way or another.

The night went on. Carl and Ang Phury had fallen alseep and, after several hours, even the Nepalis were quiet. I lay awake, watching the stars fill the sky as the cloud cleared from the valley. It was a familiar pattern. I knew the morning would be fine.

JAMES: *3 February 1992*

I managed to doze for a couple of hours very late in the night and was woken early as the others stirred. Carl was trying to use his small radio again without success but he appeared pleased with the clear weather. I asked him about the helicopter ride. My terror of heights would have to be ignored as I was told there was no means of being winched straight up into the helicopter. I would have to dangle below.

'You'll have a five-minute ride back to Talu,' I was told.

'I've got to urinate, Carl.' He did not reply. I said it again, this time emphasising I could no longer get up. Carl was obviously not keen to be part of my nursing care and said something to the villagers. Two of them leapt to their feet and, between the three of us, I rose slowly and took a few unsteady paces to my latrine. My friend with the straw hat stood by my side, my arm around his shoulder and his around my waist, enabling me to stand while I relieved myself. I was impressed by the gentle care this man took of me. He laid me slowly back down on my bed as if he were handling an infant.

Then the howling returned. All the men jumped up and ran into the clearing, leaving me by myself. I lay there, apprehensive. Some of the men came back and Carl said they had signalled the helicopter which would return shortly with the rope. 'The other guys out there are clearing an area in the snow where we can harness you.'

'What will be, will be,' I decided.

As the howling reached fever pitch Carl shouted some instructions in Nepali to one of the villagers who picked me up easily and carried me on his back. The men held me up and Carl fastened the harness. I had a hood covering most of my face with just a little peephole through which one eye could gaze. I watched Carl deftly tie the dangling rope to the harness in what appeared to be a very simple knot.

'Are you sure that knot's okay?' I asked Carl. There was no response. 'The knot's okay, isn't it?' I repeated loudly, concerned by its simplicity.

But Carl was stepping away and I could feel my weight being taken up by the harness, away from the supporting arms of the villagers. There was a moment where it seemed the helicopter struggled to lift me before I rose rapidly, dangling below in the freezing winds with the noise of the chopper shrieking in my ears.

As I swung in a pendulum motion, the harness cut into my groin and armpits. I peered through my little hole at my rock which was quickly growing smaller. At last I was escaping the prison. I looked up to see the most spectacular view I have ever seen. The peaks of the Himalayas in the distance were catching the first golden rays of the rising sun. When I looked down again, the dense forest had been replaced by cleared farmland and we were nearing a small village. Many Nepali were standing around the huts watching. The helicopter descended until I was within reach of the villagers. Five or six men grabbed hold of me, one of them struggling to undo the harness. I lay back, bewildered by the crowd trying to help and shouting excitedly.

Eventually I was free of the harness and being carried by the men towards another helicopter. The villagers were rushing in now and touching me, talking in Nepali. One man seemed to be in command and he spoke fluently in English, trying to make me feel more at ease. 'Welcome back to the land of the living. Just relax, they're touching you for good luck. Everything will be all right now, mate.'

I was put in the back seat of the second helicopter. There was still a crowd anxious to observe the event. The man who'd spoken introduced himself as Tom. I could see the tears in his eyes as he repeated Carl Harrison's sentiments about the work that had gone into looking for me.

The pilot climbed in and Tom introduced him as Colonel Pun. The colonel was grinning from ear to ear as I shook his hand feebly and thanked him. I asked if we should wait for Carl but Tom said he thought it was important they get me to Kathmandu as soon as possible.

As the helicopter took off, Tom asked if I would like some food. I replied I would really like some tea and he produced a thermos of warm, sweet, Nepali tea. I sipped it slowly, watching the ground speed below me. The noise made it hard to talk. I had two more cups of tea before asking about food. A white box of sandwiches was produced. I watched the big bank of clouds covering the Kathmandu valley grow larger and carefully picked away, selecting only bits of the sandwiches I felt were safe to eat. I chose a little bit of tomato, some bread and I really couldn't say no to a small piece of chicken.

We broke through the dense cloud and I could see the low buildings of Kathmandu. I looked for familiar landmarks without success. It seemed like another lifetime when I had last seen Kathmandu.

When we reached the airport there was another crowd of people. I searched their faces for Joanne. 'Where's Joanne?' I asked Tom. He pointed to a figure that blended in blurrily with all the others present.

'Wave to her,' said Tom. As I did, tears started to flow again. I could see a woman waving back wildly with both arms.

The helicopter touched down lightly and I could see Joanne being held back by a couple of people until the rotor blades slowed. Tom jumped out of the front seat to help me out. The people beside Joanne released her and I staggered forwards. I threw my arms around her neck and we both wept.

JOANNE: *3 February 1992*

The night of Sunday 2 February was one of the longest of my life. Having heard nothing from the search party on foot meant I didn't really know what to think or hope for. There was a good chance that this stranded person could be James, but the logistics were dumb-founding. How could someone withstand sub-zero temperatures with no food, no fire and scant clothing for the forty-two days since James was last seen?

I really felt like talking to Calum. I wanted to share my anguish with him. Maria was marvellous. She persuaded me to try to sleep and tried to keep my mind off the possibilities but it was no use. I tossed and turned all night.

My greatest fear was that whoever it was would not last one more night. How could I ever live with myself if the search party reached the cave to find a body? How could I ever tell my parents that James had been alive the day before but had died with a search party on the way? Maria tried to reassure me, pointing out that if he'd had the strength to signal the helicopter he would hang on for us, especially given the boost in morale that he must have felt. I accepted this but the 'what ifs' kept circling through my brain. I did a fair bit of praying that night, willing James not to give up.

I was ready to go by 5 a.m. It was still dark and very, very cold. The radio operator was just turning on the receiver and still rubbing the sleep out of his eyes when we arrived. There had been no further trans-mission. Word had spread that something was going on. There seemed to be lots of people around. There was nothing for Maria and me to do but wait and speculate. Two hours later, there was still no news. Colonel Pun's second-in-command appeared. I pounced and grilled him on all the possible reasons Colonel Pun hadn't contacted us. Obviously the poor man had no more idea about any of this than I.

As it got lighter, it became apparent that there was a lot of cloud overhead.

'Great!' I moaned to Maria. 'It's probably snowing buckets in the mountains. No one will get near this person for weeks.'

The major declared that he would take a training flight up to Talu to see how things were going. I watched the little Alouette take off. It headed in a different direction where there was a tiny gap in the clouds. I watched until it was a speck in the distance and sent silent prayers up with it.

Within ten minutes the major called in. He was out of the

Kathmandu valley and the weather was marvellous. The skies were completely clear.

And so we waited. I fidgeted and fretted, unable to stand still yet scared to move away in case word came through. The major transmitted again. The other helicopter had taken off from Talu and was also in the air. I could feel my pulse hammering. My palms were damp with sweat. I knew that, after all this time, I would hear something definitive in the next few seconds.

'Ground control this is army two-nine. Ground control this is army two-nine. Come in ground control.' My heart leapt to my throat. It was Colonel Pun's helicopter.

'Army two-nine, this is ground control. Go ahead,' responded the radio operator.

'Ground control, is Joanne there?' The radio operator moved so I had access to the microphone. I could feel my legs shaking and tears welling in my eyes.

'This is Joanne speaking, over.'

'Joanne, this is Colonel Pun. We have found your brother and he is alive. I repeat, we have found your brother and he is alive. Over.'

It took a second for the words to sink in and then I started to sob. Those were the only words I had wanted to hear for the past five weeks. I felt a combination of euphoria and relief. I was so happy. I was unable to continue talking. Maria and I hugged each other. The radio operator looked confused. I guess from my reaction, he could not make out whether the news was good or not. Quickly, I tried to regain composure.

'Colonel Pun, is James okay?'

'Joanne, I repeat we have found your brother and he is alive.' I could not make the Colonel understand my question. He continued, 'We are going to winch him from the cliff back to Talu and bring him back to Kathmandu. Over.'

'I understand, Colonel. Over and out.'

At that point, reality started to sink in. What sort of shape would he be in? Was he conscious? Would he recognise me? What injuries could he have? Would he need emergency evacuation to Bangkok? We set to practicalities. Maria quickly phoned Auli. We'd need the embassy vehicle immediately. She phoned Dorrilyn and Dr Pandey. They would be with us in twenty minutes. We also alerted Patan hospital.

'Ground control this is army two-nine. Come in.' I was put onto the receiver again.

'Colonel Pun, this is Joanne. Go ahead.'

'Joanne, we have got James in the helicopter and have just taken off from Talu. He seems perfectly all right. We will be landing in Kathmandu in twenty minutes. Over.'

How could someone who'd been lost like that for forty-three days be 'perfectly all right'? 'Colonel Pun, how is James? Is he conscious? What is his state of health? Over.'

But the colonel still failed to understand and repeated the same message. I gave up and said, 'Okay, Colonel, I understand. See you soon. Over and out.'

That twenty minutes seemed an eternity. All the people we were waiting for seemed to take forever to arrive. The four-wheel drive was first to come. Auli and Larry were there with Dorrilyn. Embraces were exchanged all around. These people had all been a part of the search since the beginning and, like me, they were overwhelmed.

'It's a miracle,' I said to Auli. 'I just can't believe it.' We had found blankets from somewhere and I was pacing around the edge of the tarmac clutching one, casting anxious glances into the sky, as if by watching for it I could make the helicopter appear sooner. Dr Pandey and Dorrilyn discussed medication and what procedure they would take. I heard the beat of the helicopter blades but the craft was still invisible because of the low-lying cloud and smog. I started to cry again. Dorrilyn put her arm around me.

'You've got to be strong,' she said.

'I know,' I whispered. 'But what sort of state will he be in?'

'You've found him and he's alive. That's what matters right now.'

The helicopter came into view. Still a long way off, but getting closer every second.

'Look!' said Dorrilyn. 'Someone's waving! Wave back!'

'It can't be James waving,' I said. 'How could he be waving?'

'Wave back,' she insisted. 'He'll want to see that.'

I began to wave but started crying as the helicopter lumbered to the ground. There were hundreds of people on the tarmac. It seemed they had come from everywhere. I waited impatiently for the blades to slow but Tom had already jumped out of the helicopter. He stood in front of it, arms outstretched as if to say, 'Look what we've brought you!'

Still crying, I approached the side door of the chopper. Tom slid it open and there was James. I knew instantly that it was James and that moment I really did believe that he'd been found. He looked old and wizened. His skin was stretched taut across his face and his forehead was furrowed deeply with lines. He had a bright red beard, possibly three centimetres long. His hair was greasy and he was filthy. He was impossibly thin, skeletal. He looked at me and I sobbed his name.

He started to cry too and got out of the helicopter to take a step towards me. We embraced and I told him I loved him. He said, 'I can't believe you're here. Thank you. Thank you so much.'

'Don't,' I said. I looked beyond James and saw Colonel Pun, Captain Koirala and Tom. Although they were all grinning from ear to ear, the shine of tears glistened in their eyes.

EPILOGUE

JOANNE:

It was not until 14 February, St Valentine's Day, that James and I arrived back in Brisbane. The eleven days after James stepped out of the helicopter at Kathmandu airport had been, in many ways, as trying as the weeks that preceded them. The fact that James had survived and our family was waiting for us were all that kept me going. I had never been so elated, exhausted, anxious, grateful or confused and angry.

Looking back, I can't really remember going from the tarmac to the back seat of the embassy's four-wheel drive. One minute I was virtually holding James up and the next he was stretched across the back seat of the vehicle, leaning on me. Larry was driving with Auli beside him and Dorrilyn was crouched in the rear of the car, leaning over the back seat, monitoring James's pulse and blood pressure. Dr Pandey had performed a quick examination and we were on our way to Patan hospital.

I had recovered from the initial shock of his appearance. It had nearly broken my heart to see my strong and athletic brother reduced to this bedraggled, wizened skeleton. His hair was matted and every crease in his skin filled with dirt and grit. His fingernails were black with grime and even inside his ears was caked. His lips were parched, cracked and ulcerated and the straggly red beard aged him greatly. His skin was taut across protruding facial bones and his green eyes seemed enormous. I could feel his ribs and shoulder bones through the padding of his jacket. I estimated he would have lost some thirty kilograms. He had a very distinctive smell, a musty mixture of sweat and smoke, of dirt and hay. It had deeply permeated all his clothes. We talked all the way to the hospital, both periodically breaking into tears. But he was quite lucid. I told James all the family were fine.

'Gaye said to tell you she loves you and she wants to marry you,' I said. I told him they did not know he had been found.

'How on earth did you hold on for all that time, James? How did you do it?'

'I didn't do anything, I just sat there,' he replied. 'I can't believe you found me. I can't believe you kept looking all that time.'

At the hospital there seemed to be people everywhere, all watching us with curiosity. Dr Garlick, the medical superintendent, was waiting. He had James taken straight to an examination room – very basic by Australian standards – with Dr Johnson, a younger man with an English accent.

'I'm afraid I'm very dehydrated,' James said. 'Do you think I could have something to drink?' Someone was sent to bring James some tea.

Dr Johnson wasted no time inserting a drip into James's arm. His temperature was so low, it didn't even register on the medical thermometer and his blood pressure dropped about 55 millimetres mercury with any change in posture.

I had to suppress a gasp when James's shoes and socks were removed. His feet were blue and felt like blocks of ice. They had a thick crust of dead skin. I watched Dr Johnson as he checked them out. To my relief, he didn't seem too appalled. The pulses were apparently good which meant they still had some blood supply.

James had slurped his way through three cups of tea by this stage and asked for a soft drink. He gulped one down in no time. Moments later he vomited the whole lot back up again.

I guess some twenty minutes had elapsed since we were first admitted to the hospital. The basic examination indicated that James was in reasonably good shape all things considered.

'Is he going to be all right?' I asked the doctors.

'I don't see why not,' Dr Garlick responded.

'In that case, I need a phone, please.'

I explained to James I was going to call Mum and Dad. He asked me to tell them he loved them very much. As Dr Garlick led me through the corridors to his office I still could not shake the feeling I was in a dream. I seemed incapable of taking in my surroundings. I had no idea of where we were in the building or where we were heading. I really could not believe that, after all this time, I was about to make this call.

My fingers were shaking as I dialled. I waited impatiently for the beeps signifying the international connection. Dad answered.

'Ken Scott speaking.'

'Dad, it's Joanne here.'

'Joanne! How are you?'

'Dad, I'm good. I'm really good. I've got the most wonderful news. We've found James. James is with us and he's alive.'

There was a moment of silence and then Dad repeated, 'You've found James and he's alive,' as if he could not quite believe what I had just told him. 'He's alive.' I thought I could hear his voice break. 'After all this time. He's alive!'

'Dad, it's a miracle.'

'Where was he?'

'To the south-west of Gopte, perched under a rocky overhang trapped on a mountainside.'

'That's wonderful. That's just wonderful.'

My mother shrieked, 'I can't believe it!' before lapsing into hysterical sobs of joy.

Within an hour or so, James had been set up in a room on the second floor. The basic nature of the rooms made me wish again we could leave Nepal immediately, although Dorrilyn said that it was far better than would be found at Bir hospital.

James's room had two beds. The other was occupied by a young man who coughed constantly. As is customary in Nepal, he always had several relatives sitting around him. The only way we could separate them from James was with a curtain. The relatives chatted loudly and came and went continuously. This made it very difficult to get any peace.

An electric blanket was placed on James's bed and a bar radiator nearby. Dr Zimmerman, James's physician, arrived. Of course, James had met him before. Mark Zimmerman had taken James and Tim on ward rounds nearly two months before. He must have been appalled at how James had deteriorated. He explained that he thought James had suffered an area of cerebral ischaemia, a stroke.

It is no fun to be caring for a critically ill patient in a Third World country. During the search I had felt a huge onus to find out what had happened. Now I had an even greater responsibility. Having found James alive and having given renewed hope to Gaye and my parents, I had to get him back to Australia alive. The time in Patan hospital was a nightmare.

For three or four days, James was extremely emotionally unstable. One minute he would be on top of the world, the next he would be down in the dumps, crying his heart out, even saying he wished he could be back under his rock. It cannot be easy to go from six weeks of solitude and believing you were most likely going to die into the hub of hospital activity. His vision had worsened to the point where he could no longer discern faces. Shortly after Dr Zimmerman had examined James, he had changed his diagnosis. James's visual problems might be a result of thiamine (vitamin B1) deficiency. If thiamine is not given promptly, irreversible brain damage can occur. As soon as Mark Zimmerman made the connection, James was given thiamine injections. The combination of impaired sight, emotional fragility and an organic brain dysfunction stemming from malnutrition generated quite a paranoia. James would react with trepidation when people entered the room, calling out, 'Who is it?' or 'What do you want now?' It was essential that someone he knew and trusted be with him at all times. Dorrilyn and Anne-Maree Young took it in turns to help me.

Fortunately, the other occupant of the room had volunteered to move out for he was not comfortable sharing a room with a Westerner. This meant we had the room entirely to ourselves, a great luxury. I slept on a wooden cot on the floor. Tom and Maria had brought in a mattress with blankets, towels and urns of water.

One day a nurse came in to try and take James's electric blanket away. I yelled at her, demanding to know what she was doing. She said another patient needed the blanket. With complete disregard for the other person, I refused to let her take the blanket away. As far as I was concerned, James still needed it and he was going to have it. It was not my problem if there were not enough electric blankets to go around.

Re-feeding had to be planned carefully. Introducing foods without thought to the chemistry involved could have brought on anything from heart failure to death. James's diet consisted of clear fluids for a couple of days, followed by soups and thicker broths. The next transition was breads and pastas with small amounts of egg and vegetables. I remember one day being sure that Dr Zimmerman had said to 'get James into the eggs'. By 11 a.m. James was forcing down his sixth boiled egg. Dr Zimmerman came in on ward rounds and James and I proudly related how successfully he was consuming the eggs. The physician's eyes widened.

'I said no more than three eggs throughout the day,' he told us. James paid severely with terrible stomach cramps later.

All the broths, soups and food were provided by Maria, Val Garlick, Anna Johnson and other concerned women. I don't know how I would have ever coped without their help and support. James reminded me of a young bird or animal on demand feeding. Every two to three hours, day and night, he would want food or fluids. This made for very interrupted nights. His feet were also distressing him. The pain started during his first night in hospital. He was almost crying in distress, thumping the pillow in frustration. Pethidine injections and rubbing his feet seemed to help. I had barely slept since the night of 2 February, leaving the hospital only briefly once a day to have a hot shower, change clothes, drop off laundry and pick up more food and water for James (we had decided it would be safer not to depend on hospital food and water). A couple of days after James was rescued I was massaging his feet and fell sound asleep sitting on the stool at the end of his bed. It was continually suggested I should go back to Blue Mountain to sleep but I refused. I was too scared that something would happen to James while I was away.

We may well have exasperated the nurses with our exacting questioning but we had good cause. Dorrilyn had caught one nurse about to take James's temperature orally after the same thermometer had been used to take a rectal temperature on another patient! Nevertheless, I was very happy with the standard of medical treatment James received at Patan. We were extremely fortunate to have such knowledgeable and caring medical staff to look after us.

When James was being examined or wished to talk to someone alone, I would wander up and down the corridors of the hospital. At night there would be people outside the rooms of relatives lying on the hard, cold floors with blankets over them. Spittoons were placed strategically and the sound of people hawking reverberated around the building. There frequently was one young man who would try to keep his son entertained in the corridor. His wife was in hospital having suffered third degree burns to much of her body. This man was nursing her and trying to look after their son. Another girl of perhaps twelve or thirteen used to smile shyly at me from under a red shawl. She was nursing her dying grandmother. Sometimes I would see whole families sitting anxiously outside the operating theatres.

James and I were both getting some counselling at this stage. He had to make some huge psychological adjustments. It took him days to come to terms with the fact that he was probably going to live and needed help to overcome the guilt he felt. It would take a long time for him to recover from everything.

We were under strict instructions from James's doctors that he not be allowed many visitors or a lot of outside intrusion. A stream of people kept wanting to see him, ranging from people who had helped in the search to other Australian tourists who had heard he had been rescued and was in hospital.

On 18 January, James's disappearance had made headlines across

Australia and my parents had been touched by the concern people had shown. In addition to the support of friends and relatives, there had been letters of sympathy coming in from all over the world. We wanted all these people to know as soon as possible that James had been found alive. Mum and Dad decided that the best thing to do was to notify ABC radio and the local Brisbane paper, the Courier Mail. It certainly worked. Within less than an hour, the televised broadcast of an international cricket match had been interrupted to say that James had been found. We had no inkling of the storm that would quickly follow.

People's reactions were touching. I have heard stories of complete strangers breaking down in tears. Gaye was at work when the news came through. She was in the middle of giving a tutorial when the head of the college came and told her to phone her mother at home. She braced herself for the news that a body had been found. Like my mother, Gaye's first reaction was shock and disbelief.

Andrew Ross was also at work when Beverley phoned him. He merely said that it was good news and hung up. Andrew had spent so long preparing himself for a body to be found, it took him a few minutes to register what Beverley had said. He rang my father because he could not believe he had heard the news correctly. As soon as Dad confirmed James was alive, Andrew left work to spread the news and start celebrating.

A friend of Auli's told her a matter of days before James was found that he had dreamt James was alive in a cave. Back in Australia, one of the men James used to work with had been explaining to his nine-year-old daughter that James had gone to Heaven. The little girl had suddenly spoken up. She said, 'You're wrong, Daddy. James is not in Heaven but they have to hurry up and find him.' And of course the words of Thrangu Rinpoche, the lama I had seen at Boudha on 11 January, still rang in my ears. He had indicated the right area and told me I would meet my brother again.

On the afternoon of 3 February, after my father had spoken to the paper and the ABC, the university switchboard was jammed with incoming calls. The calls were from a variety of people – friends, associates, relatives – but, even at that very early stage, a significant number were from the media. At the university, journalists flocked for an interview.

When my parents eventually got home, their house was flooded with people. First were Gaye, Beverley and Andrew's parents, but then some of James's friends dropped in, quickly followed by the media who wanted to film the celebrations. The telephone never stopped ringing and it was after 11.00 p.m. before the camera crews and photographers left. One reporter tried to drag my father away from the telephone whilst I was talking to him.

Next morning, Tuesday the 4th, my parents were woken at 4 a.m. by a call from a journalist, the first of a relentless stream. By 8 a.m. two television stations had camera crews banging on the front door. At work the stairwells were filled with media people wanting interviews. The journalists barged into the lab, unplugging scientific equipment at random, so they could use their electronic gear. All work in the laboratory ground to a halt.

In Nepal the phone calls from journalists started at 5 a.m. on the morning of 4 February. I had not slept for forty-eight hours at that point. The nurses on the ward could not speak English well enough to decipher any more than that the call was from Australia. Thinking it must be my parents, I went to the phone. It was a journalist from the ABC. He got fairly short change because of the time before I answered several questions. All this went on tape without my being aware of it. From that point on the phone barely stopped. Dorrilyn and I took it in turns to answer. One station wanted me to drop everything at the hospital and do a satellite link-up. I told them that after all we had been through, I was damned if the first time I saw my parents was going to be in front of thousands of people. Dr Garlick arrived and said he had been getting calls since 4 a.m. Tom and Maria were also inundated.

The situation worsened over the next few days as journalists and camera crews from all over the world descended on Patan hospital. James was in no fit state to be interviewed and neither was I. We could understand why there was so much attention and I repeatedly told journalists that we would be more than happy to tell the story eventually. The most important thing, at that time, was James's health and getting him back safely to Australia.

The question of money raised its head quite early in the piece. I was called from James's room into the nurses' station to answer another call from Australia. It was someone from a well-known current affairs show, offering me $50,000 for the story. I told them that no matter how much they wanted to pay, we were not going to talk with them or anyone until James was well enough. Back in Brisbane, television stations and magazines were contacting my father from Wednesday the 5th, offering incentives to sign exclusive rights contracts. They were told to discuss it with us once we had returned to Australia and James was well enough.

At this point we began to see that the story could be worth something. No one had received payment for any interviews at this stage. James was concerned about the money that had been spent – at least $50,000. Selling the story could be one way of paying back the search costs.

The lengths to which journalists went to try to get a story astounded me. Someone tried to steal James's medical records. Photographers tried to get in through the windows of his room. Reporters masqueraded as James's travel insurers. I refused to talk to any of them. In typical style, it took the Nepali press several days to cotton on to the fact that there was a story. They barged into James's hospital room. I had to force them out bodily. The poorly written article that appeared in the Rising Nepal the next day was highly sceptical about James's ordeal and claimed I refused to talk to them as I 'was not in the mood'.

When reporters tried using the expenses involved in getting here to persuade me to give an interview, I pointed out that I had never invited them over! It also seemed bizarre that I had struggled to keep people interested in James for weeks and now everyone was interested to the point of endangering James's life. I was sure they would not have been interested at all if we'd only found James's body.

I felt very resentful that I was being subject to so much extra stress and I could not understand why my parents could not get them to stop. I phoned Calum and my father in a very distressed, exhausted state, almost on the verge of emotional collapse. I pleaded with them to do something about the press. That night, Wednesday the 5th, my father appeared live on a national current affairs show and made a public appeal for the media to back off. He explained how I was being plagued by the press day and night and that I just wanted to concentrate on getting James home. This appeal was ignored.

The same evening, my parents went to bed at midnight, having had an emotional day of interviews and phone calls. The phone rang shortly afterwards. It was a reporter wanting to know how he felt to hear that his son had just gone into renal failure. For some reason, the reporter wanted a reaction to this question. James had not gone into renal failure at all.

It was probably 6 February when my parents realised things were out of hand. The offers they were getting for exclusive rights to the story were becoming more and more impressive. I was obviously having difficulty coping. The whole family was being plagued day and night. Patan hospital was being affected. Some reporters were just wandering from room to room in the hope of finding James, intruding on critically ill people. The doctors treating James believed his health was at risk. He was still in a very delicate emotional state and extremely susceptible to infection. His vision was very limited and he was on four-hourly pethidine shots to try to control the pain in his feet. We needed help.

Andrew Ross spoke with a solicitor friend who suggested that Dad contact publicity agent Harry M. Miller. He would have preferred to use the university and let them earn the commission but that had fallen through. When Dad called, Harry said he had been waiting to hear from us and would be willing to act as our agent. Miller was not concerned about having anything in writing: his only stipulation was that he would do all talking to the press.

My parents did not issue any further press interviews. They would have preferred to keep everyone informed, but the invasive nature of the media meant it was impossible to achieve this on an informal, low-key basis.

The name, Harry M. Miller, was vaguely familiar. I was less than cordial during our first conversation, a three-way telephone link-up with Harry in Sydney and Dad in Brisbane.

Harry said, 'I know what you're going through. They're all sharks and vultures.'

'Yeah, well,' I responded, 'I'm sure you're no bloody better. What do you want?'

Despite my rudeness, Harry persevered and explained his role. It was two-fold: first to get the press to give us some peace at least until James was safely home and, secondly, to try to help us recoup the costs of the search. He quickly decided he had to come to Kathmandu. Coincidentally, he was to arrive on the same flight as our medical evacuation team.

Other issues had complicated matters. James told me about the photographs he had asked to have taken under the rock. His camera and other personal belongings had been taken to Auli's house. The embassy had had the film developed. I have been assured it was a dreadful mistake but, somehow, a photograph of James dangling from the bottom of the helicopter was leaked to the world media. James had, of course, not seen the photos and was very concerned that there might be some graphic shots of him in an awful state. He did not want our parents and Gaye to see a photo of when he was first rescued before they had seen he was safe!

A day or so later, probably some three days after James's rescue, I was at Blue Mountain for my daily shower. Carl Harrison was also there, discussing the press with Tom. As someone who makes a living from guiding treks and expeditions around Nepal, it was natural Carl should want some publicity out of this. So, I was not overly surprised when he told me that he was going back to Talu the following day with a team from Australia's *A Current Affair*, or that he was being paid for this interview. We still had the advertised reward of $3000 to distribute. I asked Carl if he would take the money up to Talu and share it between himself, Ang Phury and the Talu villagers. To my way of thinking, this was the best way to handle the reward. Having heard James's story, I realised that, had it not been for the two villagers who kept trekking on that afternoon, no one would have reached James that evening. Tom told me earlier that, as soon as they knew someone had been sighted, he had tried to organise a party to go up on foot from Talu. Carl had said, however, that no one should go up until he returned from Kathmandu. Once the helicopter arrived back at Talu, the weather prevented it from flying up to rescue James. He wanted to hold off in the hope that the cloud would clear and allow him to rappel from the helicopter. Tom had felt it so unlikely that the weather would improve and so important that someone reach James that day that he had threatened to take five villagers from Talu and go up himself. At this, Carl had agreed to go. Tom had told me that the main motivation behind the villagers' willingness to go up was the reward. Carl and Ang Phury had been hired by me which would, stictly speaking, preclude them from the reward. I thought the fairest thing was for them all to share it. Carl's response shocked me.

'The Talu villagers are not entitled to any reward,' he told me. 'They did not find James. I found James.' He went on to say that all the people of Talu wanted was to hear their names on radio and a copy of the photos that were taken under the rock. Carl's attitude annoyed me. Obviously, I would have to sort that out myself. I could certainly arrange for the villagers to be thanked on radio but how was I going to get time to get the photos developed? I handed the negatives to Carl and asked him to return them to me after he had made copies. I saw Tom wince. Little did I know that Carl had come into Tom's office stating that he was tired of everyone else making money out of this and he was going to as well. At that point we had not made a cent out of it. Tom had charged *A Current Affair* for an interview he did with Colonel Pun but the fee was donated to my parents to help with the search costs. Once Carl had the negatives he said, 'These negatives belong to me.'

'They don't,' I replied. 'They were taken on James's film, using James's camera and at his request.'

211

'It was my idea to take the photos,' Carl said. I could see no way to get the negatives back. I could not understand his behaviour. James was devastated when he learnt what I had done. He asked how he had looked in the photos. I had seen the shots, but in my mental state I had not noticed what they were of!

It was three days after his rescue before James felt able to talk with Mum, Dad and Gaye. (The press were lining up for interviews with him before he had spoken to his own family!) The first conversation was very draining. After that, he tried to talk to them daily. We were also being sent faxes from Australia, mainly get well messages, but some also contained newspaper articles. I used to censor them slightly. One day, when I had stepped out briefly, James saw a cartoon that depicted him in a hospital bed and Dr Garlick saying to reporters, 'I'm sorry. He's not well enough to talk to anybody for under $100,000.' This left him distraught and made me realise how right we had been to shelter him from the press.

The media did not like the intervention of Harry Miller, probably because he makes their job more difficult. As soon as he became involved, everything quietened dramatically for us. If the media phoned, we just told them to ring Miller. To my relief, I was able to get some rest. The hospital was able to return to normal and my parents were left alone. With their access restricted, some journalists fabricated or invented stories of their own.

The question of the story being a hoax gained momentum after we asked Miller to help. A number of newspaper articles and current affairs shows had spoken with so-called mountaineering experts, and the end products seemed to concentrate on the fact that James was not as well prepared for the trek as he might have been and that, because the story was so amazing, it could not be true. In the show Carl Harrison did with *A Current Affair*, he stated that James made 'all the classic mistakes' and that he had been ill-prepared for the conditions. Having played such a major role in the whole episode, Carl had a right to express his opinion publicly. What astounded us was the way in which a number of other people immediately jumped on the bandwagon. The *Adelaide Advertiser* and *A Current Affair* interviewed a member of the Nepal-Australia Friendship Society who claimed James 'could almost be charged with attempted suicide'. He said he could not understand 'his foolhardiness' and thought he 'was lacking something upstairs'. He also was quoted as having said 'I just can't see how he'd survive after ten days at the most under the conditions he faced'. The man knew few of the facts or circumstances of the story but his words were given weight by the press. In the same article someone, reportedly a member of the SAS, was quoted as saying that he 'found it very hard to believe' and that he 'doubted anyone could survive by eating snow'. Another article in the *Courier-Mail* quoted the Sydney Honorary Royal Nepali Consul-General as saying, 'It's very odd that someone who was in good health couldn't make contact with someone in the mountains.' In the same article the head of World Expeditions was reported as saying James had been trapped by a colossal snowstorm near the Ganja La Pass. James was nowhere near the Ganja La Pass. In a later article in the *Sunday Mail* entitled, 'Trekkers Puzzled as Scott under Snowline', the same man reportedly claimed that James was only half a day's walk from Tarke Ghyang and he was under the snowline. Phedi is a common village name in Nepal and he had the wrong Phedi! He was also quoted as saying, 'Scott was a medical student and he didn't even have a medical kit.' We were so incensed by what was printed that we rang this man ourselves. He said that he hadn't spoken with a journalist for a long time and that he had been quoted completely out of context.

The *Rising Nepal* published an article entitled 'Scott the Stoic or James the Joker?' in which they suggested James had been cared for by 'a svelte, sexy, she-Yeti' who 'stumbled on the lost wanderer and promptly fell in love. The cupid's victim played nurse to this medical graduate and kept him alive with yak meat and snug embrace.'

My first meeting with Miller was at the Yak and Yeti Hotel. I had come from the hospital and was laden with thermos flasks and food containers. I was not looking my best. I tried to phone his room from reception but could not get through so I went straight up and pounded on his door. He answered, clutching a cordless phone in one hand.

I suspect we were both a little surprised at the appearance of the other. He invited me in and offered a cup of tea. The first thing I asked him was just who was paying for him to be here. He replied he was paying for himself. Slightly mollified, I got down to business. He advised me that the best way of ensuring a hassle-free trip home was to sign a press contract as soon as possible. A number were in the offing. I had a slight problem with this, as James was not well enough to sign or even consider any of this. I was taking on the responsibility of signing for him. Knowing James was a considerably more astute business person than I, I could not help but have some doubts as to whether I would make the best decision. The proposals were explained and I said I would think about them. Within twenty-four hours, a deal had been signed with *60 Minutes*, but not on the basis of money. We actually had a higher offer from another programme but *60 Minutes* was prepared to hold off interviewing James until he was well. We also signed a deal with the London *Daily Telegraph* and Fairfax papers in Australia. Of course, the deal in any such contract is for exclusivity. That means, once you sign, you are not at liberty to speak to any other press or to be photographed by anyone except those with whom you have the agreement. That suited us down to the ground. The money from these contracts was enough to return every cent that had been donated towards the search and rescue. In the case of donors who did not wish to have their money refunded, the equivalent sum was given to Patan hospital.

One newspaper claimed that James had been offered two million dollars to name the brand of chocolate he had. The interest in the type of chocolate stunned us. It had all been eaten by the second day he was lost and had no bearing on his survival yet reports came out saying how James had survived on snow and chocolate. Why did people not ask what type of sleeping bag he had or the brand of the anorak? These items helped him to live.

I could not wait to get back to Brisbane. Once I got home, my responsibilities would be over. I had heard of all the celebrations back home and felt a little resentful that everyone else could celebrate while I was left coping in Kathmandu. Auli had held a party at her place on the night of Saturday the 8th. I expressed my appreciation to all the searchers who had risked their lives in the search. I really felt that, without the team effort allowing areas to be ruled out and all leads to be investigated, we would never have found James. Later on, Debbie Harrison took me aside and complained that I should have thanked Carl personally. This was after he had behaved so ungraciously about the reward and had taken the negatives. I disagreed. When I asked Carl again to return the negatives, he refused. He said he didn't want other people making money out of them. 'Fine,' I replied, 'let's burn them.'

Carl refused. I said, 'Okay, Carl, if you're going to keep them, at least promise me you won't sell them.' He agreed. Carl also visited James before we flew out. James asked that, if Carl was going to keep the negatives, he at least should be able to get a copy of the photos any time he wanted. Carl told him that would be fine.

Eventually Wednesday came, the day of the medical evacuation, and we boarded a Thai Air flight to Singapore. On the plane, the staff were wonderful. In an evacuation, a stretcher is fitted across nine seats in economy at the rear of the plane. The stretcher is then screened from public view by curtains. James, Dorrilyn and the doctor were loaded first. The Australian nurse from the evacuation team and I completed departure formalities for the others. I said goodbye to all the friends I had made and tears of relief filled my eyes as we took off.

One would think that people would respect the privacy of an invalid travelling behind curtains. To my amazement, several people took it upon themselves to peer through and see what the curtains were shielding. One tall, fat man chose to do this while directly opposite me. I punched him hard in the arm and told him to piss off. He didn't argue.

Even at Bangkok there were intrusions. Once the plane was clear of passengers, we took down the curtains. It was too hot to leave them in place. Suddenly, two men came racing down the aisle, saying they knew our family and wanted to talk to us. They were journalists from the *Courier-Mail*. They had hidden in the toilets of the plane in the hope of getting a photograph and interview. James told them that he'd 'had a pretty shitty six weeks' and just wanted to be left alone. They were quickly despatched.

Our stopover in Singapore was amazing. The reception from the press brought the ambulance to a standstill. Reporters swarmed the hospital to the point where we had to smuggle James out in the morning through the morgue.

The following morning, our Qantas flight touched down at Brisbane airport. I did not know where my family would be or what plans had been made. A representative of the Federal Airports Corporation had come on board. He was amazed by the number of reporters crowding the airport arrivals section and lining the road. He had arranged for one cameraman to be on the tarmac. By this stage, I was fed up with cameras. I said we would refuse to get off the plane unless he was taken away. We were all highly emotional at finally being back in Brisbane and I did not want our private emotions displayed on film.

Dorrilyn, James and the doctor left in the first ambulance. At James's request, a blanket was held up to protect his privacy. A second ambulance was there to carry the medical evacuation team's gear. On every evacuation, thousands of dollars of equipment is carried to cater for all possible circumstances. It is quite routine to have two ambulances to meet a medivac patient.

By this time, I was so tired I could hardly stand. To avoid the crowd of reporters, John, Robbie and Calum met me at the rear door of the luggage area. It was marvellous to see them all again, especially Calum, but I was so tired and drained I must have almost seemed in a trance.

What we had encountered in those few days was a taste of things to come. The headlines for 14 February centred around a supposed security row over James's transportation to the Royal Brisbane Hospital. It seemed the ambulances had raced with sirens blaring, even going on the wrong side of the road to get round a traffic light, with a large police escort. On arrival at the RBH, cameramen had been 'jostled' by hospital security staff. Miller was blamed for all this. An official investigation later revealed he had nothing to do with it. Apparently a number of police had headed to the scene of their own volition. The hospital had every right to keep the media off its premises and protect a patient's request for privacy. The media made a bigger fuss about the events involved in James's transportation to hospital than was really warranted. Their noses were probably out of joint at not being permitted to intrude on a very private occasion.

We did interviews with Eric Bailey from the London *Daily Telegraph* who did a wonderful job. We were less than impressed with the *60 Minutes* effort. Hours of taping for my segment came down to a few minutes of insipid journalism. James came out of hospital for the day to complete the filming which was supposed to take only forty minutes. Some three hours later they were still going. James was tired and wanted to stop. He was told there were just another two or three questions. At that point, the interviewer let loose with a series of antagonising, accusatory questions that culminated in James losing his temper, calling the interviewer some well-deserved names and nearly collapsing with anger. We calmed him down and took him back to hospital immediately. We refused to have anything further to do with either the interviewer or the producer of those segments. It was a mystery to us why, with the wonderful story they could have had, they chose to produce two pointless, banal pieces.

We also learnt about 'spoiler' articles. The papers and television programmes that have not bought the exclusive rights produce articles in opposition. Some of these are quite clever. The day my story came out in the newspaper, the rival paper ran a headline about 'Our Real Iceman'. It was about someone who had crossed Antarctica. On the same day a number of opposition papers ran long articles which claimed to tell James's story of how he survived, even going to the extent of writing what they felt he was thinking and saying to himself.

Readers not knowing any better would have believed it all. It was amazing what they managed to produce when neither James nor I had said a word to them. In an attempt to get a story, one reporter even went to the extent of phoning James's medical student friends in the hope of 'digging up some dirt' on James.

It is, however, easy to concentrate on the negatives rather than the positives. We also had some very encouraging letters sent to newspapers and some wonderful editorials written. A lot of the articles were quite positive. As James's health improves and he talks freely with people, reports have continued to be favourable. Letters bearing good wishes from all over the world arrived. Some, merely addressed to 'James Scott, Himalayan Survivor, Australia', have found their way to my parents' house.

By the end of April, we had paid back every cent that went into the search, something that we would never have been able to do without the media interest. We had a thanksgiving party at the farm and invited everyone who had supported us throughout those traumatic months.

James and I have both done public speaking to raise money for Patan hospital. Ingo Schnabel of the Himalayan Dog Rescue Training Centre has also asked us to help him establish the James Scott Search and Rescue Academy at Sundarijal. James donated his straw hat for auction at the RBH fair to raise money for the hospital.

The negatives that Carl Harrison took turned up in the office of a French magazine. Thanks to the London *Daily Telegraph*, they were returned before they could be published.

The reward money has been distributed to the villagers of Talu who will use it for the benefit of all who live in the village. They have invited James to visit them in a year or so to see what good has come from it.

At the end of the day, in spite of all the negativity, disbelievers and stress, there is much for which to be thankful. For five weeks we went through the hell of believing that James was dead and that we would never know what had happened to him; that he would become another statistic in Nepal and we would have to get on with life without him. James and I both managed to overcome the odds, to ignore the obstacles and to rise above the negativity. I know I am very proud of what I achieved in Nepal and of James. One thing has been made very clear to us: with the love and support of family and friends, with help from God, determination and confidence in one's own ability, it is possible to achieve what no one thinks you can. In our case, the reward for all this was the most wonderful thing: James is still with us.

EPILOGUE

JAMES:

Sixteen months have passed since I was medically evacuated. After the drama of the journey home, it was a welcome relief to reach RBH. I was taken into one of the cubicles in the emergency department where I was finally reunited with my parents and Gaye. Although I had spoken to them at length over the phone, it was almost unbelievable to actually be with them. Everyone seemed a bit apprehensive at first, choosing their words carefully, fearful I might become upset. I still had feelings of guilt about all the suffering I'd caused them and for a time the conversation was a little stifled. It wasn't long before we all relaxed, talking and joking as if everything was normal. For a brief period I was just plain James Scott once more and it was wonderful to be with everyone I thought I'd lost forever.

The weeks following my rescue were almost as challenging as the forty-three days on the mountain. To recuperate physically and mentally was difficult. I had unrealistic expectations of my recovery, believing that I'd be back to my normal state of health within a couple of months. Mentally, the recovery was rapid. Initially, I had a compulsion to talk to everyone about everything. I'm sure they grew quite tired of listening but everybody was very patient. Gradually the urge faded and after a month, I was back to normal conversation. Apart from the first few days after my rescue, there were no nightmares. Nor did I have any long-standing emotional scars that the media said would haunt me for years to come.

The skin continued to peel away from my feet, but new skin had grown underneath. I had some cold injury, but very early during my recovery I was reassured that no amputations would be necessary. The pain was controlled by more modern medications available in Australia and after several months it eased to a mild tingling. My feet lacked sensation, a result of vitamin deficiency. Injections and tablets of multi-vitamins replenished my stores and feeling gradually returned. Four months after I'd been rescued, my toes could feel what they touched.

The exact amount of weight I lost will never be known. I wasn't weighed until the second day, after I'd been fully rehydrated through an intra-venous line. The scales tipped just over sixty kilograms; the fluid that would have been restored to my body was anywhere between three and five kilograms. The measurements didn't matter. In my emaciated condition, I still had trouble lifting one leg off the bed. A physiotherapist designed a weight-training programme to help. I spent days struggling with empty or light-weight dumbbells, but slowly the muscles returned. It was three months before I was back to my original weight, being very careful to adhere to a low fat diet. This was to avoid obesity, a common complication following prolonged starvation. Nine months after my rescue I was approaching my original strength and build.

I had a marked deficiency in my balance, which would cause me to walk slowly with my legs wide apart. I couldn't stand with them together without swaying. My balance is still not perfect but you would have to look very closely for a long time to know. Nevertheless, every step is taken with care and thought to avoid tripping or staggering.

The only other residual handicap is my vision. I now spend every waking moment watching the world bounce up and down, with one image sitting slightly above the other. A part of my brain which controls the movements of my eyes has been damaged, another result of Vitamin B1 deficiency. My eyes constantly oscillate up and down in their sockets. This was a torment as I couldn't even recognise faces. How would I ever return to my studies? It was several months before I could read without feeling nauseous as the words bobbed up and down on the page. But even this has healed with time, to the extent where I have been able to cope with my final year of medicine. I am also back at karate and, despite the abnormalities in my sight and balance, I am able to train hard at the sport I enjoy so much.

I am grateful that I have emerged from this ordeal relatively unscathed. I am also thankful God provided me with sufficient recovery to resume a normal life. Other people seem to worry more about my minor handicaps than I do. I am just thankful to be as well as I am, considering the punishment my body took.

I am still astonished by the reception I received from the Australian media. The initial articles which aimed to discredit my story generated a lot of scepticism and hostility. Views voiced by ill-informed individuals were soul-destroying. My only desire was to be left in peace with Gaye and my family and friends. As my health improved, I was prepared to be interviewed and talk to journalists, who would subsequently publish more accurate articles. The influence the media had over the public and the power they possessed shocked all those who were close to the family.

At the time of writing this, I am aware that many people remain sceptical of my story. I am yet to have someone directly confront me with this view but occasionally friends relate back how they overheard people expressing their doubts.

This scepticism is something I can understand. It is human nature to form opinions on the few threads of information that we are given and often we are reluctant to change our views. So often it has been written that I survived on snow and chocolate bars. Such a simplistic summary of my survival techniques will of course raise questions.

In marked contrast, from the day I returned to Brisbane, letters of congratulations and encouragement started arriving. For every critical comment I heard or read through the media, many more letters of support arrived.

The ordeal has provided me with a new perspective on life. I spent forty-two days without food, warmth or company. Every night I battled cold, pessimism and depression. Back home in an Australian summer, surrounded by loving friends and family, Gaye and I were about to marry. My life is now full of all sorts of pleasures. What does it matter what others think when I have everything I could ever want?

Joanne, Gaye and I returned to Nepal in November 1992. It was a wonderful trip, giving me the opportunity to meet and thank many of those involved in the search and rescue. Tom Crees still went out of his way to help us any way he could. It was terrific to see Graeme and Auli from the embassy and thank them in person for all they did. We organised to have a drink with Graeme at Tom and Jerry's. At one point he told me how he was very pessimistic about my chances as soon as he was told of my disappearance. Despite a view he held secretly to himself, he had always been there to make the search possible. I am very touched by the concern he showed Joanne and my family and the efforts he made to find me.

The only time our trip was marred was during a meeting Gaye and I had with the Australian Ambassador. We went with the intention of thanking him for the help the staff at the embassy gave Joanne. He levelled some unwarranted criticisms towards me, Joanne, my family and several other individuals central to the search. We left the meeting with a very sour taste in our mouths.

This was the only down point of what was otherwise a very enjoyable time. *60 Minutes*, who'd sponsored our return, took us up to Talu where we got a warm reception. We returned to the rock after an arduous climb. It was the same cold and barren area albeit with less snow. The film crew's usual joviality left them as they took in the shelter and its surroundings.

One of the most frequent questions I am asked when public speaking is 'How have my own values in life changed since the ordeal and have these new values faded with time?'.

It is a very difficult question to answer. I can say for certain that my belief in God has strengthened enormously and I am certain He exists.

I also know how important it is to treat others well. Unlike Pip in *Great Expectations*, I was lucky enough not to be tormented by the way I had acted towards people.

I also realised how important those closest to me are. This I have not forgotten. Nor is it likely ever to fade from my memory. To lose one close friend or family member is a tragedy. To lose everyone is beyond comprehension.

Finally I believe that whilst in the mountains, I reached a pinnacle of purity that I will never touch again while living in Western society. My existence became so primitive that the lust and greed we all have at times for money and material possessions was replaced by a desire for the basic necessities of life. All that I wished for as I battled through those days was some food, warmth and love. Never before had I appreciated just how beautiful a small bird could appear. I'd never really taken in the majesty of a clear starry night. I had been so humbled that something as simple as a few hours of sunlight would fill me with warmth and gratitude. Now that I am back home with everything I could ever possibly need I can't derive the same pleasure out of such basic events. But I still appreciate the strength these things gave me when I had no other pleasures.

There remains one last question: what is it that allowed me to survive for forty-three days in such inhospitable conditions, where it is commonly believed that it is impossible to stay alive for more than a week? There is no simple answer. My attitude throughout the ordeal was generally one of hope and optimism. I did all that I could to rise above the difficulties I faced and tried to clutch at any straws available to me. I had some medical knowledge that helped prevent frostbite and hypothermia. I had six years of karate training which provided me with both mental discipline and muscle for my body to feed off.

There is only one thing of which I am certain. There is nothing extraordinary about me. Before these terrible events occurred I would not have believed for a moment that I would be capable of overcoming such seemingly impossible odds. Yet I am still alive to tell the tale. The lesson I have learnt from this whole event – simplistic as it might sound – is that no difficulty is impossible to overcome. There is no challenge in life that is too hard to confront. I am just an ordinary person who

221

fell into an extraordinary situation and, with the help of many others but especially Joanne, we achieved a remarkable outcome. It is my wish that my experience will serve as an inspiration to others to overcome life's obstacles. For it is only by overcoming difficult challenges that one truly appreciates the rewards that life has to offer.